THE EMPEROR'S NEW ROAD

THE EMPEROR'S NEW ROAD

China and the Project of the Century

JONATHAN E. HILLMAN

Yale

UNIVERSITY PRESS

New Haven and London

CSIS | CENTER FOR STRATEGIC & INTERNATIONAL STUDIES

Published with assistance from the Mary Cady Tew Memorial Fund.

The Center for Strategic and International Studies (CSIS) is a
bipartisan, nonprofit policy research organization dedicated to
advancing practical ideas to address the world's greatest challenges.

CSIS does not take specific policy positions; accordingly, all views
expressed herein should be understood to be solely those of the
author.

Center for Strategic and International Studies
1616 Rhode Island Avenue, NW
Washington, DC 20036
202.887.0200 | www.csis.org

Yale University Press books may be purchased in quantity for
educational, business, or promotional use. For information, please
e-mail sales.press@yale.edu (U.S. office) or sales@yaleup.co.uk
(U.K. office).

Set in Janson type by IDS Infotech Ltd., Chandigarh, India.
Printed in the United States of America.

Library of Congress Control Number: 2020933559
ISBN 978-0-300-24458-8 (hardcover : alk. paper)

A catalogue record for this book is available from the British Library.

This paper meets the requirements of ANSI/NISO Z39.48-1992
(Permanence of Paper).

10 9 8 7 6 5 4 3 2

Contents

Preface

TRAPPED IN NO MAN'S land, somewhere between China and Kyrgyzstan, I had time to think. Border guards at checkpoint five of seven had just started their lunch break, and I had to wait for their return. A few days earlier, I had attended the first Belt and Road Forum in Beijing, a massive and tightly choreographed celebration of Xi Jinping's signature foreign-policy vision for connecting China and the world. But on China's border, things were moving slowly, if at all. As minutes stretched into hours, the idea for this book was born.

In Washington, DC, and other Western capitals, policy makers heard about the forum in Beijing. They read about dozens of foreign leaders showing up, over sixty countries signing onto China's effort, ancient trade routes being revived, and other grand claims, often the same ones that Chinese state media tout. They saw maps of new economic corridors running outward from China. All these details add to an image of China as cunning, strategic, and marching in lockstep toward midcentury.

They missed the lunch breaks and border delays. From afar, the challenges standing in the way of China's global ambitions, including actual mountains, look smaller. Ironically, given an abundance of suspicion, relatively little has been done to check whether actions on the ground are advancing these ambitions. Quite understandably, most people cannot spend time crossing China's borders by car, foot, and boat or climbing onto its trains and docks in other countries, as I have done while writing this book. These pages share those glimpses of ground truth.

When the border guards returned several hours later and waved my vehicle through, arriving in Kyrgyzstan was something of a homecoming. In 2009, I lived in Bishkek, Kyrgyzstan's capital, as a Fulbright scholar. I was fascinated by how Central Asia reflected and balanced outside influences. I was greeted by Asians who prayed to Allah, drank vodka, spoke Russian, ate Turkish food, listened to American music, and traded Chinese goods. I came to appreciate how the world's crossroads provide a checkup of the global order.

Kyrgyzstan is different a decade later. Gone is the U.S. military base that served as a hub for troops and supplies going to Afghanistan. China's presence has poured out of the bazaars and into new roads, fiber-optic cables, and power projects. Xinhua, the Chinese state-media outlet, has opened a "cultural center" in Bishkek that sells copies of Xi Jinping's writing. Yet the Kyrgyz people are hardly sold. Rather than warming to Xi's call for a "community of common destiny," many are wary of China's influence and appalled by its internment of ethnic minorities.

This landscape, as I have tried to show it, has much in common with the past, but it is more complex than any "Great Game" or imperial contest. While the United States mostly complains these days, China is forging ahead. But it is not doing so alone or uncontested. Japan, India, Russia, and many others have their own designs. Far from being pawns, smaller countries are often the most pivotal players. Many of them have far more recent experience dealing with outside powers than China has acting as one. The road is theirs, as I hope it will remain for years to come.

PART I

Empire Strikes Back

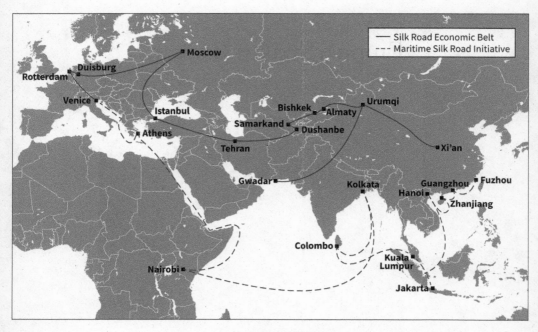

China's Belt and Road Initiative

Center for Strategic and International Studies, Reconnecting Asia Project; Xinhua

CHAPTER ONE
Project of the Century

T HE ORCHESTRA STRUCK UP as the People's Leader entered the cavernous hall. As he strode down the red carpet, entourage at his back, his hundreds of distinguished guests stood and applauded. They fell silent when he took the dais.

"Dear friends," he said, looking out at the sea of visitors. "This is indeed a gathering of great minds."

In flattering them, he flattered himself. His friends numbered royalty, presidents, merchants, and intellectuals and were a Noah's ark of nationalities: Asians, Arabs, Africans, Europeans, Persians, and Russians. From all corners of the world, they had trekked to his court. Some came to pay tribute. Some came to trade. Others, like me, came out of curiosity.

It was a scene that Marco Polo might have recognized from his travels during the thirteenth century, but it was May 14, 2017, at the Belt and Road Forum in Beijing. President Xi Jinping stood before nearly thirty heads of state and delegates from over 130 countries. "In the coming two days," he explained, "we will contribute to pursuing . . . a project of the century."

But that was an understatement. China's Belt and Road Initiative (BRI), pursued to its end, stands to become *the* project of the century. Its size and reach are staggering. China has promised to

3

spend $1 trillion building new roads, railways, and other infrastructure beyond its borders. Adjusted for inflation, that is roughly seven times what the United States spent through the Marshall Plan to rebuild western Europe after World War II. It is five times as much as the Trump administration proposed and failed to persuade Congress to provide for infrastructure within the United States. The contrast is striking: the world's leading power no longer leads, while its rising power charts a course to the center of everything.[1]

It is impossible to fathom the BRI without a map. When Xi announced the BRI in 2013, it had two key aspects: an overland "belt" across the Eurasian supercontinent and, somewhat confusingly, a maritime "road" across the Indian Ocean and up to Europe via the Suez Canal. Originally called "One Belt, One Road," its purported aims are to deepen trade, investment, policy coordination, and even cultural ties. These new connections all have one thing in common: they lead to China.

Xi's vision is constrained by neither geography nor even gravity. Since its announcement, the BRI has stretched into the Arctic, cyberspace, and outer space. The list of participants has grown to exceed 130 nations and includes not only China's neighbors but also most African countries and even countries in Latin America.[2] After Governor Jerry Brown of California visited China in June 2017, Chinese state media mischievously speculated that California could join.[3]

The same forces that powered China's meteoric rise are now being channeled through the BRI and beyond its borders. Over just a decade, China went from having no high-speed railways to having more than the rest of the world combined. Increasingly, Chinese companies challenge those from Japan, Europe, and other advanced economies for projects in world markets.

The BRI also provides a runway for China's bloated state-owned companies to take off and parachute into new markets. Between 2011 and 2013, China used more cement than the United States required during the entire twentieth century, and its ability to build now outstrips its domestic needs.[4] Home to seven of the world's ten largest construction companies, China desperately needs to ensure paychecks for its millions of workers.[5] The BRI is their safety net.

The BRI has become more than a policy—it is a brand. With such large amounts of investment available, central and local governments, private firms, and nonprofit organizations are incentivized to repackage their work around the BRI. Over one hundred Chinese think tanks are dedicated to studying it. In China, there are "Belt and Road" fashion shows, music festivals, and art exhibits. Belgrade's annual marathon was added to the Belt and Road Marathon Series. This race was different. "It does not focus on the competition level, but more on friendship, cultural exchange and promoting economic growth," an organizer explained.[6]

But for all the attention the BRI receives, it remains poorly understood. A major challenge is that the BRI label evades classification. There is no official definition for what qualifies as a BRI project. There are Chinese-funded projects in nonparticipant countries that share many of the same characteristics. The BRI was officially launched in 2013, but projects that were started years earlier are often counted. China's lending is opaque, leaving observers to piece together bits of information from public sources and keeping many details secret.[7]

The effort is undeniably bold, and it has been compared to *xieyi*, a traditional Chinese painting style that uses broad brushstrokes to capture emotions rather than minute details. In 2018, at a speech marking the fifth anniversary of the BRI, Xi called for moving from that style to the *gongbi* style, a realistic technique that produces meticulous paintings.[8] It was a clever way of acknowledging that many details still needed to be worked out. When viewed up close, the BRI begins to lose focus.

Grasping in the Dark

As in the parable of the blind men and the elephant, observers have struggled to describe the BRI because they have latched onto different parts of this beast.[9] Some feel a gift horse, and they are content to accept it with flaws. Many of China's partner countries have few options for meeting their investment needs. Developing Asia alone needs $26 trillion in infrastructure investment by 2030 to maintain growth and adapt to climate change.[10] China cannot satisfy those needs, but it is going boldly into markets where few others dare to go.

Some feel a beast of burden, a force to pull their own agendas. Multilateral institutions see an opportunity for global development and a chance to expand their own budgets. At the Belt and Road Forum, the World Trade Organization signed an agreement with China, as did the World Bank, the World Health Organization, and other international agencies. Top officials at the United Nations (UN) have embraced the BRI, declaring that it supports the UN's 2030 development agenda and even producing a cartoon that extolls its benefits.[11]

Some feel a golden goose. The CEO of the German conglomerate Siemens has called the BRI "the next World Trade Organization." Herbert Smith Freehills, an elite international law firm, has assembled a working group of over eighty lawyers for BRI projects.[12] The management consulting firm McKinsey has found opportunities on both sides of the negotiating table, advising Chinese state-owned companies as well as recipient countries on major deals. HSBC and other major financial institutions have assembled BRI teams to source deals and make friends in Beijing.

Some feel a trojan horse. When HSBC's official Twitter account asked, "What do you think of when you hear the term Belt and Road?" it opened the floodgates to a wave of negative responses, which included "Imperialism," "neocolonialism," and "China exporting debt," among others.[13] Twitter is full of snark and outrage, but U.S. government warnings about the BRI are not so different. "China is diligently building an international network of coercion through predatory economics to expand its sphere of influence," then-acting U.S. Secretary of Defense Patrick Shanahan said in 2019, pointing to suspicious port investments in the Indian Ocean.[14]

Some sense that the elephant is white. Fitch, the ratings agency, was one of the first dissenting voices to suggest that economics might be taking a backseat to politics along the BRI. "Chinese banks do not have a track record of allocating resources efficiently at home, especially in relation to infrastructure projects—they are unlikely to have more success overseas," it pointed out.[15] Leaders are eager to announce new projects to reward supporters and cement their legacies. China's massive firms are happy to build them, regardless of their commercial or strategic value. Both sides exploit the lag between opportunity and accountability. When the bill comes due, it will be someone else's problem.

There are elements of truth to each of these perspectives, but none fully captures the creature in question. No single perspective can. The BRI is a global initiative, but its contours depend on local context. Some projects help development. Others serve China's strategic aims. Some will do both. Other projects will fail outright. If the BRI is a painting, each country is a unique canvas, shaped by geography and colored with its own history and culture. Seeing the BRI as it is requires traveling to the places where it is unfolding. Discerning its unique qualities, and imagining what it could become, requires an appreciation for what has come before it.

The Education of a Rising Power

Weaving together history and fieldwork in sixteen countries, this is a book about China outside of China.[16] It provides a middle view that is often missing between cotemporary high-level views of China's foreign activities and the messier reality on the ground.[17] I focus primarily on the Eurasian supercontinent because it has attracted the majority of Chinese investment and construction spending since the Belt and Road was announced.[18] It is also where most of the world's people and economic output reside. Many hot spots and flagship projects are included, but more places surely deserve attention.

This book, at its core, is about power. I focus on China's infrastructure projects because they are the carrot for convincing countries to participate, the spoils for China's national champions, and the source of the West's greatest anxieties about the BRI. Every project is a negotiation, and the most contested are windows into society. They reflect the ambitions and flaws of their designers. They are conduits for resources and symbols of prestige. They can reshape relations within and between countries, for better or worse.

The painting that emerges in these pages is not the one of global goodwill promoted in Beijing, nor the one of strategic cunning perceived in Washington. From sweeping maps to individual investments, relatively little has been done to verify whether China's activities actually match its aspirations. The challenge is understandable. The BRI is opaque and vague by design. But grasping in the dark, many observers have imposed order where it does not exist. Chinese officials have only a loose grip on the brush, and others have been happy to fill in the details for them. That is changing, as China learns, but the difficulties it faces are enormous.

Around the world, China is retracing the footsteps of colonial powers and repeating their mistakes. Cleverly, Chinese officials cloak their efforts in "Silk Road" caravans and other romanticized images of ancient times, but as Chapter 2 argues, there is a more recent period that urges caution. During the great-power competition that lasted from the mid-nineteenth century to World War I, western powers pursued major infrastructure projects to expand their influence at the expense of indigenous people, the environment, and economic stability. As a weaker state, China resisted strategies similar to those it now employs as a rising power.[19]

Despite these imperial echoes, this is not a story about China's domination but its education as a rising power. China's tool of choice, infrastructure, is appealing to developing countries but incredibly difficult to deliver. Even in the best business environments, most large projects cost more than expected, take longer than expected, and deliver fewer benefits than expected. Infrastructure is often touted as a solution to society's employment and productivity woes, but the reality is that done poorly, projects destroy more value than they create.[20]

I once put that argument to a room full of Chinese officials responsible for planning the BRI's initial stages. I had been asked to come and present my research on their initiative. It felt like being asked to tell Thomas Edison about lightbulbs, but I wanted to see how they would react. The answer? Blank stares. Apparently, the notion that bad projects might ultimately leave people and places worse off just did not compute. After all, China's own rise has been fueled by dramatic infrastructure spending. Its top leaders have all ascended in a system that rewards GDP growth, which they have learned to boost through building infrastructure.[21]

These incentives favor quantity over quality, masking longer-term costs. Within China, "ghost cities" artificially boost growth figures and then sit unused. The same playbook that Chinese planners have used at home, where they have fewer checks on their authority, faces even greater challenges abroad. Risks are so high and widespread along the BRI that three out of four participating countries have sovereign-debt ratings that are either junk or not rated.[22] As the financial and reputational costs of failed projects mount, China is beginning to appreciate why Western countries pool their resources through the World Bank and other multilateral institutions and put safeguards in place.

"The Asiatic Invasion"

A century ago, the British geographer Halford Mackinder, sometimes called the father of modern geopolitics, pondered, "Is not the pivot region of the world's politics . . . that vast area of Euro-Asia which is inaccessible to ships, but in antiquity lay open to the horse-riding nomads, and is to-day about to be covered with a network of railways?"[23] That prediction did not foresee World War I, which derailed not only Eurasian railways but global integration more generally. Suddenly, Mackinder's words sound plausible again. Thanks to generous Chinese subsidies, regular railway services have sprung up to connect nearly sixty Chinese cities with nearly fifty European cities.[24]

If China is answering Mackinder's question, the consequences could be monumental. He believed that Eurasia was the "geographical pivot of history" and that whoever controlled its heartlands controlled the world. In truth, what Mackinder called the "world island" never stopped mattering. Two decades ago, the former U.S. national security advisor Zbigniew Brzezinski argued, "Eurasia is thus the chessboard on which the struggle for global primacy continues to be played."[25] At the time, China was a regional power mostly confined to the Far East. It is now a global power pushing west.

For China, Europe is the prize at the end of the supercontinent, but as Chapters 3–5 explain, treacherous terrain stands in the way. The challenges begin at China's doorstep. As I learned when crossing Central Asia's borders on foot and while hitching a ride across the Caspian Sea, the BRI is a middleman's dream. Its megaprojects offer ample opportunities for bribery, kickbacks, and theft. These challenges are hardly limited to Central Asia. Indeed, the problem is not simply corruption where China aims to go but how it aims to get there: building massive projects with little transparency and accountability.

Corruption is a feature, not a bug, of the BRI's design. As a former president of China Export-Import Bank said in 2007, "We have a saying: If the water is too clear, you don't catch any fish."[26] Giving Chinese companies an advantage by limiting outside scrutiny and competition might seem clever but could backfire spectacularly in the future. When projects are poorly chosen—because of political or corrupt considerations—and do not generate sufficient returns, recipients struggle to pay back loans. Scandals reveal the true beneficiaries of these deals, and popular resentment grows. When the water is murky, you cannot see the bottom.

Russia is the gatekeeper for China's overland ambitions, straddling as it does eleven time zones across the top of the Eurasian supercontinent and with deep ties to Central Asia; no other country is better positioned to spoil China's eastward expansion. But Russia, economically and diplomatically isolated from the West, has few options. Xi and Putin have met over thirty times while in office, elevating their countries' relations faster and higher than ever before. They now tout a strategic partnership, relishing the alarm this triggers in Western capitals.

But one of the most visible symbols of the two countries' economic partnership, a new bridge across the Amur River, hints at lasting divisions. Separated by less than a mile, each side feels like a different world. When I visited, the Chinese were amused that a foreigner was interested in their project. On the Russian side of the bridge, soldiers informed me that it was a "strategic project" and strictly off-limits. Thanking them, I turned to leave. "But you are already here," their leader pronounced, turning my sightseeing trip into a day-long interrogation. U.S. policy makers could use Russia's insecurities to stoke competition with China, but unintentionally, they have been pushing these historical enemies together.

Central and eastern Europe are the bridgehead to Europe. To make inroads, China brings together seventeen central and eastern European heads of state every year. This "17+1" format, which includes EU and non-EU members, is deceptively designed. It gives the outward impression of multilateralism, but in practice, Chinese officials use these gatherings to strike bilateral deals. China's checkbook disproportionately favors the non-EU governments, where investment rules are less transparent and open, causing European officials to worry that China is creeping through a "Balkan back door."

China's divisive push into the European Union's neighborhood could eventually help unite it.[27] The EU has ramped up investment screening, branded China a "strategic competitor," and launched its own connectivity initiative.[28] These are small steps; but they reflect a growing consensus, and their direction is clear. Some EU officials are beginning to view China's economic toolkit as seriously as they view Russia's military. Mackinder would recognize this threat as an opportunity, a common cause around which to rally. "European civilization is," he argued, "the outcome of the secular struggle against Asiatic invasion."[29]

"The Pivot upon Which Everything Turned"

Alfred Thayer Mahan, the most influential American strategist of the nineteenth century, would view the BRI's maritime activities with suspicion.[30] Unlike Mackinder, Mahan believed that history hinges on control of the sea. In his landmark study on sea power, Mahan approvingly quotes George Washington writing to Benjamin Franklin that "naval superiority . . . was the pivot upon which everything turned."[31] The most important source of that power, Mahan believed, was the tendency to trade. As the world's largest trader and home to the second-largest merchant fleet, China has already arrived as a commercial naval power.[32] Given that 90 percent of world trade travels by sea, the BRI's maritime dimensions are likely to be more consequential than its overland dimensions. In that respect, we are still living in Mahan's world, not returning to Marco Polo's anytime soon.

China's path to the sea is contested, however, as Chapters 6–8 explain. Its overland and maritime ambitions converge in South and Southeast Asia, where it faces fierce competition from regional powers. Australia, Japan, India, and the United States are all working to provide alternatives to Chinese investment. Still, China is often its own worst enemy. Where the facts on the ground have not suited its position, it has changed the ground, creating artificial islands in the South China Sea and militarizing them with runways and missiles. Most countries want China's investment and trade but find its increasingly aggressive behavior alarming. China's partners might be smaller, but they are no less savvy. Many have far more experience dealing with outside powers than China has experience acting as one.

In Southeast Asia, China is pushing to forge new north-south connections, while Japan is defending its east-west connections. Southeast Asian countries have turned this contest into their own investment buffet. No one knows the game better than Mahathir Mohamad, Malaysia's former prime minister, who courted Japanese investment when he first took office in the 1980s. "The powerful will take what they will, the weak will yield what they must," Mahathir reflected in July 2018, paraphrasing the Greek historian Thucydides to describe the challenge that China presents.[33] But Mahathir was being sly and downplaying the strength of his hand. In Southeast Asia, the powerful pay what they must, and the weak take what they can.

In South Asia, the flagship of China's BRI may become its greatest test. Xi has put his personal stamp on the China-Pakistan Economic Corridor (CPEC), traveling to Islamabad in April 2015 to cement the two countries' "all-weather strategic cooperative partnership" and sign a host of agreements. But after ballooning to a mythical $100 billion, CPEC has drifted back to earth and delivered only a fraction of its initial promise. Dangerously, China is betting it can succeed where the United States and international community have failed for decades.

If Chinese loans were cigarettes, Sri Lanka's Hambantota Port would be the cancerous lung on the warning label. Mahinda Rajapaksa, Sri Lanka's blindingly ambitious prime minister, borrowed heavily to build the port and other projects that carry his name and are hardly used. After China took a controlling ownership stake and a ninety-nine-year lease for the port, U.S. officials seized on the example to illustrate the perils of China's "debt diplomacy."[34] But these critiques give China too much credit and overlook the agency of recipient countries, where most solutions reside. The true story of Hambantota Port, as Chapter 8 recounts, is more chaotic than strategic and more Shakespearean drama than spy thriller.

Risk and Reward

Warnings about the "next Hambantota" miss an even bigger prize: digital infrastructure. Mackinder and Mahan, for all their wisdom, did not live in a world of airpower, let alone cyber power. While

Western capitals debate the risks of allowing Chinese technology into their next-generation wireless networks, Chinese firms are rapidly connecting the world's next-generation markets, as Chapter 9 explains. In East Africa, Chinese firms are laying underseas cables, equipping cities with surveillance cameras, and building wireless networks. On Maslow's hierarchy of digital needs, network security is secondary to cost, positioning China's tech champions to grow globally even if their Western presence withers.

New connections, physical and digital, also produce unintended consequences. Eurasia's ancient routes carried not only silk and horses but also Mongol invaders and the bubonic plague. Recent viral outbreaks have been concentrated in areas of Asia where burgeoning animal and human populations live in close proximity and which China aims to develop and connect with the world. Britain's vast telegraph network carried not only colonial commands but also nationalists' potent ideas for change and became "the means of challenging and undermining the very empire that created it," as the historian Daniel Headrick writes.[35]

Given this certainty of surprise, the BRI's sheer scale demands attention. If China succeeds, it will become the most central node in global flows of goods, data, and people. Chinese technical standards, for everything from high-speed railway systems to wireless networks, will become more widely adopted, as will Chinese preferences for environmental and social safeguards, or the lack thereof. China's military will benefit from expanded global access, and its diplomats will have more levers for influence. China will be stronger to impose its will, and the world will be weaker to resist. Over the longer term, the sum of these changes is not simply a world revised but a world remade. The Middle Kingdom will have returned.

But China is more constrained than its imperial predecessors were, as Chapter 10 explains, and it will struggle to turn Xi's grand vision into reality. China can co-opt, coerce, and gradually revise the status quo, one artificial island or highway at a time. But like a vampire at the door, China must be welcomed in by its hosts. By necessity, China's imperialism is incremental and relies on economic means. It is also more vulnerable to scrutiny, and in the coming years, more observers will throw light onto China's opaque practices. In response, China may end up embracing some of the standards it now resists—not out of goodwill but out of self-interest.

Ironically, if the BRI is overhauled, Western policy makers might eventually regret that Chinese officials took their advice.[36] A more focused, higher-quality effort could turn China from a lender of last resort into a preferred partner. It could spread Chinese influence in more targeted areas, from setting technology standards to swaying foreign capitals. It could limit China's losses. Above all, it could demonstrate that China is succeeding where other great powers have failed.

What is already clear is that the BRI is no Marshall Plan. It is much easier to rebuild developed economies, as the United States did in western Europe after World War II, than to develop economies. The Marshall Plan was a focused effort, concentrated on a narrow set of countries, spanning under five years, and involving a finite set of activities. Since leaving the station, China's BRI has become a gravy train without a conductor. Its fevered pace has already exceeded China's ability to accurately measure, let alone manage, these activities. Corruption and rent-seeking are thriving in the chaos. Conceptually, China's BRI is closer to the War on Terror: poorly defined and ever expanding.

There is no end in sight. Domestically and internationally, Xi has support to forge ahead. A pledge to pursue the BRI was added to the Chinese Communist Party's constitution in 2017, suggesting that Xi's vision could extend even beyond his lifetime tenure. At the second Belt and Road Forum, in 2019, Xi addressed an even larger audience of country representatives and heads of state. Unlike the War on Terror, of course, the BRI speaks more directly to the aspirations of developing countries. With few alternatives for investment, even leaders who shook their fists at the BRI while campaigning for office took the stage in Beijing to applaud it.

As long as China has the wallet and the will to build new connections beyond its borders, it will have opportunities to do so. The question is whether the BRI will add to China's power or detract from it. That hinges on China having the discipline to choose the right projects and walk away from the wrong ones. In the BRI's first six years, its mission has not merely creeped but cascaded. Mistakes were surfacing even before the coronavirus pandemic paralyzed the global economy in 2020, exacerbating the BRI's pre-existing conditions and revealing how the very connections it aims to strengthen carry both promise and peril.

As the following chapters show, the BRI is an imperial project in the rewards that China could reap as well as in the risks it faces. Before all roads lead to Beijing, Xi may be overreaching.

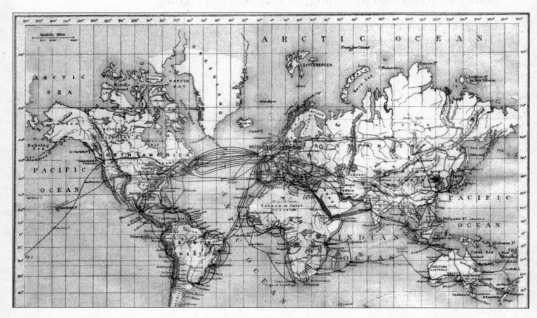

Eastern Telegraph Company's System and Its General Connections, 1901
A.B.C. Telegraphic Code, 5th ed.

CHAPTER TWO

Imperial Echoes

Technology and the Struggle for Control

I F YOU LISTEN CLOSELY, history sometimes more than rhymes. The trick is knowing where, or rather when, to put your ear. Quoting famous explorers like Marco Polo and Ibn Battuta and flashing images of camels and desert caravans, Chinese officials have cloaked the BRI in romanticized notions of the Silk Road. The ancient silk routes set a high-water mark for connectivity in their time, but they were primarily a continental phenomenon focused on overland trade as opposed to a truly global phenomenon where maritime trade dominates, as it has since the sixteenth century. It is a brilliant marketing device, but in critical respects— politically, economically, and technologically—it is misleading.

A more accurate—and alarming—parallel is the great-power competition that lasted from the mid-nineteenth century to World War I, an imperial contest masterfully chronicled by the historian Daniel Headrick.[1] Many of the BRI's key technologies—deepwater ports, high-speed railways, and fiber-optic cables—are direct descendants of technology that Western powers leveraged during this period to expand their access to foreign markets. The costs, unintended consequences, and challenges faced by strong and weak states are telling as well. The world's ruling and rising powers pursued major infrastructure projects to expand their influence at the expense of indigenous people, the environment, and economic stability. As a weaker state, China resisted strategies similar to those it now employs as a rising power.[2]

The echoes are loudest on the ground, where China is figuratively and sometimes literally retracing the steps of imperial powers. In 2018, China began manufacturing a new fiber-optic cable, the Pakistan and East Africa Cable Express, or PEACE, which will become the shortest route for high-speed internet traffic between China and Africa.[3] A century and a half ago, Britain was wrapping the world with telegraph cables to protect its colonial interests, including one through Gwadar, the same port town in Pakistan where China's new cable will begin. China now operates Gwadar's port as part of the China-Pakistan Economic Corridor, a risky endeavor examined in Chapter 7.

Kenya is another primary stop on the PEACE cable. In 2017, it opened a $3.3 billion railway, its most expensive infrastructure project since independence, built with Chinese financing and by Chinese contractors. As Chapter 9 explains, the railway shuttles passengers from Mombasa to Nairobi, running alongside a railway built by the British in 1901 and, over the objections of environmental groups, through Kenya's national parks. Privately, World Bank officials say it would have been cheaper to upgrade the British line. A leaked report from Kenya's auditor general has warned that defaulting on these loans could allow China to take control of Mombasa Port.[4]

Sri Lanka has become the poster child for risky borrowing along China's BRI, a controversy that Chapter 8 examines. In December 2017, a Chinese state-owned enterprise took over a deepwater port in Hambantota, a small fishing town on Sri Lanka's southern coast. The port was never intended to be Chinese owned and operated, but it was Chinese financed and built, adding to a debt that Sri Lanka could not repay.[5] China now has a ninety-nine-year lease, the same length that Britain once secured for Hong Kong. No one needs to draw this connection for Sri Lankans, who won their independence from British colonial rule seventy years ago.

These flagship projects are just a few episodes in China's BRI, a global drama that is still unfolding, yet they evoke familiar plotlines. Since ancient times, infrastructure has been not only a feature or by-product of empire but also a tool for imperial expansion.[6] Rome built a network of roads to carry commerce, information, and the most formidable soldiers in antiquity across an expanding domain. The same road network that Darius the Great used to control the Persian Empire in the fifth century BC was used by Alexander the Great to conquer it two hundred years later. At the height of the ancient silk routes, the Mongol Empire established a network of postal roads that carried messengers and envoys.

Two challenges run through this history to the present, and technology is at the center of both. Great powers face the challenge of improving connectivity while maintaining control. For most of history, physical distance and terrain shaped communication possibilities. The time to send a message from one town to another was the time it took to travel, on foot or horseback, between those towns. Transportation and communication infrastructure were one and the same. The emergence of the telegraph broke that relationship, leapfrogging communication ahead of transportation for the first time. But far from resolving the tension between connectivity and control, the telegraph and its successors have only further complicated it.

Weaker states face the challenge of developing economically while maintaining their independence. Infrastructure projects hold out the promise of growth, connecting communities and serving as the backbone of modern economies. Foreign powers can offer financing, expertise, and technology that would otherwise be unavailable. But foreign assistance rarely comes without strings attached, and the construction of a project is not the same as transferring the knowledge required to build and operate it. The promise of new infrastructure is almost universally attractive, but for states courting foreign investment, the benefits are easy to exaggerate, while the true costs and risks are often downplayed.

The most striking change is that China, having played the role of the weaker state, is now grappling with the challenges that accompany its rising power and expanding global footprint. The script has been flipped, although as with all historical comparisons, there are important differences. New technologies open avenues for influence, while international institutions and norms moderate today's global connectivity competition.

To understand these challenges, there is no better year to begin than 1869, when three megaprojects shrank the world. The U.S. transcontinental railway, the Suez Canal, and the Indo-European Telegraph leveraged new technologies to carry people, goods, and information faster than ever before. In the West, these projects are popularly remembered as symbols of progress. In hindsight, the story looks very different, not only from the perspective of the weaker states, which often sacrificed political autonomy for relatively little economically, but also from the vantage point of the great powers themselves, whose overwhelming drive to build and expand concealed risks lurking beneath the surface. Every connection brings disruption, and no one foresaw how these projects, and the new technologies they harnessed, would unfold.

"A Province Conquered"

Cannons erupted on November 17, 1869, as a French imperial yacht *L'Aigle* (the *Eagle*) was scheduled to begin the first journey through the newly created Suez Canal. Empress Eugenie, the wife of Napoleon III, was sitting aboard. Behind the French yacht, a flotilla of forty ships carried European diplomats and royalty, including the emperor of Austria, the crown prince of Prussia, and the princes of the Netherlands and Hanover.[7] The idea of linking the Mediterranean and the Red Sea had captivated rulers from the pharaohs to Napoleon, but the former considered it impossible and the latter too costly. The project became the world's most expensive infrastructure project after a decade of deal making, construction delays, and cost overruns. Finally, the moment had arrived.

The Suez was so historic that a representative from the Vatican blessed the canal a day before its opening. "A time has arrived which is not just one of the most solemn of the century," he began, "but also one of the greatest and most decisive that mankind has seen since the beginning of its history here." The canal was bringing the West and the East closer together, and he speculated that political harmony could follow. He concluded by urging, "let us turn our thoughts not just to the image of each country but to the grandeur of the whole of humanity."[8]

That message evaporated literally overnight. Under the cover of darkness, a British naval ship, the HMS *Newport*, maneuvered out of its assigned spot. When the sun rose, it was sitting at the front of the line, ahead of even the imperial French yacht, and positioned so it was impossible for other ships to pass. Empress Eugenie was forced to watch the British ship glide into the canal first. The ship's captain, George Nares, was officially reprimanded but privately praised by his superiors and later promoted. From the moment the canal opened, rather than moderating the global competition for influence, the Suez only intensified it.

The Suez was also a massive bet on technological trends. When the project began, most of the world's ships were powered by wind. Twenty years after its completion, steam power was dominant on the world's seas, a trend the canal both harnessed and accelerated.[9] It was also steam power that carved the canal out of the desert. Specially designed dredges pumped mud out of the canal, barges shuttled heavy equipment, and locomotives replaced camels and mules. Much of the work was carried out in previously inaccessible areas and sweltering heat. "The Suez Canal is not only a waterway, it is a province conquered from the desert," bragged a former general counsel of the Suez Canal Company, which built and operated the canal until the 1956 Suez Crisis.[10]

Few projects in history have bent geography as the Suez did. Previously, a ship sailing from Asia to Europe was required to go around the Cape of Good Hope, a distance the canal cut in half. As a correspondent for the *New York Times* noted, "It is to Europe what a new Pacific Railroad . . . is to the United States."[11] The canal was many things: a marvel of modern engineering, a giant shortcut for commerce in a flattening world, and a fast lane for European powers to push farther into Asia.[12]

The canal brought the world closer together, but it delivered surprisingly little for Egypt, the country at its center. In the 1850s, to finance a modernization push, the Egyptian government ventured deeply and dangerously into international capital markets. If Egypt's rulers were aware of the risks, the outside money was too tempting to refuse, and they basked in the attention that came with announcing new projects. Mohamed Sa'id Pasha, the khedive of Egypt and Sudan when the canal was started, arranged for Egypt's first loans and spent lavishly. When he died in 1863, the government's debt had risen to five times its tax revenue.[13] His nephew and successor, Isma'il Pasha, continued the spending spree, including borrowing $1 million for the canal's opening celebrations.[14]

Both Sa'id and Isma'il had promised that the canal belonged to Egypt, but the deal to build the canal was designed to extract local value rather than create it.[15] The ninety-nine-year concession agreement was slanted toward the Suez Canal Company, which assumed all costs but gained the lion's share of future earnings. Under the deal, Egypt received 15 percent of the company's annual profits, the company's founders received 10 percent, and its shareholders received 75 percent. The route for the canal had not been decided, but the agreement gave the Suez Company expansive land rights and twenty thousand unpaid laborers each year.[16] The company was assuming a great risk, pioneering the largest infrastructure project in history; but its powers were vast, and the potential rewards were far from equitably shared.

Nor was the technology that created the canal meaningfully diffused among the greater Egyptian population. The Suez Company complained that local staff lacked essential skills, and rather than train them, it preferred to recruit workers from Europe.[17] At the canal's blessing, the Vatican representative claimed, "Egypt, destined to reap the first of the fruits of this great labour, will call you the one who brought about her renaissance, and history will reserve a glorious and truly earned page for the Khedive Ismail."[18] Egyptians benefited from improved water systems but gained only a fraction of the human capital they had been promised. Like the canal itself, the technological "renaissance" ran through Egypt, but it was not diffused throughout it.

Meanwhile, Egypt's infrastructure binge was eroding its sovereignty. Its external debt increased twenty-three-fold between 1862 and 1875, when Egypt was forced to sell its 45 percent stake in the Suez Canal to Britain.[19] After Egypt went bankrupt the following year, representatives from Britain and France were put in charge of the government's revenue and expenditures. In 1882, Britain invaded and colonized Egypt.

The canal's impact on global trade was unexpected. To the horror of the canal's French backers, British ships captured most of the gains. As steamships became dominant, Britain had the ship-building capabilities and capital to expand its fleet. France and other European governments, including Italy, Russia, and Austria-Hungary, all expected that their proximity to the canal would come at Britain's expense. But Britain's distance from the canal proved a boon. Its ships had better-balanced flows of goods, especially to the East, where they carried manufactured goods and textiles from India. British ships carried 60 percent of the canal's total tonnage during its first year of operation and 80 percent in 1880. The canal was "cut by French energy and Egyptian money for British advantage," the *Economist* quipped.[20]

The Suez intensified foreign competition in China. Thanks to the canal and the rise of steamships, Western merchants were able to reach China faster and fill their ships with greater volumes of goods, putting pressure on the existing system of treaty ports.[21] That commercial pressure, which brought more steamships and foreigners to China's shores, and subsequent military action expanded the number of ports in the following decades. Fifty years later, there were thirty-two ports open to foreign trade, and by 1917, the number had ballooned to ninety-two, including sixty-nine formal treaty ports.[22] Naturally, foreign competition did not stop at the water's edge.

Greater activity at China's ports increased the demand for access to its interior. Chinese authorities sought to limit foreign access to the treaty ports, but as foreign trade increased, so did requests for better infrastructure to support the ports. Western traders wanted railways to shuttle cargo and raw materials, especially coal to fuel their ships and telegraph lines to communicate with the mainland and receive orders from home.[23] Both technologies were popular in the West, but the Chinese government rightfully viewed its foreign backers with suspicion. In London, a Chinese diplomat was alarmed to discover a public report with a map that included a proposed railway network running through his country. "Then I first realized that their ambitions were not limited to occupying the treaty ports," he later wrote.[24]

China's ambitions are now being questioned as it pushes into ports around the world. In Greece, China has used its checkbook to take the port of Piraeus, as Chapter 5 details, accomplishing what the Persian King Xerxes failed to do with overwhelming force twenty-five hundred years ago. China's projects in Pakistan, Kenya, and Sri Lanka—mentioned earlier and examined in greater detail in Chapters 7, 8, and 9—illustrate its growing reach and associated risks. In Djibouti, China has built a shipping terminal next to its first military base on foreign soil, and U.S. officials worry it will take control of another shipping terminal, as Chapter 9 also explains. China does not "occupy" these ports in the same way colonial powers did, of course, but the BRI's aims are even more expansive.

"The People Insist"

Six months before the Suez Canal bridged two seas, a connection forged of steel caught the world's attention. On May 10, 1869, Leland Stanford, a California business magnate, drove a golden stake into the ground at Promontory Summit, Utah, connecting the Union Pacific and Central Pacific railways and completing the world's first transcontinental railway. For a country that had been at war with itself four years earlier, the railway was a potent symbol. The United States was healing divisions, racing west to fulfill its destiny, and conquering time and space with new technologies. Only later would the railway's true costs become clearer.[25]

The United States' transcontinental railways were not kind to those who lived in their path or to those who built them. Carrying troops and settlers, the railways expedited the breakup and deaths of western Native tribes. Railway workers endured long hours and dangerous conditions for little pay. Many of them were foreign, including thousands of Chinese workers, who were discriminated against and forced to pay for their own lodging, food, and tools. Hundreds of them died.[26] Chinese workers even partially drove the final spike into the ground so that Leland Stanford and the other VIPs taking ceremonial swings would not lose any dignity, and after the ceremony, they replaced the golden spike with standard equipment.[27]

Like China's BRI, the expansion of the railroad was made possible in the first place by cozy relations between government and large corporations. In 1862, President Abraham Lincoln signed the Pacific Railway Act, which issued land grants directly to corporations for the first time. Among other subsidies, the government provided a series of land grants that, if combined today, would be larger than California.[28] But lacking transparency and effective oversight, this cooperation led to corruption. Most infamously, the construction company Credit Mobilier inflated its fees and bribed American politicians with cash and discounted stock. Among those paid were the secretary of the treasury, the vice president, and four senators. Kickbacks also secured the support of state legislators and judges, who had threatened to hold up projects.

Speed was prized above safety. U.S. land grants and loans required completing projects, which incentivized using temporary wooden structures and other short-term solutions. Railway executives publicly challenged their competitors to see who could build fastest. In 1869, the head of the Central Pacific Railroad company won a bet by pushing his workers to lay ten miles of track in a single day.[29] It was not long before the emphasis on quantity over quality showed. Bridges failed, engine boilers exploded, and trains derailed. Mismanaged timetables and single-tracked routes led to deadly train collisions.[30] During the same period in Britain, railway engineers painstakingly ensured that tracks were as close to level as possible. The process was slower and more expensive in the short term; but these projects lasted longer, and many of the bridges and tunnels that were built in Britain then remain in use today.

As more track appeared than the market needed, the value of everything the railways carried was distorted. New land was eagerly exploited, and wheat, cattle, coal, and silver production skyrocketed. Towns like Dodge City, Kansas, grew rapidly as they were connected to markets in the east of the country. Later, as the railways moved farther west and closer to sources of cattle and other commodities, many boom towns went bust. The Dakotas became a natural experiment in state support, as the historian Richard White recounts in *Railroaded*.[31] In South Dakota, railways emerged more gradually to meet demand, and farmers settled in areas that were more naturally advantageous for their crops. But in North Dakota, land grants and subsidies encouraged rapid construction, driving up land prices and oversettling less fertile land.

Early signs suggest that China's BRI will suffer from similar excesses. Between one-third and half of Chinese transportation projects in Eurasia generate little value, according to a World Bank study.[32] Another World Bank study cautioned that Azerbaijan,

Mongolia, and Tajikistan, all early supporters of the BRI, stand to lose because infrastructure costs are likely to exceed the potential gains.[33] New railway services from China to Europe, as Chapter 3 explains, often win positive headlines for China's BRI, but they are heavily subsidized and face structural challenges. In Southeast Asia, covered in Chapter 6, China is building massive railways with troubling social costs and questionable economic value.

The United States' railway misadventure shows how economic missteps can give way to environmental disasters. Land was over-farmed and overgrazed. Mining companies dammed rivers, dyna-mited mountains, and poisoned soil and water. Hunters killed buffalo for their hides and meat and merely for sport, driving them almost to extinction. The destruction that U.S. railways wrought was not ig-nored as much as celebrated. During an eighteen-month stretch, a Kansas Pacific Railway contractor, William Cody, killed 4,280 buffa-loes to feed workers, earning him the nickname "Buffalo Bill."

Just as Chinese officials dare not challenge the BRI, the United States' westward expansion was rarely questioned after it began. As *Harper's* reported in 1867, "The work is now one of such national importance that the people insist upon its vigorous prosecution as positively as they insisted on the prosecution of the last war."[34] There could be no turning back or slowing down. Main lines branched into trunk lines, which gave way to local lines. During the 1860s alone, twenty-two thousand miles of new track were built in the United States, a feat that was nearly doubled the fol-lowing decade. Construction begat construction. Few people, if anyone, understood how all the pieces fit together.

Even fewer noticed the financial risks that were accumulating. U.S. railway excesses brought the U.S. economy to its knees—not once but twice. In 1873, a European stock-market crisis led inves-tors to dump U.S. railway bonds. With railway companies unable to find more buyers for their bonds, many of them failed, as did one of the nation's largest banks. The railway bubble burst again in 1893, leading to the deepest depression up to that point in U.S. history.

Chinese workers completed the world's first transcontinental railway in the United States, but it would take another decade before China began to build its first railway, let alone a national railway network. During the 1860s, several foreign companies pro-

posed building new lines in China, but the Qing government rejected all of them. Frustrated, some Western officials took the
rejections as evidence of China's backwardness. But the Qing government's caution was much more rational, and strategic, than
Western officials realized. Chinese authorities were more concerned about foreign influence than about the technology itself.

Chinese officials understood that the railways would bring economic disruptions and could allow foreign powers to expand their
access and influence into mainland China. "If ever a railroad exists
on Chinese territory, it must be a Chinese and not a foreign undertaking," a provincial governor explained in 1865."[35] They also worried that any damage to foreign projects within China would be
used to justify intervention and to extract additional concessions.
As one Chinese official wrote, "It will ruin the field and destroy the
livelihood of our people. The people's anger will be aroused and
they will band together and fight. . . . If the foreigners claim they
can look after and protect railways, we must reply that Chinese officials cannot forbid the people [to attack the railways] and will not
pay indemnities." Those very fears would be realized decades later
during the Boxer Rebellion, when foreign powers took further territorial concessions at the expense of Chinese sovereignty.[36]

Misreading this situation, Western companies believed they
could win over the Chinese government by simply demonstrating
the railway's commercial potential. In 1873, a British firm considered giving the emperor of China a railway as a wedding present,
an idea that was publicly supported by several British nobility.
"The Emperor of China is not likely to come to Europe to see railways, so it is proposed to take the railway to him," a British newspaper explained. "If the railway itself were brought within reach of
the personal knowledge of the Emperor and his Court, the present
hesitation (and whatever there may be left of opposition) would
soon give place to an enthusiastic desire for railway travelling."[37]
The British chargé d'affaires in Beijing discouraged the idea, which
faded away as less generous schemes moved forward.

While some Western companies tried persuasion, others decided to ask forgiveness rather than permission. In 1872, a senior
U.S. diplomat in Shanghai, O. B. Bradford, began leasing land for
the construction of a "carriage road" from Shanghai's waterfront

into the city. To avoid violating a U.S. treaty with China, Bradford
sold his lease to a British firm, which concealed its true purpose
under a front organization named "Woosung Road Company."[38]
By mid-February 1878, the company laid about a mile of railway
track. Ignoring the objections of the local authorities after the
project was discovered, it imported a locomotive, began operations,
and continued extending the line until August, when a Chinese
man walked in front of the train and was killed.

Both sides were eager to defuse tensions, and they reached a
deal allowing the Chinese government to purchase the railway.
The Chinese were satisfied because they reasserted control, making the foreign project their own. The British were satisfied because they believed that the project had served its purpose. The
Woosung Road Company even made a handsome profit, in a fraction of the normal time. Before the railway was halted, it was carrying enough passengers that it became commercially profitable.
This commercial success, its British backers assumed, would naturally lead to more railway projects.

What the Qing government did next shocked the British. It
began disassembling the railway, a move that the British viewed as
the very antithesis of progress. In fact, Chinese officials had local
economic interests to protect. The railway could carry cargo that
would otherwise travel along Woosung Creek on Chinese vessels.[39]
Chinese officials also worried that foreign companies would use the
line to smuggle goods between Shanghai and Woosung and that
more railways would quickly follow.[40] In seeking to avoid the railway's disruption, Chinese officials understood the unintended consequences of railways even better than their Western counterparts did.

Recognizing that the Woosung railway was built by foreign companies to serve foreign interests, Chinese officials attempted to transform the project to better serve their own interests. They planned to
reassemble the railway in Formosa (Taiwan) to strengthen its defense
from attack. The rails were moved but never reassembled, perhaps
due to a lack of funding.[41] After the Woosung's removal, a handful of
rail projects emerged in the following two decades, but it would take
a military defeat to shift the government's position.

At the outbreak of the Sino-Japanese War in 1894, the Qing
government had less than two hundred miles of rail, and its defeat

marked a major turning point in the government's industrial policy.[42] Chinese officials singled out railways, and Japan's successful
modernization program, as a key element of national power. Tellingly, the government body responsible for China's foreign affairs
was put in charge of railway matters.[43] Just as foreign threats
shaped the Qing's early railway policy, which was mainly defensive
and sought to limit the influence of foreign powers, they brought
about a major shift at the end of the nineteenth century.[44]

That shift put China in a position that is even more familiar to
many of its partners along the BRI. Building railways required foreign capital and expertise, and China was lacking both. It began
borrowing heavily. Early loans typically had interest rates in the
range of 5–6 percent and ran for thirty years, but later commitments were higher interest and shorter duration. A particularly
egregious example was a single-year loan at 9.5 percent interest—
the infrastructure equivalent of modern payday-lending scams.[45]

As the weaker party in these negotiations, China agreed to
terms that favored its larger foreign partners. Lenders also secured
construction rights, which they used to extract additional commis-
sions for supplying materials, and rights to railway profits until the
loans were repaid. By 1931, foreign loans for railways were approx-
imately half of the Chinese government's total foreign debt, and
nearly 40 percent of those payments were in default.[46] China was
the victim of the predatory lending practices for which it is now
criticized.

"Shout It from the Rooftops"

Like the U.S. transcontinental railway and the Suez Canal, a third
global link completed in 1869 would eventually carry far-reaching
and unintended consequences. That year, as the British eyed the
Suez's maritime route to India, they were desperate for a reliable
telegraph connection.[47] In 1853, the British government had begun
connecting India's major cities, and by 1865, India had twenty-
eight thousand kilometers of telegraph. British authorities de-
pended on these lines to suppress an uprising two years later,
cementing their strategic importance to the empire. At the same
time, London was establishing itself as the central node in global

telegraph networks, but the empire lacked a fast and reliable link to its crown jewel.

The existing connection's poor performance reflected the technical challenges of early telegraphy and the Eurasian supercontinent's geopolitical landscape. In 1865, sending a message from Britain to India took five to six days and involved twelve to fourteen relay stations.[48] At each transfer station, staff received, decoded, and physically handed the message to another operator, who recoded and transmitted on the next system.[49] Sometimes messages arrived mangled by the operators who had relayed them. It was an international game of telephone before the telephone, and it was expensive to play. A twenty-word message cost five British pounds, or the equivalent of roughly US$800 today.

Early telegraph wires faced design and operation challenges. In the telegraph's first few decades, there were no international standards, and wires were produced according to various specifications.[50] Through trial and error, engineers were still figuring out what materials were best for different climates and how to protect wires against common threats, from ships' anchors to stormy seas. The first cable to India was laid in two sections, from the Red Sea to Aden and Aden to Karachi.[51] Both failed, leaving the British government to rely on a connection laid in 1865 from the Persian Gulf to Constantinople. The Ottoman Empire sat between Britain and its prize possession.

The British government blamed the countries through which the wires passed. As one member of Parliament demanded, something must be done to "avoid the delays, and errors arising from transmission at the hands of those working the present land route, comprising half-educated half-castes, Turks, Austrians, etc., who all combine in mutilating and mangling the plain English of our messages."[52] His colleagues applauded. Others pointed out the risk of espionage as messages traveled across Europe's chessboard of rivalries.

The solution was more wires touching friendly territory and dedicated operators. In 1866, a select committee appointed by the House of Commons concluded, "That, having regard to the magnitude of the interests—political, commercial and social—involved in the connection between this country and India, it is not expedient that the means of intercommunication by telegraph should be dependent upon any single line, or any single system of wires, in the hands of several foreign governments, and under several distinct responsibilities, however well such services may be conducted as a whole, in time of peace." The following year, the British government pledged to provide support for surveying new routes to its eastern colonies, negotiating access with foreign governments, and laying cables.[53]

Sensing a windfall, the Prussian firm Siemens und Halske proposed a new line through Persia and Russia that avoided the Ottoman Empire. It was a family effort for the Siemens brothers. One brother handled negotiations with Britain, another dealt with Russia, a third handled Persia, and a fourth helped automate the process for passing messages between receiving stations. The project was complete in 1869 and went into service the next year. The first message from London to Kolkata took twenty-eight minutes. Ecstatic, Werner Siemens wrote to his brother Carl, "Shout it from the rooftops that the 10 to 12 hours to the Red Sea have been beaten by our one minute to Tehran and 28 minutes to Calcutta."[54] In early 1870, a competing cable was laid via the Red Sea, touching only Egypt and further minimizing Britain's dependence on foreign territories.[55]

Before long, Britain's commercial dominance of global telegraph networks provided strategic dividends. At the turn of the century, the British government developed a separate system of cables, known as the "All Red" routes, which touched only Britain and its possessions. As the network grew, the British treasury opposed some of these projects on economic grounds. But it was largely outmaneuvered by the British Army, Navy, and other defense organizations, which "developed a virtual fetish" for the routes, as the historian Paul Kennedy writes.[56] These investments had little commercial value, but they proved prescient in the coming years as competition among Europe's great powers escalated and finally spiraled out of control.

For German officials, the guns of August were followed by a deadly silence. On August 5, 1914, a day after declaring war on Germany, Britain cut five of Germany's telegraph cables, which remained disabled for the duration of the war.[57] Britain's advantages stemmed not only from owning and operating physical infrastructure but also from the abilities of its companies and the international standards they set.[58] Britain's largest telegraph company manufactured two-thirds of the cables used during the nineteenth century and almost half thereafter. In 1896, there were thirty cable-laying ships in the world, and twenty-four were British owned.[59] Britain's monopolizing the expertise to lay cables meant that its rivals struggled to repair damaged cables.

What British officials did not foresee was the telegraph's potential to fracture their empire from the inside out. The Indo-European telegraph cable, and the vast network of which it was a part, carried not only Britain's colonial commands but also potent ideas for change. Nationalist movements used these tools in their fights for independence, and Britain's censors were unable to stem the flow of news and communication. As the historian Daniel Headrick explains, "The increasing ability of Indians to acquire and disseminate ideas and information, using the very media of communication that the British had introduced, did not make British rule permanent, but undermined it instead."[60]

The vast majority of the world's governments were eager to adopt the telegraph during the 1860s and 1870s, but the Chinese government worked to prevent and then tightly control its introduction. Considering the new technology, Shen Baozhen, the same Chinese official who later oversaw the dismantling of the Woosung railway, worried in 1865, "It will be even more difficult to prevent dissemination of unfounded rumors in newspapers, frightening people."[61] Like China's caution with railways, its initial resistance to the telegraph and eventual adoption of it were driven in large part by national security concerns.

Initially, the gravest threat was not the information carried by the telegraph lines but the foreign powers that were eager to build them. As China's leading foreign-affairs body concluded in 1870, "When foreigners are allowed to take one step forward, they rush ahead. . . . With galloping speed [they will] incessantly attempt to penetrate into the interior and with ever-changing ventures pursue their shrewd schemes."[62] Telegraph wires were even more vulnerable than railways to theft or damage, Chinese officials reasoned, and any loss could invite foreign powers to intervene directly.

Of course, the Qing government's official position reflected a variety of views, not all of them opposed to the telegraph. There was interest among China's merchant class in extending the telegraph network, for example, but there were also other reasons for opposition. Provincial officials worried that the telegraph would erode their autonomy by increasing the central government's responsiveness and demands.[63] Foreign diplomats had similar concerns. Officially, British diplomats were among the most active advocates for the introduction of telegraph lines in China. Privately, they expressed concerns about London's micromanagement of their affairs from afar.[64] The representatives of the empire loathed imperiousness when it threatened their own power.

Foreign firms pressed ahead with a series of creative, and legally dubious, attempts to land cables in China. In the late 1860s, Chinese authorities agreed to allow underwater cables that landed on ships. They may have reasoned the underwater cables were less vulnerable to theft and vandalism, or perhaps they recognized they would be unable to prevent the foreign companies from proceeding. Playing a game of red-light, green-light, the foreign firms inched closer to shore without formal permission. They moved from floating vessels to docks, to makeshift structures near the beach, and finally into the open air within the treaty ports and land controlled by foreigners. Among the first open-air cables was a line erected along the path of the Woosung railway. Chinese officials initially ordered it dismantled along with the railway in 1878 but later changed their position.[65]

By the late 1870s, Chinese officials had begun to recognize that their policy was self-defeating. Initially, they had worried that adopting the telegraph would give foreigners an information advantage. China also lacked the technical expertise to operate, let alone construct, the lines. Foreigners providing those services would have access to Chinese official messages before the intended recipients did. But foreign powers were utilizing that same technology on their shores while they relied on older methods. "Apparently the foreigners are very persistent in their intention to construct telegraph lines," Shen Baozhen wrote in 1870. "If we merely allow them to construct telegraphs on their own, then when there is a need to communicate on secret matters, they will be informed in one or two days, while after more than ten days have passed, we shall still be ignorant."[66]

Security concerns drove the expansion of China's telegraph network in the following decades. Relying initially on foreign support,

especially the Great Northern, a Danish firm, for engineers, supplies, and even teachers for a telegraph school, the Chinese government gradually developed its own expertise. New lines emerged to
help address changing security threats.[67] During the mid-1880s, re-
acting to French forces in Vietnam, China added lines in its southern provinces. A decade later, as tensions escalated with Japanese
forces in Korea, China built more lines in the north. The technology that was viewed as a dangerous back door for foreign powers
became a necessity for keeping foreign powers at bay.

But like the British, the Qing government was unable to dull the
other side of the telegraph's sword. The same wires that carried the
central government's orders also helped the revolutionary groups
that sought to overthrow it. In 1911, years of popular resentment
and government missteps exploded as Chinese military units and
provinces began breaking away from the government. The telegraph
was not the cause of the Qing's fall, but it was a consequential tool,
available to groups that protected the status quo as well as forces
fighting for change. The same events might have unfolded slowly
decades earlier, in the era of couriers on horseback, giving the government time to put down the initial uprising. But with the telegraph, news traveled faster than government forces could, and the
uprising became a revolution.[68] Having unsuccessfully fought the introduction of the telegraph, the Qing dynasty fell after adopting it.

China's Turn

China's experience as a target of colonialism may be more
important than its imperial past. During the second half of the
nineteenth century, China faced the impossible choice between
pursuing its economic aspirations with foreign investment and the
political imperative of maintaining its sovereignty. Shortly after
suffering defeats to the British, China was understandably too
defensive, favoring sovereignty at the expense of new technology
that others, including Japan, were successfully adopting. Its caution
ultimately became a liability, and it paid a price during the Sino-
Japanese War for not developing its railway system, during the
Boxer Rebellion for developing that system, and afterward when it
borrowed too heavily to catch up.

From President Xi down, Chinese officials uniformly and emphatically reject accusations of colonialism along the BRI. "No matter what stage of development it reaches, China will never seek hegemony or engage in expansion," Xi explained at the National Communist Party Congress in 2017, a line that other officials have repeated.[69] To reassure the world about China's future intentions, Chinese officials and academics reflexively point to the past, claiming that it is not in China's "DNA" to colonize other countries.[70] Of course, as the Qing dynasty consolidated power, it employed many of the same techniques for control within its expanding contiguous borders as European powers applied outside their own.[71]

Dangerously, China now confronts the challenge faced by past empires but without having made the same mistakes internationally as those that came before it. In the wake of two world wars, Western powers have established international institutions that set guidelines for foreign lending, capping interest rates and conducting environmental- and social-impact assessments, among other requirements. Chinese officials promise that they care about these objectives as well, but they have been unwilling to implement the same practices.

As Chinese officials respond to criticism about their current infrastructure efforts, they recall this history and cry hypocrisy. After all, today's developed countries were not required to meet high environmental and social standards when they were developing in the nineteenth and early twentieth centuries. Is the international community now setting a higher bar or a double standard? But this is a dangerous misreading of history. The United States, for example, developed not because of its railway misadventures but in spite of them. Had U.S. railway construction proceeded more slowly, reflecting market needs rather than insider interests, the United States would have enjoyed more of the railway's benefits with fewer of its costs.

As the following chapters show, the BRI is at root an imperial project, harnessing new technologies to old ends. Some of these are the latest generation of basic technology that was used during the nineteenth century, including automated ports, high-speed rail, and fiber-optic cables. Others could bring more revolutionary changes, including remote sensors that sweep up vast amounts of data and artificial intelligence that sorts it. There is also fundamental tension between the connectivity that Beijing claims to seek through the BRI and the control it is unwilling to give up, as Chapter 10 concludes.

Without a doubt, China's BRI will carry unintended consequences. Connectivity is often fetishized, viewed in Silicon Valley as a good in itself rather than as a means to an end. The historical record is sobering. The silk routes carried not only spices and ideas but also the bubonic plague.[72] Railways were the pride of a divided America and the catalyst for two recessions. Britain's telegraph wires provided commercial and strategic advantages before hastening the loss of its prized colonial possession. As China races forward with the largest foreign infrastructure push in history, its foreign partners, its competitors, and even its own officials will be surprised.

PART II

To Europe

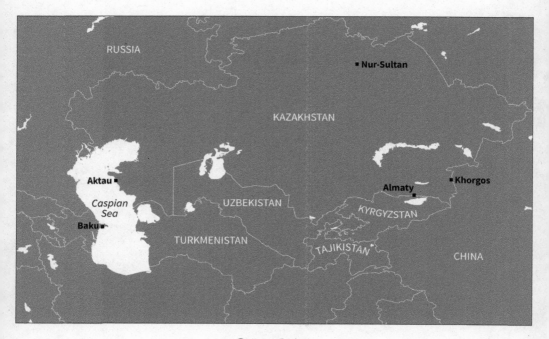

Central Asia

Center for Strategic and International Studies, Reconnecting Asia Project

CHAPTER THREE

The Crossroads

Central Asia

THE CENTER OF THE world is surprisingly close to the middle of nowhere. In human terms, the center of the world is the city with the smallest average distance to every person on the planet. It is always shifting, as populations fluctuate, but one estimate puts it at Almaty, Kazakhstan.[1] The world's furthest point from any ocean, the middle of nowhere, sits in western China, near its border with Kazakhstan. Geographers call it the "Eurasian point of inaccessibility."[2] Less than a hundred miles away, China and Kazakhstan are making a massive bet to turn that label on its head.

Early one morning in May 2017, I set out from Almaty to visit Khorgos Gateway, a massive industrial zone and logistics facility that straddles the Chinese-Kazakh border. During the three-hour drive, I saw more livestock than people on the road. Every so often, our car slowed to a halt and waited for a herd of goats or sheep to pass. Most wandered the flat green plains unattended. To the south, snow-capped mountains, part of the Tian Shan range, hung in the background like a giant's lower teeth. The highway was under construction, and smooth new segments interspersed with older stretches that seemed to have more potholes than road.

Just miles away from Khorgos, our car was stopped by police. We pulled over, joining a small line of cars. An officer approached, and rather than waiting inside the car, my driver stepped out. I watched in the mirror as he was escorted away and into the backseat of a police car. He returned a few minutes later, unfazed. I asked what happened. "Money," he said in Russian, rubbing his thumb and forefingers together as he pulled the car back onto the road. The cost was about a fifth of what I had paid the driver for the ride, and he must have priced the bribe into the fare, because he did not ask for more. The shakedown was as routine as filling up with gas.

"Welcome! How was the drive? Did you meet the police?" my host at Khorgos Gateway said with a smile. Donning orange hard hats, required for touring the grounds, we set out to see the facilities.

"New Dubai"

Before arriving, I had looked at satellite images from 2010, which showed undeveloped brown steppe. The same area is now equipped with customs and immigration facilities and dormitories for thousands of workers, although only 250 were employed in 2018.[3] Early promoters of the facility promised it would become a "New Dubai" and projected that by 2020, economic activity at Khorgos would increase twenty-fold, supporting fifty thousand jobs—a dramatic transformation that has yet to occur.[4] The nearby town of Nurkent, which had twelve hundred residents at the end of 2017, is optimistically projected to grow to one hundred thousand by 2035.[5] Kazakhstan is building it, but on this steppe of dreams, it is far from guaranteed they will come.

The lifeblood of Khorgos is railway traffic, and its beating heart are giant yellow container cranes, which span parallel sets of Chinese and Russian railway tracks. Because railways in Russia and across the former Soviet Union are wider than the standard gauge used in China and most of Europe, cargo must be swapped at the border. Popular legend holds that tsarist Russia picked a different gauge to defend against invasion. In truth, it is more likely that the decision was initially made for efficiency and safety reasons.[6] As more track was constructed, the cost of switching to standard gauge became too high.

Khorgos is a gamble that overland trade will be more competitive in the future than it has been during the past half millennium. In the late fifteenth century, the invention of large oceangoing vessels and new navigation methods made maritime trade cheaper and faster. Mercantilism and competition among Europe's colonial powers pulled commerce to the coastlines. Political disintegration in Eurasia's heartlands, which brought conflict and harder borders, reinforced this shift. Since then, trade between Asia and Europe has traveled primarily by sea. In 2016, rail carried just under 1 percent of trade between China and Europe by volume and just over 2 percent by value. Maritime shipping carried 94 percent of China-Europe trade by weight and nearly two-thirds of trade by value.[7]

Central Asia's Soviet past still casts a shadow, standing in the way of east-west routes through the region. When Soviet planners looked south, they did not see a collection of republics but a single political entity. They created road, rail, air, and energy networks running north-south with Moscow at the center. These networks were further cemented by divisions of labor that were intended to keep the republics dependent on Moscow. Rather than allowing any single place to become efficient at producing railway technology, tasks were spread across workshops in different republics, so that one handled passenger carriages, another repaired diesel locomotives, and so on.[8] Requests for repairs or new construction were routed through Moscow. As the Soviet economy slowed, so did its railways. By the late 1980s, nearly a third of railway maintenance positions were vacant, due to funding shortfalls. Fixing the railways, according to one estimate, would have taken sixty-six years.[9]

When the Soviet Union split into fifteen separate countries in 1991, these struggling but still functional networks were cut into pieces.[10] The railway from Kyrgyzstan's capital, Bishkek, to its second-largest city, Osh, passed through Kazakhstan, Uzbekistan, Tajikistan, and Uzbekistan again before finally arriving back in Kyrgyzstan.[11] Just before the collapse of the Soviet Union, nearly 150 trains ran weekly between Uzbekistan, Tajikistan, and Kyrgyzstan and other Soviet regions, mostly in what became Russia. Ten years later, only fourteen trains connected them with Russia.[12] Many of the region's flights still connect through Moscow. Due to political tensions, the first commercial flight between the capitals of Tajikistan and Uzbekistan did not fly until 2017.[13] The state-run airline of Turkmenistan, the most insular of the five Central Asian states, has direct flights to London, Moscow, and Beijing but not to the Central Asian capitals of Bishkek, Dushanbe, or Tashkent.

After the fall of the Soviet Union, proposals for rekindling "silk roads" began sprouting up, most of them as ambitious as they were underresourced. The European Union was among the first to take up the mantle, establishing an initiative it dubbed "the renaissance of the Great Silk Road." That imaginative appeal might have been lost in the effort's less silky name, the Transport Corridor Europe-Caucasus Central Asia, or TRACECA, for almost short. TRACECA was bogged down by disputes among the newly independent Central Asian governments and conflict in the Caucuses. Its focus on transport through Baku, Azerbaijan, and Poti, Georgia, was politically appealing, as the route avoided Russia, but economically uncompetitive, since it involved two ferry crossings and more tariffs.[14]

Several others joined the fray. In 1996, a United Nations committee approved adding Central Asian countries to the Asian Highway Network, or AHN. The AHN was formally launched in 1959, but having not received significant funding since 1975, it has become a loose coordinating body and observer rather than a catalyst.[15] Committee meetings are held to add or subtract priority projects from a master list, which helps share information but does not impose any requirements or restrictions on countries to integrate their efforts. Every few years, it issues an update on the status of transportation links, assuming the participating countries have provided information. This is the Silk Road by bureaucracy.

Of all the connectivity plans to run through Central Asia, the Central Asia Regional Economic Cooperation (CAREC) program is perhaps the most successful. Since 1997, it has cut transport costs and travel time across six corridors, which were developed through a collaborative multicountry process that the Asian Development Bank oversaw. Five other multilateral agencies participated in the planning and funding process as well.[16] Once these priorities were agreed on, progress was benchmarked and has been rigorously evaluated in terms of improvements in transit time and cost. China's BRI, by contrast, has thus far brought money without regional consensus building, coherent and consistent plans, or performance testing.

The U.S. Congress even joined the action in 1999, passing the "Silk Road Strategy Act." It aimed to help develop infrastructure and promote trade on an "East-West axis" but only made use of existing foreign assistance. The bill began by looking to the past. "Economic interdependence spurred mutual cooperation among the peoples along the Silk Road," it observed before asserting, "restoration of the historic relationships and economic ties between those peoples is an important element of ensuring their sovereignty as well as the success of democratic and market reforms."[17] This was the Washington Consensus repackaged as a Silk Road. The U.S. government dusted off the Silk Road label a decade later, during the war in Afghanistan, as Chapter 7 describes.

Most of these efforts continue in some form, as does the region's need for better connectivity. In Central Asia, it takes two days, on average, to travel from one main city to another in a neighboring country.[18] Everyone agrees on the need for greater connectivity, but like the Soviet planners who created the region's rusting infrastructure, each new vision reflects its authors' interests. It has proven far easier to announce new efforts than to finish existing projects or to abolish those that have outlived their usefulness. For a region with few connections, duplication is all too common.

Khorgos is itself a duplicate. To the north, there is an older railway connection at Dostyk, opposite Alashankou in China. After putting that connection on hold for years, due to Sino-Soviet tensions, it was finally completed in 1990. The first freight trains arrived in 1991, and by the time passenger trains were running in 1992, they were passing between an independent Kazakhstan and China. Curiously, this older connection receives almost no attention from Western media outlets, which publish a new piece about Khorgos every few months. The Dostyk facility is less efficient, taking about half a day longer to process each train, but as recently as 2018, it was still handling more cargo annually.[19]

Khorgos should overtake Dostyk in the coming years.[20] The railway route between Almaty and Khorgos is four hundred kilometers shorter than the distance to Dostyk. Khorgos has more advanced facilities, and if economic efficiency fails to do the trick, the government of Kazakhstan could direct more traffic from Dostyk to Khorgos, although doing so would deprive the workers and residents of Dostyk of economic activity. Most importantly of all, Khorgos has a patron in China. In 2017, at the Belt and Road Forum in Beijing, China's COSCO shipping took a 49 percent stake in the facility. COSCO's chairman, Xu Lirong, has promised to turn Khorgos into a "regional hub" and "deliver the products of Central Asia, including Kazakhstan, across the sea to the world market."[21] The image of Central Asia selling to the world is a powerful one, but nearly all east-west economic activity does not originate in Central Asia. It passes through.

"Dawn of a New Commercial Era"

China has turned east-west trains into an effective, albeit misleading, advertisement for the BRI.[22] While their role in larger trade terms remains small, China-Europe railway services have grown dramatically in recent years. As recently as 2008, regular direct freight services from China to Europe did not exist.[23] As of March 2019, they connect nearly sixty Chinese cities with nearly fifty European cities.[24] Six times cheaper than air and twice as fast as shipping by sea, rail could provide a compelling middle option for high-value goods like laptops, cell phones, and auto parts.[25] Hewlett Packard was among the first companies to experiment with direct rail shipments from its manufacturing facilities in western China to markets in Europe. An optimistic study, commissioned by a railway industry group, estimates that China-Europe rail services could double their share of trade by volume between 2016 and 2027.[26]

China provides generous subsidies for these routes, making their true economic viability difficult to assess. Subsidies vary in practice, but reports suggest they can account for up to half the total cost of shipping. From 2011 to 2016, China's provincial governments collectively spent over $300 million subsidizing China-Europe block trains, which run as a unit from origin to destination. Provincial governments were so eager to announce new train services that they were undercutting each other with subsidies. Each new service was named after its local champion, creating a long list of services and confusion among prospective customers. In 2016, the China Railway

Company stepped in and announced that all China-Europe trains would be referred to as "China Railway Express."[27]

The railways' economic outlook is cloudy, but their political benefits for China are clear. They have become one of the most visible, albeit misleading, manifestations of China's connectivity ambitions. Xinhua, China's largest state-run news agency, runs articles every few weeks about the China-Europe railways. They have been so eager to promote these routes that even trains terminating in Central Asia are described as new "China-Europe" services.[28] The image of a train traveling across the Eurasian supercontinent is savvy marketing, casting the BRI as practical, peaceful, and historic. With first-time arrivals celebrated in France, Latvia, and Finland, among other countries in recent years, it is tempting to believe that trains are replacing camels on the old Silk Road.

Even countries that have been reluctant to endorse the BRI have embraced China-Europe railways. When a train from Yiwu, China, arrived in London in January 2017, the *Telegraph* called it "a new chapter in the history of the centuries-old trading route," and the *Guardian* said it "heralds the dawn of a new commercial era."[29] In reality, the route was an adjustment from a similarly hyped journey taken between China and Spain in 2014, and the difference between the two routes exists entirely within the EU. On arriving in Duisburg, Germany, the train continued to London instead of Madrid. Given the abundance of transport services between the United Kingdom and Germany, that distinction is hardly groundbreaking.

After touring the container yard in Khorgos, we stepped into the control center. A few rows of desks, each with its own computer screen, faced a giant projector that had been divided into different video feeds. My guide toggled between them to point out the areas we had just visited. Cameras automatically catalogue the license plates of all vehicles entering and exiting the facility. Port-management software recommends how to efficiently unload trains, where to place containers, and which equipment and staff are best for the job. These high-tech features are compelling, but they also mean that fewer people are required to operate the facilities. At successful logistics facilities, cargo is abundant, and people are scarce.

On China's border and beyond, new infrastructure and stream-
lined customs have helped speed the movement of containers.
With state-of-the-art equipment, Khorgos can process a train
twenty hours faster than the older facilities at Dostyk. DP World, a
Dubai-based logistics firm, helps operate the facility, bringing best
practices with them and training local workers. A decade ago, pro-
spective shippers had to coordinate with each country the railway
crossed and navigate a mountain of duplicative paperwork. While
the process remains cumbersome, specialized companies now handle the details. In 2006, it took thirty-six days to ship a forty-foot
container by rail from Shanghai to Hamburg. In 2018, it took just
sixteen days.[30]

But these new routes face several challenges to becoming sustainable. In 2016, the EU imported over $190 billion more goods
from China than it exported to China, an imbalance that is reflected in rail transport patterns. Service operators estimate that
roughly 60 to 70 percent of railway shipments are westbound. On
those eastbound trips, containers are often empty. After arriving in
Europe, other containers are sent back to China by sea.[31] Maritime
shipping offers benefits from scale that the railways will never
match. Modern ships can carry more than a hundred times as much
cargo as a standard train. All this suggests that while rail transport
will increase, it will make up only a modest share of overall trade.

As my tour of Khorgos concluded, there was just one thing
missing: an actual train. Despite the cutting-edge systems and the
talk of Khorgos becoming the next Dubai, there was little noticeable commercial activity under way. Central Asia is second to none
in hospitality, but I suspect that my host's attention was due more
to the absence of competing obligations. My colleague who visited
in 2016 was also unsuccessful. "Maybe it will arrive later today," an
employee told him with a straight face, as they surveyed the vacant
transit zone. My hosts were not holding out hope; or perhaps their
tracking systems were more developed, and they had more accurate information. "Not today," I was told.

The gap between what Khorgos is and what it aspires to
become tests the imagination. It is a clever attempt to turn
weakness—isolation from the world's oceans—into advantage.
That ambition has attracted dozens of reporters, bringing global

attention to one of Kazakhstan and China's flagship joint projects. As the procession of these "news" pieces has continued for several years, with little actual change to report, I have occasionally wondered what fraction of traffic through Khorgos is visitors writing about it—a trend to which I have, of course, contributed.

To the credit of the facility's managers, Khorgos is always living five years into the future. The caravan of researchers and reporters passing through has created a long record of promises that have not been realized. Yet most visitors are still captivated by what Khorgos could become. Rather than question why the facility has not met its 2020 targets from years ago, journalists tend to cite the most recent year of activity and then an ambitious estimate for future growth. The project's managers are dreaming big, and some hype around the project is practical. For new routes to take off, people need to learn that they exist.

Khorgos is more compelling as a model for bringing best practices to Central Asia than as something that will bring change to the rest of the world by shifting significant amounts of trade inland. It is a priority for Kazakhstan's former president Nursultan Nazarbayev, who has a flair for starting from scratch. In December 1997, Nazarbayev moved the nation's capital six hundred miles north, from Almaty to Astana. While Nazarbayev's move was poor economics, it may have been savvy politics, helping to marginalize his political opponents and cement his hold on power.[32] In just twenty years, the city's population grew more than threefold, from 290,000 to 1.1 million people. Shortly after Nazarbayev's retirement was announced in 2019, the city was officially renamed Nursultan.

With similar zeal, Nazarbayev has carved out a special place for Kazakhstan along China's BRI. In September 2013, at Nazarbayev University in Nursultan, Xi first called for building "an economic belt along the Silk Road."[33] Kazakhstan has been at the front of those plans ever since, and Kazakh officials say, half jokingly, that their country intends to be the "buckle" in China's Belt.

More importantly, they have backed up that rhetoric with resources. The following year, in November 2014, Nazarbayev unveiled his own plan for improving Kazakhstan's infrastructure. Called "Nurly Jol," meaning "Bright Path," it entails investments of $40 billion by 2020 and aims to turn Kazakhstan into an east-west trade hub. With favorable geography and natural-resource wealth on which to draw, Kazakhstan is the best positioned among the Central Asian nations to become a hub.

"China Is Playing Monopoly"

But Kazakhstan's rising generation aspires to even more. In May 2018, I gave a presentation at Nazarbayev University, and one of the students asked a simple question with big implications: "Can Kazakhstan use the Belt and Road to become a place where people want to stay, a place that sends things to the world, rather than a place that things pass through?" If Kazakhstan's only gain from the BRI is as a transit point, the benefits will be smaller and more highly concentrated among the companies and workers providing services at the border and transportation across the country. If new infrastructure helps Kazakhstan increase exports and develop new industries by reaching more markets, a wider cross-section of society could benefit.

Kazakhstan's turn as host of the world's fair, in 2017, was an expensive attempt to move the country in that direction. Its theme, "Future Energy," was intended to rebrand the Central Asian energy supplier as an energy innovator. Nazarbayev called it "a turning point for Kazakhstan to start a completely new page in economic development."[34] Unintentionally, the big show also put the country's flaws center-stage. Its $3.5 billion price tag drew criticism in a country where the average salary is below $500 a month, and the first CEO of the expo, Talgat Yermegiyaev, was indicted for corruption.[35] A Hilton-branded hotel that was built in the expo complex was delayed and finally opened seven weeks after the expo had concluded.[36]

The pavilions, organized by each of the 115 participating countries, were perhaps the most telling.[37] The Chinese pavilion included a high-speed-railway simulator, and during Xi's visit in June 2017, he and Nazarbayev took turns stepping into the cockpit. Using a live video feed, they also "inspected" Khorgos Gateway.[38] The Russians brought a large piece of Arctic ice into their pavilion, and when Putin visited, he was given a briefing on the status of Russian nuclear icebreakers. In contrast, the United States did not even send a cabinet-level official, and federal law prohibits funding such exhibitions, placing the burden on private-sector participants.³⁹ In the U.S. pavilion, a video featured famous American inventors and showed their garages.⁴⁰ While China and Russia were reaching outward, the United States highlighted the benefits of staying home.

Great powers are playing different games in Central Asia. As the scholar Eric McGlinchey puts it, "China is playing Monopoly. Russia is playing Risk. The United States is playing Solitaire. For policymakers in Beijing, the game is business. For policymakers in Moscow, the game is existential. For policymakers in Washington, the game is an afterthought. Central Asia is material for Beijing; China can easily walk away if its natural resources and infrastructure investments sour. Central Asia is imperial for Moscow; Russia will not walk away if its influence is questioned. Central Asia is inconsequential for Washington; the United States has all but forgotten the region now that attention has shifted away from Afghanistan."⁴¹

The "game" is changing, however, as China moves deeper into Central Asia. Chinese investments and Chinese workers in Central Asia require security.⁴² In 2016, a suicide bomber attacked the Chinese embassy in Bishkek, Kyrgyzstan's capital, wounding three Kyrgyz staff. China's treatment of ethnic Uighurs could inspire more attacks from Islamic militant groups in the region. Meanwhile, each new investment makes walking away a bit more difficult, politically and financially, particularly those projects that are associated with the BRI. After winning enough rounds of Monopoly, China, like other great powers before it, may find itself playing Risk.

Evidence of this shift is already apparent in Tajikistan, where China has quietly assembled a military presence. To guard against an influx of militant groups from Afghanistan, China has built or improved thirty to forty border posts on the Tajik-Afghan border, a stretch of which Tajikistan has effectively handed over to Chinese control.⁴³ After years of free riding on U.S. military activities in Afghanistan, where U.S. forces have guarded Chinese-owned mines and other investments, China may be taking on more responsibility.

These measures are also noteworthy for what they indicate about regional relations, especially that Tajikistan is willing to host Chinese troops and that Russia has tolerated them. Hosting foreign military forces is rarely a popular option for leaders, but the area is so remote that Tajik leaders might enjoy the financial and security benefits of the base while suffering little public scrutiny. In addition to bases in Kyrgyzstan and Kazakhstan, Russia maintains a military base in Tajikistan that it staffs with roughly seven thousand troops. But Russian officials do not appear to be threatened by China's venture into a region they have dominated for so long, perhaps because it is far from Russia's borders and reflects a shared interest. All three countries stand to benefit from increased security in the area, through which militants and drugs have long flowed.

While China's security presence is a mere toehold, its economic footprint has blown past Russia's in recent years. By 2009, China had overtaken Russia as the region's leading trade partner. That year, the China–Central Asia gas pipeline, running through Turkmenistan, Uzbekistan, and Kazakhstan, was completed, pulling the region away from Russia and toward the east. China has also become the region's leading lender, edging out not only Russia but also the World Bank and other international financial institutions.[44] It has used resource-for-loan deals to secure access to Turkmen gas and Kazakh oil. Kazakhstan tops the list for China's trade and investment partners in the region, but its neighbors are also grabbing the BRI as a lifeline.[45]

In Central Asia, the competition to court China has occasionally resembled a BRI talent show. While in office, President Almazbek Atambayev of Kyrgyzstan said, "we can become an effective hub for transshipment of Chinese goods to Eurasia and Europe."[46] President Emomali Rahmon of Tajikistan has said that "Tajikistan can be a connecting bridge between China and other countries adjoining to the region" and that Chinese projects will "revive the southern branch of the Great Silk Road."[47] Uzbekistan has been the wildcard in the region since its long-standing president, Islam Karimov, died in 2016. His successor, Shavkat Mirziyoyev, has taken a warmer approach to the BRI, stating, "Uzbekistan supported the Belt and Road initiative from the start, and its delivery is an important factor in the sustainable development of our countries."[48] In 2017, President Gurbanguly Berdimuhamedow of Turkmenistan released a book titled *Turkmenistan Is the Heart of the*

Great Silk Road and made that phrase the official national slogan for the following year.[49]

Privately, of course, Central Asian officials have reservations. They say that China offers flexibility but subpar quality. "They are great at building to the budget you have. But ten or fifteen years later, you have to rebuild everything," one official told me. Several have said that their governments bargained hard with the Chinese to ensure that a high percentage of local labor is used, citing some of China's investments in Africa that primarily used Chinese workers. It is less clear whether they appreciate the dangers of unsustainable debt. Debt levels as a percentage of GDP in Kyrgyzstan and Tajikistan are among the highest of China's BRI partners.

China's growing presence also inflames popular grievances about government corruption and inequity. In 2016, the Kazakh government announced plans to extend the period that foreigners can lease agricultural land from ten years to twenty-five years. The changes became a flashpoint for broader fears about Chinese influence and grievances against the Kazakh state, sparking the country's largest protests since its independence. In Kyrgyzstan, citizens are roughly split as to whether they view China as the most important economic partner or the greatest economic threat.[50] It is difficult to disentangle these reactions, but that is partially the point. Citizens suspect corrupt bureaucrats are among the BRI's main beneficiaries.

Crossing the Caspian

A year after crossing Kazakhstan's eastern border with China, I traveled to its western border on the Caspian Sea. The Caspian is the world's largest inland body of water, five times the size of Lake Superior and larger than all of Japan. Its oil reserves have long attracted the interest of world powers, and the fall of the Soviet Union opened the door to foreign firms.[51]

Oil remains the top prize, but another contest is heating up. The Caspian is at the center of a competition to connect Asia and Europe with new railways, ports, and other infrastructure. China's BRI envisions two corridors that stretch westward and through the region to Europe. India and Russia are backing a north-south corridor that runs through Iran and Azerbaijan. In 2018, the United States finalized an agreement to send supplies across the sea to Kazakhstan and on to Afghanistan via Uzbekistan.

Like other places in the middle, the Caspian is hoisted up and held back by middlemen. Countries bordering the sea—Azerbaijan, Kazakhstan, Iran, Russia, and Turkmenistan—are jockeying to become hubs along emerging routes. Paradoxically, they are among the strongest supporters of the BRI but also harbor one of its greatest challenges. All five countries rank in the bottom third of Transparency International's Corruption Perceptions Index. Their average score is lower than sub-Saharan Africa, the world's worst-performing region in 2017.

These efforts all aim to carry goods and people faster and farther, and there is plenty of room for improvement. During my journey, time and space seemed to expand. The sea itself was calm, but crossing it required navigating confusion on its shores. Every step of the way, someone was eager to help—for a price, naturally.

My trip across the Caspian began in Aktau, Kazakhstan, a city where the streets truly have no names. Developed in the 1950s, it still uses a Soviet-era grid system that assigns numbers to districts and blocks. Upon arriving, I called the Caspian Shipping Company, which has a monopoly on Caspian ferry tickets. The next boat? Tomorrow, the day after, or maybe the day after that, I was told. Earlier travelers said it could take days.

There are no set schedules for the ferries, which carry railway cars, vehicles, and the occasional passenger. There is nothing fast or cheap about the trip. Flying from Aktau to Baku takes an hour and costs about $100. The same route by ferry takes anywhere from twenty to forty hours and costs $80. For intrepid bikers and motorcyclists, the extra time can be worth the hassle. The Caspian Shipping Company lists its ferry fleet online, but when I checked, the vessel locations had not been updated for a month. The waiting game had begun.

There are few distractions in Aktau. Lonely Planet, the travel guide, lists five "top sights," one of which is the sea and all of which can be seen during a fifteen-minute walk. Among those attractions are a decommissioned Soviet MiG fighter plane, a remnant of empire, and a statue of the Ukrainian poet Taras Shevchenko, who has become a symbol of Ukrainian nationalism.

Restless after a day and another unsuccessful call to the ticket office, I started checking the names of the ferries on a website that compiles updates from ship transponders. Strangely, two ferries listed their destination as Kuryk, located fifty minutes south of Aktau. Another search turned up an announcement about a new ferry complex there. I called the ticket office again and was assured the ferries only left from Aktau. I tried a few numbers for the Caspian Shipping Company, including, mistakenly, a "help line" that I learned is not for confused travelers but for reporting graft and ethics violations.

With some luck, I did not so much catch a boat as stumble onto one. After two days in Aktau, I set out for Kuryk, a village of less than ten thousand people that the government aims to transform into another key hub on the New Silk Road. "Now we can say that Kazakhstan is not a landlocked country and has access to all the seas, including the Persian Gulf," President Nazarbayev proclaimed at an opening ceremony in Kuryk for an automobile-ferry terminal in December 2017.[52]

The past and future collide just outside Kuryk. There is a graveyard with headstones from the 1950s and, moments later, large white letters placed on the side of the road: KAZAKHSTAN 2050. Looking across the flat expanse, I wondered how much had really changed in this area during the past eighty years and how much would during the next thirty. The hour drive was a landscape of endless lines, the most commanding of which was where brown steppe meets blue sky. Pipelines and powerlines were accents, running parallel and perpendicular to the horizon. The same flat steppe watched the Soviet Union rise and fall, watched an independent Kazakhstan emerge, and now watches as China tries to reach across the Caspian.

The port's office was not used to visitors. A customs official was explaining that they did not sell tickets, when a man wearing a dark-blue shirt with epaulets emerged from a back room. He was the dispatcher, the maritime equivalent of air traffic control. The next ferry would be leaving tomorrow, he assured me. His coworker, who I will call Amir, was also staying in Aktau and could give me a ride.

The next morning, after a few phone calls, Amir generously picked me up. We made three stops, one for food and two to pick up more coworkers. Their exact jobs were unclear, but all involved coordinating—with the government, military, shipping companies, and customers. Naturally, that involved a lot of waiting. They were required to be on call around the clock, usually only getting notice about incoming ships a day or so in advance. Each made a few hundred dollars a month. No one could say when the boat was leaving, but I was the only one worried about missing it.

Close to Kuryk, we passed yet another port. Surrounded by high fences and signs that promised, "Tough Projects in Safe Hands," it is run by the subsidiary of an Italian company. They were too rigid, one of my new companions explained, and required hard hats, speed limits for driving within the complex, and other rules. "They have their way of doing business. We have our way of doing business," he said as we swerved around potholes. A new road was being paved, he noted, but because everyone took a little piece, it was taking twice as long to finish.

We arrived, and despite not working in the ticket office, Amir eagerly secured my ticket. Three burly Russian bikers roared past us and into the hull of the ship. I boarded just as railcars were rolling on. Twenty minutes later, the deck started vibrating, and black smoke rose from the ship's twin exhaust stacks. We were off.

"Only Mother Nature Knows"

The sea was as calm as the shore had been chaotic. After land was out of sight, it was only the ship, the sun, and the sea. Commissioned in 1986, the *Professor Gül* was named after an Azerbaijani professor of geography. It stretches over five hundred feet and holds up to twenty-eight railway containers. Only a fraction of that capacity was being used on my voyage. Surrounded by nothingness and having barely caught the boat, I had a new appreciation for the influence of the people who navigate these "places in between" and the longer-term challenges they may pose for China's BRI.

After all, the BRI is a middleman's dream. Its megaprojects and multitude of new connections offer ample opportunities for bribery, kickbacks, and theft.[53] The world's most corrupt sectors are construction, transportation, and extraction, which includes oil and mining. The BRI has a heavy focus on all three.

The problem is not simply corruption where China aims to go but how it aims to get there: building massive infrastructure projects with little transparency and accountability. Large infrastructure projects provide ample opportunities for skimming. One expert has identified thirteen reasons why construction is prone to corruption, including the size of projects, government involvement, the number of contractual links, the project's complexity, the concealment of work, and entrenched national interests, among other factors.[54]

Allegations of corruption related to Chinese projects have already shaken the region's governments. In Tajikistan, a major highway financed by the China Development Bank was allegedly used to funnel millions of dollars to associates of the Tajik president's son-in-law, Jamoliddin Nuraliev.[55] The road was upgraded in 2010 and turned into a toll road, ostensibly to repay the $280 million loan. The contract was awarded to a company called Innovative Road Solutions, which had no experience operating roads and was registered in the British Virgin Islands. It was exempted from several taxes, and the government initially claimed that its ownership was a "trade secret."[56] A government official who spoke out against the contract was fired, and a journalist reporting on it was sentenced to twelve years in prison, a decision that was later revised to a fine and community service.[57] The road was a triple loss for Tajik citizens, who were not employed in large numbers to build it, have to pay more out of pocket to use it, and will likely have to pay again through public taxes since toll receipts are going to a tax haven rather than paying down the loan.[58]

In Kyrgyzstan, Chinese-financed projects have been inflated to enrich local elites. For one road project, cement was billed at $1.10 per kilogram, when it could have been obtained for $0.07 on the local market. Chinese contractors and Kyrgyz officials overseeing a power-plant project in Bishkek, financed by a $386 million loan from China's Export-Import Bank, authorized invoices for $320 pliers and $1,600 fire extinguishers, among other inflated expenses. Months after opening, the plant had an accident that left Bishkek residents without heating. "About 90 percent of the necessary materials and equipment were bought at an elevated price," its director later said.[59] Thirty people were arrested on corruption charges related to the project, including a Chinese contractor and two Kyrgyz former prime ministers, and five criminal cases have been launched.

In many of the countries that China's Belt and Road aims to connect, these problems are endemic and will not simply fade away, as Alexander Cooley, who directs the Harriman Institute at Columbia University, has cautioned.[60] Nor are solutions easily imposed from the outside. This is a lesson that the United States has learned, painfully and expensively, in Afghanistan, where large U.S.-funded projects have sometimes enriched elites, stoked corruption, and exacerbated rivalries.[61]

Of course, Chinese companies are not alone in being accused of peddling influence. But authorities in the United States and the European Union are more vigilant in policing their own companies abroad. China adopted a foreign-bribery law in 2011 but has done little to enforce it. Chinese companies are also among the least transparent according to a study of one hundred companies in fifteen emerging markets.[62] They have been willing to operate with fewer strings attached, even picking up projects that have been abandoned by the World Bank, Asian Development Bank, and other more stringent lenders for corruption violations. Chinese officials chalk some of this up as the cost of doing business.

China's largest lenders prefer operating in the darkness, and their sheer size makes this a global problem. China Development Bank and the Export-Import Bank of China have grown to hold more than twice the assets of major Western-backed multilateral development banks and lend more to developing countries.[63] Their projects are publicized after contractors are picked, and loan terms are rarely released. The calculus behind these decisions might seem pragmatic: more opportunities and fewer obstacles equals greater influence.

There are upsides to Beijing's no-strings-attached approach, but it also carries the seeds of its own destruction.[64] It deals with partners as they are, without imposing difficult governance reforms. Washington's Silk Road Act, for example, included among its priorities developing rule of law, independent judiciaries, and transparency in the region. Without conditions, Beijing is freer to go where it wants, and its dealings can be more transactional. When doing business in difficult places, it can press its advantage, ensuring that Chinese companies and workers are the first to benefit. China may ask less of its partners up front, but it also takes more.

A willingness to handle huge deals opaquely provides even more opportunities for political leverage. By agreeing to inflate project costs, for example, Beijing can funnel money to its friends in high places. A backroom deal can itself become a source of leverage, since either side could make demands and threaten to expose the other. But Beijing holds the stronger hand. Given the immense demand for infrastructure, China has more countries courting its investments than its partners have alternative sources of investment.

This cynical approach may sound cunning, but it is fraught with risk. Putting aside its economic costs, corruption stokes resentment. Requiring assessments for financial, human rights, environmental, and other impacts is highly pragmatic. These assessments require additional time, but they minimize well-documented risks associated with projects. When ignored, those risks can come back to haunt leaders, especially those in more democratic states. Billed as a decades-long effort to unite the world, the BRI is already generating pushback, as subsequent chapters explain.

As the sun began to set on the Caspian, the *Professor Gül's* engines pushed us forward at a leisurely ten knots, or eleven and a half miles per hour. The crew followed a strict schedule, rotating shifts and eating at set intervals.

Yet no one would venture a straight estimate about when we would arrive. The ship's junior engineer, a cadet at the Azerbaijan State Marine Academy, said he had made the crossing over two hundred times. He recounted delays at sea and in port, where congestion can cause ships to wait for up to a week before they dock. The weather could turn ugly, too. In 2003, a ferry crossing from Aktau to Baku sank, killing forty-three of the fifty-one people on board.

What I mistakenly took for nonchalance was prudence. Twenty hours and two bowls of borsch into our voyage, the wind picked up as we approached Azerbaijan. The ship anchored frustratingly close to the coast and waited for better weather. I asked the chef how long it would be. "Only mother nature knows," he laughed. We eventually pulled into Alat, a port near Baku, around two a.m. the next morning.

From dock to dock, the trip took about thirty-two hours. That is hardly a revolution in today's world of just-in-time delivery, but it could become an improvement over the status quo, especially if backers of the new port can deliver their promise of an eighteen-hour crossing. Even greater gains could be achieved by reducing the waiting time on land.

But not all inefficiencies are accidental or easily fixed. The art of the middleman is turning uncertainty into advantage. The more complicated the process, the more value middlemen offer as guides. The more choke points, the more opportunities to take a cut. It is easy to criticize corruption. It is another thing to persuade people making only a few hundred dollars a month to give something up in the hope that greater company profits will trickle down.

Corruption looks ugly when it is wearing handcuffs, but usually it wears a friendly face. When my boat finally arrived in Azerbaijan, I cleared customs and asked a security guard how to get a taxi to Baku. Realizing that I was not among the normal passengers, neither on vacation riding a motorcycle or bike nor on business escorting cargo, I expected lots of questions about the nature of my trip. Why take a day-and-a-half boat ride when I could have taken an hour flight?

But the guard was not the least bit interested in why I was there, only where I was going. He took out his cell phone, dialed, and spoke a few words in Azerbaijani. Turning back to me, he said, "My cousin can drive you. Twenty-five dollars?"

Legend:
- ☐ Eurasian Economic Union Members
- – – Power of Siberia pipeline

Yamal LNG

RUSSIA

BELARUS

KAZAKHSTAN

KYRGYZSTAN

ARMENIA

Blagoveshchensk-Heihe
Bridge

Russia

Center for Strategic and International Studies, Reconnecting Asia Project; Gazprom

CHAPTER FOUR

The Gatekeeper

Russia

"**I**T IS PROHIBITED TO visit this place," the Russian soldier said, flipping slowly through my passport as if it held a secret.

We were sitting in a small room with two large windows overlooking an unremarkable construction site, a flat expanse of brown dirt in Blagoveshchensk, a city in Russia's Far East. The wind carried the crack and clang of power tools toward us, and Russian workers in hard hats ambled by in ones and twos. They were building a bridge into Heihe, China. The two cities share a river, called the Amur in Russian and the Heilongjiang, or "black dragon river," in Chinese.

They also share a bloody past. Blagoveshchensk literally means "city of good news," but its defining moments have been decidedly otherwise. The city was founded as a military post in the mid-nineteenth century after two treaties demarcated the river as the border. During the Boxer Rebellion in 1900, Russians expelled ethnic Chinese from the city, forcing them at bayonet point to cross the river without boats. Five thousand Chinese men, women, and children were killed.[1]

In 1969, U.S. officials watched with white knuckles as Soviet and Chinese troops clashed farther downriver. "A major conflict developing between China and the USSR," one U.S. State Department official warned, "might well extend into other areas of the world and indeed threaten a large portion of the world's population."[2] Cooler heads prevailed, but Soviet-Sino mistrust simmered; and the split provided the window for Henry Kissinger and Richard Nixon's opening to China.

Chinese and Russian officials now boast of building bridges across their borders, literally and figuratively, as part of a strategic partnership. First proposed in the late 1980s, the Blagoveshchensk-Heihe bridge was finally started in 2016.[3] It has become a symbol of warming relations between the owner of the world's largest nuclear arsenal and the world's second-largest economy.

Straddling eleven time zones across the top of the Eurasian supercontinent and with deep ties to Central Asia, Russia is the gatekeeper for China's overland ambitions. No other country is better positioned to spoil China's BRI. China needs Russia's cooperation, but a century of conflict and competition leaves a deep layer of mistrust and suspicion.

"Why are you here?" the soldier asked.

"I would like to see the bridge," I replied, reaching back to my college language classes and coming up with a jumble of Russian words.

"Why do you want to visit the bridge?"

"I would like a photo."

"It is not allowed. What is the purpose of your visit?"

"Tourism."

"How long are you in Russia?"

"Only today."

The breeze was cool outside, but the air inside the temporary building was stifling. I was sweating in a T-shirt and had no idea how he was holding up in his forest-camouflage uniform.

"It is prohibited to visit this place," he repeated.

"It's OK," I said, standing and reaching for my passport. "No problem."

"This is a strategic project."

"It's OK, no problem, I leave now."

"But you are already here."

"I don't understand."

"Do you need a translator?"

"It's OK, I am leaving."

"No, you must answer my questions," he insisted, laying a blank sheet of paper on the table and uncapping a pen.

My stomach dropped. What began as a casual inquiry directed from me to him—a request to see the bridge—had boomeranged back and was quickly becoming an interrogation.

"Most Trustworthy Strategic Partners"

The paranoia that courses along Russia's borders is as real and powerful as the Amur itself. Russia is the world's largest country by landmass, and across the centuries, its rulers have risen and fallen on their ability to defend its difficult borders. During the thirteenth century, the Mongols invaded Russian lands from the Central Asian steppe. Over the past four hundred years, most of Russia's threats have come from the west, where large plains allowed European armies—the Poles, Swedes, French, and Germans twice—to penetrate deep into Russian territory.[4] As the U.S. diplomat George Kennan wrote in his famous 1946 cable, often remembered as the Long Telegram, "Russia has never known a friendly neighbor."[5]

The collapse of the Soviet Union exacerbated Russia's worst fears. It shrank the buffer zones between Russia and its competitors to the west. As newly independent countries joined the European Union and NATO, the Kremlin saw that space shrink further. "This is not just a psychological issue for us," Russian intelligence chief Yevgeny Primakov, who would become foreign minister and prime minister, warned about NATO expansion, "It's a security question."[6]

Several American experts saw the danger, too. Expanding NATO, Kennan warned in 1997, "may be expected to inflame the nationalistic, anti-Western and militaristic tendencies in Russian opinion; to have an adverse effect on the development of Russian democracy; to restore the atmosphere of the cold war to East-West relations, and to impel Russian foreign policy in directions decidedly not to our liking."[7]

While Western capitals were celebrating the triumph of democracy and free markets, policy makers in Moscow felt that their weakness was being exploited. "It was not the process of expansion that would have to take Russia's position into account but Russia that would have to adapt to the process," Primakov later wrote.[8]

Russia's heightened insecurity on its western flank compelled it to improve relations to the east. In the early 1990s, Russian and Chinese officials began working to resolve long-standing border disputes. The process was painstakingly slow. A final agreement, struck in 2008, settled outstanding claims over a shared border running over twenty-six hundred miles and set the stage for further development. Russian Foreign Minister Sergei Lavrov said at the time, "All the conditions are created for the Russian-Chinese border to always be one of stability, openness, friendship, development and prosperity."[9]

Heaping praise on each other, Putin and Xi have rapidly elevated their countries' relations.[10] While in office, they have met over thirty times, and every time, it seems, they declare that their friendship has grown even stronger. In July 2017, Putin bestowed Russia's highest state award on Xi and feted their "comprehensive partnership and strategic cooperation."[11] Echoing those sentiments, Xi said that China and Russia are each other's "most trustworthy strategic partners" and that relations are "at their best time in history."[12] Returning the favor, Xi conferred China's inaugural Friendship Medal on Putin in 2018.[13]

They know the West is watching. "We came to let the Americans know about the close ties of the armed forces of China and Russia," the Chinese defense minister Wei Fenghe said during a visit to Moscow in 2018.[14]

Nor is the romance purely rhetorical. At the United Nations, China and Russia have used their seats on the Security Council to oppose international interventions. They have staked out similar positions on North Korea, state control of cyberspace, and other areas, often contrary to U.S. interests. Their joint military exercises expanded to European waters in 2017, and the following year, Russia included several thousand Chinese troops in its largest exercise since the Cold War.[15] Russia and China have signed energy deals, launched joint projects in the Arctic, and even announced a joint aerospace company that aims to compete with Boeing and Airbus.[16] To hedge against U.S. sanctions, Russia has been shifting its foreign currency reserves into Chinese currency.[17]

By most measures, lumping Russia and China together is overly generous to Russia. Russia has nuclear weapons but also a one-trick economy focused on energy exports, a rusting military, and a declining population. Russia's illegal behavior can be seen around the world, from its illegal annexation of Crimea and support for Bashar Al Assad in Syria to its meddling in U.S. elections. But decades from now, U.S. officials may come to regret pushing historical enemies together through chest-thumping public statements, sanctions, and tariffs.

A deeper Russian-Chinese partnership would be Kissinger's worst nightmare realized. An unflinching objective of U.S. foreign policy since World War II has been to prevent the domination of the Eurasian landmass by a single power. Historically, rising powers reaching for that mantle have sparked conflict and brought the world to war with them. China is the most likely challenger, and the most alarming interpretation of the BRI is that it is China's roadmap to hegemonic power. Xi now holds the keys in the form of investment and respect that Putin, economically and diplomatically isolated from the West, craves.

Russian officials were suspicious when the BRI was announced. "We understand this Chinese initiative as just another attempt to steal Central Asia from us," a senior Russian official told Alexander Gabuev, a scholar at the Carnegie Endowment.[18] Officials in Russia's security agencies were more concerned than their economic counterparts, but three economic risks colored their impressions, as Gabuev recounts. They worried that the BRI could undermine Russia's proposed trade architecture for the region, undercut the Trans-Siberian Railway by routing trade around Russia to Europe, and dominate access to raw materials and infrastructure contracts in Central Asia.

But Moscow was also running out of options. In 2014, in the wake of the war in Ukraine, Russia was increasingly isolated and vulnerable given its dependence on Western energy markets, investors, and technology.[19] Around this time, the Kremlin conducted its first comprehensive assessment of the pros and cons of partnering with Beijing. Partnering with China posed long-term risks, including new dependencies on a larger partner, but it was the only viable path available to reduce Russia's western vulnerabilities. The assessment

concluded that the benefits, particularly in the short term, out-
weighed the risks.[20]

Moscow's calculus will change if China becomes more threatening or the West becomes more welcoming.[21] As China's economic
footprint grows, so will its security footprint. Sightings of Chinese
military vehicles and construction in Afghanistan's Wakhan Corridor, as well as a Chinese military base and border posts in nearby
Tajikistan, show that this expansion is already under way, as Chapter
3 noted.[22]

American policy makers could use these developments to stoke
Russo-Sino competition, but they have been doing the opposite.
"Moscow and Beijing share a common interest in weakening U.S.
global influence and are actively cooperating in that regard," the
U.S. Defense Intelligence Agency concluded in a 2017 report.[23]
The Trump administration's *National Security Strategy* singled out
China and Russia as competitors that "challenge American power,
influence, and interests, attempting to erode American security and
prosperity."[24] These lines might win applause among some U.S. audiences, but they are also a rallying cry for China and Russia.
There is nothing strategic about pushing U.S. competitors closer
together through tough-sounding public statements.

"Eurasian Union"

Putin and Xi have also promised to "link" their signature economic
visions. Putin's vision is the Eurasian Economic Union (EAEU),
which aims to integrate Russia and four former Soviet states in a
single market for goods, services, capital, and labor.[25] A "Eurasian
Union" was first proposed by Kazakhstan's President Nursultan
Nazarbayev in 1994. Putin revived the idea with an op-ed written
in 2011, when he was prime minister and planning his return to
the presidency. The EAEU, he explained, was an opportunity to
make the most of a common Soviet heritage and learn from the
European Union's mistakes.[26] His pitch was intended to resonate
with Russian nationalists hoping to forge a distinctive path between East and West.[27] From the beginning, Putin's conception of
the EAEU was more about Russian politics than about regional
economics.

But like the BRI, the five-country EAEU has been less impressive in practice. Russia, Kazakhstan, and Belarus formed the initial grouping in 2014. In 2015, Armenia joined mainly for security assistance from Russia. Later that year, Kyrgyzstan joined and quickly regretted its decision, which required raising tariffs with countries outside the group, including China. In 2016, Kyrgyzstan's exports dropped by 30 percent, imports dropped by 8 percent, and overall GDP dropped 2 percent.[28] The most telling sign of the EAEU's struggles is the lack of interest among other countries in joining. Russia has courted Tajikistan and Uzbekistan as well as Moldova, Georgia, and Ukraine. A few countries have signed on as observers, but as of 2019, none were taking serious steps toward full membership.

Geography, however, demands that China deal with the EAEU. Three of the BRI's six proposed economic corridors pass through it. The China-Mongolia-Russia Economic Corridor (CMREC) includes a route through China's Manzhouli and Russia's Zabaykalsk, cities on opposite sides of the border. While the China–Central Asia–West Asia Economic Corridor (CCWAEC) does not include Russia, it passes through EAEU members Kazakhstan and Kyrgyzstan en route to Iran and Turkey. The third corridor, the New Eurasian Land Bridge, connects China and the European Union, by way of Mongolia, Russia, and Belarus.[29] These corridors are still in their infancy and need Russian-Chinese cooperation to grow.

Economics aside, Putin and Xi have strong political incentives for casting their visions as complementary. In Xi's opening remarks at the first Belt and Road Forum, he listed the EAEU first among policy initiatives with which the BRI had enhanced coordination.[30] Putin reciprocated and listed the BRI first among "integration formats," which he said could be combined to build "a larger Eurasian partnership."[31] Putin's call for a larger or "greater" Eurasian partnership is an unsuccessful attempt to combine the EAEU and BRI into something of which Moscow would have greater control.[32] The concept treats Russia and China as equals, despite their economic disparities. Xi has been happy to play along, because Putin's rhetoric softens suspicions that the BRI is a tool for extending Chinese influence into Central Asia.

Both leaders are critics of the Western-led economic order, and talk of "linking" the BRI and EAEU helps position them as leaders of an alternative approach. Xi made headlines at the 2017 annual meeting of the World Economic Forum, when he warned against protectionism and sounded like a bigger proponent of free trade and liberalization than some of his Western counterparts.[33] Putin has made similar comments, including at the first Belt and Road Forum, when he pointed to "the crisis the globalization model finds itself in."[34] Neither has offered a coherent alternative, but their criticism of the status quo resonates with many developing countries.

Putin and Xi's shared narrative is clever and opportunistic. It appropriates Western language about globalization and stokes resentment in many of the places that have benefited from globalization the most. Even if it does not yet offer a solution, it presumes that any solution should be defined in contrast to the West, in essence defining the problem as the West. Their message is made louder by the West's relative silence. With the United States and the European Union consumed with domestic challenges and relatively disengaged, Russia and China are attempting to lead a conversation about globalization.

"Welcome to Russia"

Despite this common cause, the China-Russia partnership still has an artificial flavor, supported more by leaders on high than by organic developments on the ground.[35] Outside the Heihe airport is a massive bush shaped as two bears, a panda and a grizzly, holding hands. Closer to the city center, near duty-free shops that cater to Russian tourists, there is more greenery shaped as two large doves with state flags unfurling toward each other. In this awkward romance, state media even trumpet Chinese-Russian marriages as evidence that their partnership is succeeding.[36]

In theory, Xi's and Putin's economic visions could be complementary. The BRI puts a greater emphasis on hard infrastructure, while the EAEU puts a greater emphasis on "soft" infrastructure, the rules and regulations that govern movement and commerce. Unnecessary paperwork, redundant checkpoints, and other frictions at the borders account for up to 30 percent of export value within the EAEU.[37] There is no doubt that Asia, and particularly

Central Asia, where China and Russia's visions overlap, could use both hard and soft upgrades.

But as I was beginning to appreciate, cooperation in third countries is unlikely to take off without addressing issues at their own border, where mistrust still rules.

"How much longer?" I asked the guard. "Ten minutes? Thirty minutes?"

"How many hours—that is the question. Do you want a translator?"

"I don't understand. I need to leave."

"We will get the translator. Sit here," the guard said, pointing to a chair as he left the room.

Given his concerns about security, it was an interesting choice. Facing a window, the chair offered a front-row view of the construction site. As I watched, the movement of yellow machines—trucks, a crane, an excavator—slowed. A few minutes later, a stream of workers filed out through the room behind me, a turnstile clicking as each walked through. It was lunch time.

The translator, whom I will call Nadia, arrived about an hour later. She was accompanied by a local policeman, let us call him Dimitry, whose silent grin suggested that he was amused.

NADIA: They say, you do not have permission to visit this place.
ME: I asked to visit, and when they said no, I asked to leave. I didn't know it was illegal to ask.
NADIA: They say, even if you did not know the law before you broke it, you have still broken it.

After some back-and-forth, I agreed to pay a small fine, the equivalent of fifteen dollars, to expedite the process. I stood up, took out my wallet, and prepared to leave the place like it was a restaurant that had served up a bad meal—except the waiters were carrying guns. They might appreciate a more generous tip, I thought. A hand descended on my shoulder.

"First, the official report must be written," the soldier explained. He began slowly and painstakingly filling out the report by hand. A few paragraphs in, after making a spelling mistake, he ripped up the paper and started again.

The longer the soldier worked on his opus, consulting my passport and Nadia every few minutes, the more visibly bored, and friendly, Dimitry became.

DIMITRY: Where in the United States are you from?
ME: Washington, DC.
DIMITRY: I love the Washington Capitals. Ovechkin. Kuznetsov. Orlov. The best.
ME: They are the best.

I hadn't followed the Capitals closely but knew those were the Russian players who led them to a Stanley Cup.

DIMITRY (smiling): The best.

Finally, the soldier picked up a stack of papers, tapped them neatly on the desk, and stood up.

ME: Can we go now?
NADIA: They say they need another document. Their colleague will bring it from the headquarters.
ME: Do you have computers?
DIMITRY: Welcome to Russia.

Sweating, I checked my phone: two p.m.—four hours until the last ferry left from Blagoveshchensk. I planned to return to Heihe later that afternoon after visiting the bridge and walking around the city. My flight to the United States was leaving the next morning from Heihe, where I had left my suitcase.

"Entrepreneurs of the Amur"

Taking a quick trip between Russia and China sounds preposterous, but it is way of life for a dying breed of entrepreneurs. In 1992, China opened a free-trade zone to promote cross-border trade, and every morning, people from both sides make the journey across the river as part of a small but thriving suitcase trade. To avoid customs taxes, Chinese entrepreneurs in Russia often employ Russian citizens to hand deliver items. In downtown Blagoveshchensk, a bronze statue of a man carrying an oversized suitcase in one hand and another on his shoulder was built in the 1990s to commemorate the suitcase traders. "For the hard work and optimism of the entrepreneurs of the Amur," its inscription reads.

The Amur's new entrepreneurs are not so different. Earlier that morning, in Heihe, I watched a stream of young Russian men file out of a duty-free shop and stagger toward the ferry terminal with overpacked nylon duffle bags in both hands. Behind the terminal, a Ferris wheel juts into the sky, an attempt to keep visitors a bit longer. A truck pulled around the back of the ferry terminal, and men rushed to transfer its bags onto the ferry before we pulled away. Other than a few gray Russian patrol boats doing their rounds, the river was empty.

The ferry ride takes only ten minutes, but bureaucracy stretches the journey closer to two hours. After buying a ticket and clearing customs, passengers wait for the next boat. Chinese and Russian passengers are grouped separately. Whether for efficiency or something else, the segregation felt odd for these "most trustworthy strategic partners." It was enforced by signs and halfhearted staffing. I was directed to join the Russians.

In the winter, the ferries are replaced by pontoon bridges, a floating design that dates back to 480 BC, when Xerxes marched his Persian army across the modern-day Dardanelles. The bridges are limited in the weight they can hold and must be set up seasonally. These limitations are strengths for anyone uncertain about the value of stronger links. The pontoon bridges are also inexpensive and can be easily removed. When the new bridge between the two cities is finished, it will be a more permanent fixture.

Separated by just over one thousand meters, the Chinese and Russian sides of the bridge are different worlds. A day earlier, on the Chinese side of the bridge, my driver parked on the bank of the river alongside the construction site. A civilian guard emerged from a small shack. We shook hands, and he gave an approving nod after I asked to take a photo. I walked down to the water's edge. In contrast, Russian security is so restrictive that locals often travel to

China to fish the same river. Before leaving, I asked to take the guard's picture. He smiled and agreed. My interest in the bridge was not a threat but a compliment validating its importance.

Touted as symbols of cooperation, transport links also reveal the limits of China and Russia's partnership. There are only four active railway crossings between Russia and China.[38] The United States–Canada border is roughly twice as long but has more than six times as many railway crossings.[39] The first Russia-China railway bridge, linking Tongjiang in China with Nizhneleninskoye in Russia, has proceeded in starts and fits.[40] Construction on the Chinese side was completed in 2016 and outpaced the Russian side, which was not finished until 2019. Until then, satellite images showed a structure stretching from Chinese territory and ending part way over the river. China was waiting for Russia to meet it halfway.

Far Eastern Promises

Well before the BRI, Chinese and Russian officials announced hundreds of joint projects with great fanfare but little follow-through. In 2009, Presidents Hu Jintao and Dmitri Medvedev released a list of 205 joint projects.[41] By 2015, only 19 projects were under way.[42] Part of the problem is that failed proposals are often repackaged as new offerings in the hope that foreign investors will see merit when domestic investors, including the government, did not. The list of challenges deterring foreign investors from the Far East is long: corruption, weak property rights, small market size, and poor infrastructure. In 2017, it attracted only 2 percent of China's foreign direct investment into Russia.[43]

China towers over Russia demographically, and nowhere is this more apparent than in the Far East. The Far East encompasses nearly a third of Russia's land but barely 5 percent of its population. In contrast, China's Northeast is overbrimming with labor and short on land. The population of China's Heilongjiang province alone outnumbers Russia's entire Far East by more than six-fold.

Russian officials have pointed to these disparities to stoke fears about migration. As Putin warned in 2000, "If in the near future we do not make real efforts, then even the primordially Russian population in several decades will speak mainly in Japanese, Chinese, and Korean languages."[44] The Russian government has even offered free plots of land to entice more Russians to settle the Far East, and it requires foreign investors to employ Russian citizens.[45]

But a Chinese migrant wave will not be washing across Russia's borders anytime soon.[46] Most Chinese, like most Russians, prefer living in Russia's western cities, where more jobs are available. Declining wages in Russia are another deterrent, especially when average salaries can be higher in China.[47] The same conditions that deter Russians from the Far East also limit its attractiveness to Chinese.

China's and Russia's biggest moves have been in the energy sector.[48] China is the world's largest energy importer, and Russia is one of the world's largest owners and producers of oil and natural gas. China's hunger for resources aligns with Russia's need for investment, and their shared energy interests have been advanced through several multidecade deals. In 2010, their first major joint infrastructure project, an oil pipeline from Skovorodino in Russia to Daqing in China, was completed.

In 2014, after a decade of negotiations, Gazprom and China National Petroleum Corporation struck a thirty-year, $400 billion agreement for natural gas. A new pipeline, the Power of Siberia, stretches three thousand kilometers from gas fields in eastern Serbia to the Chinese border at Heihe. It is Russia's most expensive project since Soviet times. Constructing roughly two kilometers each day, workers braved subzero temperatures, and even bears, to ensure its completion in 2019.[49]

Russian policy makers touted the new pipeline as evidence of their options. "Barack Obama should give up the policy of isolating Russia: it won't work," said Alexei Pushkov, head of the Russian Duma's foreign affairs committee, after the deal was concluded.[50] China, however, took advantage of Russia's lack of alternatives and drove a hard bargain on the price of gas and the pipeline's route.[51] Nor will Russia enjoy the leverage that it does over smaller states that rely on its energy exports. The opposite is more likely: China has more options for purchasing energy than Russia has options for selling it.

Farther north, China also wants Russia's help in providing access to the Arctic.[52] In 2018, China released its first official Arctic policy, which reiterated the claim that China was a "near-Arctic power." It has proposed building a "Polar Silk Road" from China, through the Arctic, to northern Europe. China is willing to pay. The China National Petroleum Corporation (CNPC) and China's Silk Road Fund have stakes in Russia's Yamal liquid-natural-gas project, which started operations in December 2017. Cooperation could extend to building a port in Arkhangelsk, on the White Sea, and a railway from the port to central Russia. Commercial transport through the Arctic is not likely to become profitable for decades, raising suspicions about military motives.[53]

Trade policy is another avenue for integration, but China and Russia's recent efforts have been as much show as substance. In 2015, the conclusion of negotiations for the U.S.-led Trans-Pacific Partnership galvanized them to pursue their own trade deal.[54] Three years later, China and the EAEU signed a trade and cooperation agreement that improves customs and trade procedures.[55] One Russian official called it "a major step towards the alignment of the EAEU and China's Belt and Road Initiative," but it does not lower tariffs.[56] The EAEU's defensive interests stand in the way of any deeper, more meaningful economic arrangement. China would be its largest trading partner, by far, and EAEU policy makers want to limit the impact of more Chinese exports on their domestic industries.

A considerably more ambitious approach would be establishing a free-trade area under the Shanghai Cooperation Organization (SCO). The SCO began with a focus on border disputes and security issues, but it has taken on a broader mandate and greater economic focus in recent years. Both Russian and Chinese officials have mentioned the SCO as a preferred mechanism for coordinating the EAEU and the BRI, and the organization's 2015 development strategy mentions "developing common approaches to the Silk Road Economic Belt Initiative" among its goals.[57] But the EAEU and SCO members do not overlap neatly, with the latter including a number of additional states. When Pakistan and India, two countries with high tariffs and political tensions, joined the SCO in 2017, a free-trade zone became even more unlikely.

Of course, China could join the EAEU. But it is impossible to imagine either Moscow or Beijing supporting this level of integration. Moscow dominates the EAEU in economic and political terms, and admitting China would undercut that influence. Indeed, it would be more accurate to say that the EAEU would be joining China, which is more than seven times larger in economic and demographic terms than the EAEU members combined. China, for its part, would have little to gain from binding itself to the EAEU's higher tariffs and rules.

Plenty still divides Russia and China. Beneath the endless mutual praise and talk of partnership, they are fundamentally unequal, with China towering above Russia in economic and demographic terms. Even the language they use to describe their partnership is telling. Chinese officials speak of *dui jie*, or "docking," the BRI and EAEU. Russian officials use the word *sopryazhenie*, which means "coupling," suggesting a more equal partnership that is at odds with reality.[58]

The greatest barrier to deeper integration is a similarity: Russia and China are unwilling to give up much control. Both visions aim to enhance a single state's influence. The EAEU puts Moscow at the center, while the BRI puts Beijing at the center. Both visions also maintain a defensive posture domestically. The EAEU protects Russian industries, while for all the talk about BRI promoting connectivity, China uses capital controls that limit financial flows, internet restrictions that limit information flows, and security policies that limit the movement of people and goods. Both governments favor domestic stability and self-preservation above all else. Greater connectivity could bring more growth but also more disruption and less control.

The Last Boat

There was no illusion about who was in control, as my time with the Russian border guards stretched on. "We will go get the document," the soldier announced. Apparently "we" included me, so I very reluctantly piled into a van with three soldiers and Nadia. "You don't need that," one of the soldiers said as I reached for the seat belt. "That is not against the law?" I asked. "Not when you're with us," he said. Dimitry followed in his car. The ride was only fifteen minutes, but it was in the opposite direction of the city. It was four p.m., and my chances of catching the ferry back to Heihe were dwindling by the minute.

The border guards' local command post was on a dirt road, off poorly maintained roads, behind a makeshift wood and wire gate. As we approached, the soldiers let Nadia and me out of the van and continued past the gate. We sat in Dimitry's car with the doors open, flies buzzing in and out. I was not the only one checking my phone. Dimitry and Nadia had other places to be as well. Dogs barked from within the compound.

Around 5:15 p.m., the soldiers emerged with more papers. Nadia explained that they were identical copies of the report from earlier, only the handwritten parts had been typed up. I initialed and signed a Soviet-sized stack of papers.

NADIA: They say they can make a second copy, if you would like.

ME: No, thank you.

DIMITRY: To get more paper, they may need to cut down a tree.

Suddenly, without ceremony, we were done. We closed the doors, and Dimitry sped away. As he accelerated, driving fast over the dirt road, I wondered whether he was eager to get home, putting on a show, or actually helping me catch the boat. Around 5:45 p.m., the city emerged. At 5:56, we arrived at the entry to the ferry. I jumped out and ran for the departures building. But at 5:58, the door was locked. I banged on it. A customs official emerged, opening the door just long enough to announce: "The next boat is tomorrow morning, 8:30 a.m."

If only the bridge had been complete. It could turn a two-hour ferry and customs process into a twenty-minute drive, boosting the flow of goods and people across the river. Like all new connections, these changes would force the beneficiaries of the current system to adapt. The suitcase traders might be replaced by truckers. If enough people opted to drive, the dingy restaurant and hotel where I spent the evening, both located near the ferry terminal as many others were, might struggle to stay in business. Most of all, if the bridge were complete, it would not be a restricted area. I might not have spent the day with the Russian border guard.

But as I was reminded the next morning, scrutiny was never far away. Before catching the first boat to Heihe, I had to clear customs. After looking through my passport for several minutes, a Russian official picked up a phone. Moments later, a plainclothes security agent was questioning me in a back room. When I was finally cleared to depart, the dull thud of my passport being stamped sounded to me like a slot machine hitting the jackpot.

An hour later, I arrived in Heihe, never happier to be on Chinese soil. I handed my U.S. passport to another understandably confused customs official, who called his supervisor. The supervisor took a quick look at my visa, smiled, and waved me through. Like the reception on each side of the bridge, the contrast was telling. Naturally, both sides were surprised to see an American amid the steady stream of Russians and Chinese. The Chinese were amused. The Russians were alarmed.

Central and Eastern Europe
Center for Strategic and International Studies, Reconnecting Asia Project

CHAPTER FIVE

The Bridgehead

Central and Eastern Europe

"I THINK, MAYBE, YOU MIGHT prefer taking the bus to Budapest," the receptionist at the Moskva hotel in Belgrade said politely. Most people do. It is faster, and the air-conditioning works. But I was there for the train, a route made famous by Agatha Christie's 1934 novel *Murder on the Orient Express* and more recently by China's controversial push to build a faster line. The $3 billion project, China's first railway in the EU, has become a testing ground for whose rules will prevail in eastern and central Europe.[1]

No one is yelling murder yet, but in 2017, the European Commission launched an investigation into the bidding process around the Belgrade-Budapest railway. At question is whether the Hungarian government awarded the contract to Chinese firms without an open competition, which is required by EU law. In response, Hungary held a new tender for the project. The winner is hardly reassuring: a Hungarian-Chinese consortium that includes a company owned by Lorinc Meszaros, a childhood friend of Hungary's Prime Minister Viktor Orbán.

Officials at the European Commission in Brussels and those in western Europe—especially Germany and France—worry that Chinese investments are eroding unity within the EU and weakening

79

the states on its eastern fringe. "They try to import their way of life, and this means a combination of capitalism and political dictatorship," EU Commissioner Johannes Hahn, who oversaw the accession process of new members and relations with those bordering the EU, said of China. "This will be one of the great challenges of Europe."[2]

Others have been even more blunt. "The initiative for a new Silk Road ... is not a sentimental nod to Marco Polo, but rather stands for an attempt to establish a comprehensive system to shape the world according to China's interests," Germany's Foreign Minister Sigmar Gabriel said at the Munich Security Conference in February 2018. "This has long since ceased to be merely a question of economics. China is developing a comprehensive systemic alternative to the Western model that, in contrast to our own, is not founded on freedom, democracy and individual human rights."[3]

Those concerns are spreading.[4] EU leaders, after withholding their judgment, have begun openly criticizing Xi's vision. France's President Emmanuel Macron has said that the BRI cannot be "one-way."[5] Britain's Prime Minister Theresa May, to the dismay of her hosts, abstained from signing a memorandum of understanding (MOU) during her visit to Beijing in January 2018.[6] In April 2018, the German newspaper *Handelsblatt* reported that all but one of the national EU ambassadors to Beijing signed onto a report criticizing the BRI, noting that it "runs counter to the EU agenda for liberalizing trade and pushes the balance of power in favor of subsidized Chinese companies."[7] Hungary was the lone holdout. More surprising is that Greece, which has often stood with Hungary to soften EU criticism of China, joined the statement.

Feeling neglected by western Europe, central and eastern European countries have increasingly turned toward China for investment, particularly after the 2008 financial crisis. The Czech Republic's President Miloš Zeman has offered his country as China's "unsinkable aircraft-carrier."[8] In 2016, Greece's Prime Minister Alexis Tsipras said his country could "serve as China's gateway into Europe."[9] Hungary's Orbán has put it even more bluntly: "If the EU cannot provide financial support, we will turn to China."[10]

China has been happy to oblige. Its direct investments in Europe have risen from less than $1 billion in 2008 to a record $42 billion in 2016. Chinese investments have since pulled back, due to

China's own limits on investment outflows as well as increased scrutiny from outside, but Europe remains a major focus. China's wallet has been welcomed, particularly by non-EU members, because it can dispense cash faster and with fewer restrictions.[11]

For China, central and eastern Europe are a bridge into the EU, the grand prize at the opposite end of the Eurasian supercontinent. Chinese contractors have struggled to gain a foothold in the EU market, where projects require rigorous risk assessments and most countries already have access to competitive financing. In 2009, the China Overseas Engineering Group (COVEC) became the first Chinese firm to win a contract for building a European road. COVEC's bid for the project, a highway linking Warsaw and Berlin, was shockingly low—less than half of what the government had budgeted. After winning, COVEC claimed that materials were unexpectedly expensive and quickly ran into cash-flow problems. Poland canceled the contract, making China's first foray an embarrassing failure.

Officials in Beijing have not forgotten that episode, and the Belgrade-Budapest railway offers a chance for redemption. Both parts of the railway are valuable to Beijing. The Hungarian portion is China's first railway project within the EU.[12] It is a training ground for Chinese state-owned enterprises to meet EU requirements and prove they have what it takes to compete against Western companies on their home turf. It also strengthens ties with Hungary's leadership, which has been willing to weaken common EU positions toward China.

The Serbian side of the railway provides an opportunity for China to deepen economic and political ties with a country that could become part of the EU. Although Serbia is an EU candidate, it is not bound by the same procurement regulations that Hungary and other existing members must uphold. When and if Serbia and other central and eastern European countries accede to the EU, Chinese firms already based in those countries could ride more easily into the EU market. In recent years, Chinese infrastructure investments have been disproportionately concentrated on Balkan states aiming to join the EU.[13] "It would not be immodest or wrong to call Serbia China's main partner in Europe," Serbia's minister for construction said in 2017.[14]

"The Iron Road"

Despite the attention that China's Belgrade-Budapest line has received, it is hardly Serbia's first shady railway deal with a foreign power. That would be its first railway as an independent country, started after the 1878 Congress of Berlin, which included a special committee to oversee the construction of a regional railway. The project was a matter of international concern because since the 1850s, European powers had sought to establish a railway connection with the Ottoman Empire. When the Russo-Turkish War ended in 1878, Serbia sat between two empires, the Ottoman Empire and Austria-Hungary, and the shortest route between them ran through it.

Having made the railway a priority, European powers jockeyed to influence its route. Austria-Hungary and Russia viewed the railway in zero-sum terms. Austria-Hungary's diplomat in Belgrade explained the stakes to his superiors at the Ministry of Foreign Affairs: "Russia, if it was to get the railway in Serbia, would receive in the south of our Kingdom a permanent and reliable observer, a force, a new agitator on our southern border, in the end it might get allies in Serbia." Officials in Russia, for their part, viewed the railway as an opportunity to stop the spread of Austrian-Hungarian influence in Serbia.[15]

Within Serbia, the project was praised and vilified. Establishing a railway, some Serbian elites had long argued, was a key to modernization. "Serbia will collapse, unless an iron road is constructed over it!" Prince Mihailo Obrenović, Serbian royalty, worried in 1865. Others saw another avenue for foreign influence. "In the Iron Road, which will pass through the heart of Serbia, I see that fierce dragon, which will... swallow thousands of families whose grandfathers and fathers made all sacrifices for the freedom of this country," an opponent of the railway later warned.[16]

The dragon, of course, was not China but Austria-Hungary. Serbia, lacking sufficient funds as it does today, looked for outside investors. Austria-Hungary, its imposing neighbor and historical aggressor, was offering the best financial terms for the railway. Critics of the railway argued that it was not a pressing need and that rather than enriching Serbians, the railway would subjugate them. As one Serbian economist warned, "All that our railway could export is raw materials, which are required by the Austrian-Hungarian factories. And once we have finished exporting raw materials, then we shall become laborers of foreign factory owners and capitalists."[17] The opposition also pointed to missing links in the bigger proposed network, which no one could guarantee would be built, making the railway's outlook even more uncertain.

Secrecy and bribery moved the railway along. Recognizing that Austrian companies would probably win any open tender for the project, Serbian officials held secret negotiations with Russia, which could not afford to finance the project but wanted to build it. Both sides agreed that, after securing financing from France or Britain, Serbia could hand over construction to a Russian firm. But the deal fell apart. Société de l'Union Générale, a French bank, eventually won the concession for the line, after bribing members of the royal family. It went bankrupt in 1882, less than a year after construction was started, and Serbia appointed another French bank in its place. After becoming operational in 1884, the railway generated losses for the state, which was forced to pay the guarantees it had promised its creditors.[18]

Belgrade's first railway station was completed shortly after the line, and its grand yellow facade evokes the era when the train was cutting-edge technology. The building also reflects the city's traumatic history. Infrastructure is often the first target of military operations, and Belgrade's position at the crossroads of empires has meant that its railways and bridges have often come under attack. German forces damaged the station in 1941, during the early days of World War II, and Allied forces followed suit in 1944, when the country was occupied. In 1999, NATO munitions hit the Chinese embassy in Belgrade, an accident that pushed China and Serbia closer together. The city has been destroyed and rebuilt some forty times.

"The Biggest Transportation Disaster"

After 134 years of operation, Belgrade's main station was shut down in July 2018, just days before I arrived. Eventually, it will reopen as a museum.

The new station, still under construction when I visited, is an outcast. It was built in an impoverished area with the assumption that the building blocks of city life—apartments, offices, restaurants, and shops—would be developed around it. But little has sprouted, and the station remains disconnected from the rest of the city. Travelers using it must take a bus or cab. "It is the biggest transportation disaster in Belgrade," Vukan Vuchic, a Belgrade native and leading transportation expert at the University of Pennsylvania, told me.[19]

Inside, the station was a bunker of cold gray concrete and blue construction tarps. The only decorations were graffiti on the train. Bubble letters, large and neon, covered a train several tracks away. The spray paint occasionally crept up past the lower paneling and onto the bottom of each train's windows. The station was eerily quiet, especially for a weekday morning. Rather than history, what one feels when entering is a suspicion that you are about to make a cameo in *Saw*, the horror-film franchise.

Where it matters most, though, the new station seems to be getting it right. There is an information booth staffed and ready to point travelers toward the ticket office. Before boarding the train for the nine-hour journey, I asked one of the staffers whether there was food on board. "No, that's the café," he said, pointing to two vending machines on the side of the track. I paid for an instant coffee, and brown liquid dribbled out of the machine and into a thin plastic cup. Hand burning but unwilling to drop the only caffeine in sight, I climbed aboard.

I was not expecting to bask in the luxury of the famous Orient Express, with its white tablecloths and wooden paneling. In 1882, the first Orient Express service that left Paris offered oysters, soup with Italian pasta, turbot with green sauce, fillet of beef, "chaud-froid" of game animals, lettuce, chocolate pudding, and a buffet of desserts.[20] The Orient Express was never a single line but a series of lines that stretched from Paris to Istanbul. Like the proliferation of "New Silk Road" initiatives in recent years, the Orient Express was such a captivating brand that it was appropriated, reused, and ultimately overused. The last regular train that could claim to be a part of that network made its final run from Vienna to Strasbourg in 2009.[21]

The mustachioed hero in Christie's thriller, the detective Hercule Poirot, would find few people to question but plenty of clues on today's train. Climbing into a first-class cabin on the first train of the day, I found crumbs from previous company sprinkled across the seats. Other than the staff, the only other living thing I saw were flies. Chewed gum had colonized the air vents beneath the windows. The carpet was brown and rough, showing some stains and surely hiding lots more. Molder on the Orient Express.

Shabby but punctual, the train departed at 7:42 in the morning and soon passed through the area where China and Serbia held a ground-breaking ceremony for the new railway in November 2017. "I hope workers from the two countries will work devotedly and complete the project with high quality," a Chinese official remarked after the ceremony. But when I visited that site, there were no noticeable signs of significant construction. After initially promising the project would be completed in 2017, officials have delayed it several times.[22]

The train is so flawed that, accidentally, it offers something priceless and increasingly rare. It is a tired rumbling box with signs advertising Wi-Fi that does not exist. The outlets do not work. Out the window, flat fields of wheat and sunflowers repeat endlessly. What you see in the first hour is what you get for nine hours. Few services provide such a complete escape from distraction, and when almost everything else does not work, the mind really does.

The new railway has suffered from creeping requirements. Officials promise it will be "high speed," even though original plans indicated a target well below two hundred kilometers per hour, the generally accepted threshold. Some reports have suggested they are considering further upgrading the project to hit that mark, which would inevitably upgrade the project's price tag as well. The current train could certainly benefit from greater speed. In a world where most forms of transportation have become faster, the Belgrade-Budapest line has actually regressed. In the early 1980s, the train took roughly six hours, a third less than it takes today.[23]

But beyond a certain point, the allure of speed often reflects the triumph of politics over economics. Politicians love to announce big projects, which attract media coverage and advance legacy-building efforts. There are usually other options, of course. For existing railways like the Belgrade-Budapest line, investing in upgrades and better operations and maintenance can be more cost-effective than starting anew. Those prudent decisions should be cheered by taxpaying citizens, but the theater of politics often demands more. It is hard to hold a ribbon-cutting ceremony for a maintenance job.

High-speed railways are doubly tempting because they tap into what sociologists call the "technological sublime," the thrill that planners and politicians get from delivering the latest technology and in some cases even pushing technological boundaries.[24] Superlatives often accompany new projects—the longest bridge, the fastest train, the tallest building—and can influence design choices. The technological sublime is baked into the very name of high-speed rail, which evokes images of sleek futuristic trains zipping from one city to another. Having built more kilometers of high-speed rail domestically than the rest of the world combined, Chinese firms are eager to feed these temptations.

As China aims to dominate other advanced technology and manufacturing sectors, high-speed rail is a cautionary tale for its Western competitors. After launching joint ventures with Canadian, German, French, and Japanese companies, Chinese firms were able to acquire the capabilities and technical knowledge to start producing their own high-speed rail technology. In 2010, one industry expert estimated that 90 percent of China's high-speed rail technology was derived from foreign partnerships or equipment.[25] Driven by quarterly earnings, Western firms failed to appreciate, or simply could not resist, the longer game that China was drawing them into. These deals provided foreign firms with access to China's large domestic market, but the gains were temporary.

Many of China's early partners became its competitors, and since then, many have become its collateral damage. In 2005, the German conglomerate Siemens entered into a joint venture with China National Railway Corporation to provide $919 million worth of trains for the Beijing-Tianjin high-speed railway.[26] During the railway's construction, the Chinese partner mastered the German firm's technology and deployed an "indigenous" version at one-third the cost, raising red flags that Siemens' intellectual property had been compromised.[27] When a follow-on project was announced in 2008, China's Ministry of Railways insisted it use "Chinese" technology, awarding the $5.7 billion contract to China

National Railway Corporation.[28] The accusations have come full circle as Chinese researchers have even accused foreign companies of stealing Chinese rail technology.[29]

Despite the political appeal of high-speed railways, they are rarely profitable.[30] As a rough rule, the proposed route should be between two hundred and five hundred miles in length. Outside that range, shorter routes are often better served by standard rail or buses, and longer routes are better served by airplanes. Most new routes cost at least $10 million per mile to build and rely on government subsidies to operate. To break even, high-speed railways require at least six million passengers a year under relatively optimistic assumptions about construction cost and time savings.[31] Since the first high-speed railways emerged in France and Japan in the early 1980s, only two high-speed rail projects have become profitable, and a third has broken even.[32]

The Belgrade-Budapest line seems destined to join that loss-making list. Even though its length, roughly 220 miles, is within the appropriate range, it will struggle to serve enough people. Attracting six million passengers would require every man, woman, and child in Belgrade and Budapest to buy two tickets each year. More often, annual passenger volumes must exceed nine million to break even. Tamas Matura, an assistant professor at the University of Budapest, estimates that the new line will take twenty-five hundred years to make a profit, without factoring in maintenance costs.[33]

Despite the uncertainties of the railway—or perhaps because of them—Hungarian, Serbian, and Chinese officials are already looking south. They have suggested that the railway will become part of a corridor linking another historic destination turned flagship BRI project, Piraeus Port in Greece, with European markets farther inland. Ships from China will dock at Piraeus, and their cargo will be carried by rail to Budapest, passing through Belgrade along the way. Chinese officials have dubbed it the "China-Europe Land-Sea Express Line."[34]

But like Serbia's first railway, the idea depends on other railway links being built in the coming years. Standing between Belgrade and Piraeus are hundreds of miles of railways in Serbia, Macedonia, and Greece that require upgrades. Practical concerns aside, the idea is undeniably clever and, like other parts of the BRI, has an imaginative pull. It has also been called the Balkan Silk Road, and realistic or not, it has the benefit of associating the uncertain Belgrade-Budapest railway with Piraeus, which has already established itself as one of China's most commercially successful projects.[35]

"The Dragon's Head"

When I visited Piraeus Port in October 2018, its staff was recovering from hosting a much more important visitor. A few days earlier, China's transportation minister, Li Xiaopeng, toured the facilities by boat. At the time, his three-year budget was larger than Argentina's annual GDP. Chinese officials use Piraeus as a showpiece, allowing party leaders to bask in its success and hosting foreign officials from Africa and elsewhere to give them a glimpse of what partnering with China might accomplish. When Xi visited in November 2019, he called it "the dragon's head" for China in the region.[36]

Well before Piraeus became part of China's BRI, it was center stage for the rise and fall of great powers. In the fourth century BC, the Athenian general Themistocles persuaded his government to create a naval fleet at Piraeus. The decision was criticized at the time as wasting public resources but vindicated when Persia's King Xerxes attacked Greece in 480 BC. In one of the first large naval battles in history, Themistocles lured the Persian fleet into the narrow waters at Salamis, where his vastly outnumbered Greek fleet sank three hundred Persian ships. After growing into a commercial hub, the port was destroyed during the Peloponnesian War, when Sparta defeated Athens. It was rebuilt under Alexander the Great and then destroyed again by the Roman Empire. Not until Greece's statehood in 1832 did the port begin to reemerge.[37]

China took the port without violence, though not without opposition. In 2014, after leasing a container terminal at Piraeus five years earlier, the Chinese shipping giant COSCO reached a deal to buy a majority stake in the port. Led by Alexis Tsipras, the left-wing party Syriza opposed the deal along with other proposed privatizations, which it pledged to freeze and renegotiate on better terms. When Syriza took power in 2015, its shipping minister announced on his first day in office, "The [port] selloff stops here."[38]

But under pressure from Greece's "troika" of creditors—the European Commission, the European Central Bank, and the International Monetary Fund—Tsipras accepted the deal and only made changes at its margins. Investors applauded Tsipras for this reversal, and union workers protested outside his office.[39]

Few projects under the BRI banner have achieved Piraeus's commercial success. In 2018, its container traffic increased more than fivefold over 2010 levels, when COSCO first took over the management role from Greek companies.[40] A Greek company still runs one of the three terminals, but most of the gains have occurred in the two Chinese-run terminals. When I visited, a long line of trucks was backed up beyond the entrance to the Greek-run terminal, while those entering the Chinese terminals cruised smoothly into the facilities.

The port's increase in performance has not come without controversy. Its workers union has gone on strike several times and has alleged that COSCO is not fulfilling its labor-protection obligations.[41] The new management team paid for 110 workers to retire early, roughly a 10 percent workforce cut.[42] Previously, port authority workers were allowed to work from 7:30 a.m. to 3:00 p.m., and now they are required to work standard business hours, 9:00 a.m. to 5:00 p.m. Of course, many of these adjustments are not unique to Chinese ownership and could have happened under other private owners.

EU authorities also suspect that a criminal smuggling network has shifted to the port. In 2018, they began investigating whether Chinese companies are systematically underreporting the cost of imported goods to avoid EU taxes. The EU's antifraud office has fined the Greek government €200 million for poor regulation and oversight.[43] In Piraeus, as elsewhere, better connectivity not only brings more "nice" things but also opens the door for illicit activities.

Undaunted, China is eager to expand further. It aims to turn Piraeus into the largest container port in the Mediterranean by 2020 and has already moved into second place, behind Spain's Port of Valencia. In October 2019, the Greek government partially approved COSCO's master plan for turning old warehouses into luxury hotels, adding new storage and logistics facilities, and building a cruise terminal service center with duty-free shops.[44] COSCO also wants to invest an additional €300 million to build a fourth container terminal.

As one of China's most successful projects, Piraeus also shows the limits of using foreign infrastructure in general and ports in particular to promote goodwill. Sometimes commercial success is at odds with public sentiment, especially when higher productivity means fewer workers. Touring a modern port is like watching a giant mechanized symphony: there are smooth, coordinated movements and very few people. Piraeus operates its container terminals as semiautomated, which it justifies on safety grounds but has the benefit of employing more workers. The port's top leadership is mostly Chinese, but the workers are overwhelmingly Greek. The tension between productivity and employment is not unique to foreign infrastructure projects, but foreign owners are an easier target for public protest. Beijing can lose in the public eye even when its projects succeed.

Greek citizens, like so many others, hold conflicting views about China.[45] On the one hand, a majority of Greeks view China positively as an economic partner. On the other hand, they view China's rise as negative for the European Union as a whole. Complicating matters is resentment among Greeks about the choices they face. After mandating that Greece sell state assets, EU officials express concern about China's growing investments there.

This ambivalence gives local politicians the ammunition they need to create obstacles to the port's expansion. Greece's Central Archaeological Council designated large swaths of Piraeus a heritage site in April 2019, threatening to prevent further construction at the port due to Greece's strict archaeologic protections.[46] By design, these threats are likely to yield only minor adjustments. Politicians benefit from publicly standing up to China and being seen to protect Greek heritage and culture. In the process, they may also compel China to increase its investments to win their approval.

"Balkan Back Door"

Whether the Belgrade-Budapest railway ever reaches Piraeus, it has already become a flagship project for China's regional engagement. Every year since 2012, sixteen central and eastern European heads of state, including eleven EU members and five non-EU members, have assembled around China. Originally called the "16+1" format, the group expanded to include Greece in 2019.

This regional grouping is both less and more than it seems. At first glance, it is tempting to dismiss it as a hollow talk-shop. Almost every year, statements note that cooperation will be conducted in accordance with each country's "respective laws and regulations," an attempt to reassure Brussels that EU rules are not being undermined. The group has accomplished little of consequence since it was formed in 2012. Confusion about its purpose is evident in the struggle to describe it. It has been called a mechanism, a format, a framework, and a platform, among other things.

What all these labels fail to capture is China's ability to effectively exercise its power bilaterally under the cover of a multilateral veneer.[47] Bringing together many countries, this grouping gives the outward appearance of inclusivity and consensus building. In statements, the participants affirm their commitment to principles such as openness and transparency and genuine multilateral institutions like the World Trade Organization and the United Nations.[48] "We need to uphold multilateralism," China's Premier Li Keqiang told attendees in 2018.[49]

Beneath the surface, China's 17+1 format is fundamentally different from the multilateral practices and institutions it claims to uphold. China and its partners do not subscribe to a common set of rules that has any significant impact on their behavior. Nor is anything of consequence done by consensus. China's multilateralism through the 17+1 format and the BRI more generally lacks depth, and it relies on stroking egos and dangling bilateral deals. Call it "flatteralism."

Most of the time, the 17+1 equals two: China and the smaller country with which it is negotiating. It is an equation that has worked well for Beijing, which has used its economic power to divide the EU's current membership and deepen roots in candidate countries. In 2016, Hungary, Croatia, and Greece helped soften an EU statement on China's claims in the South China Sea. Similar tactics have blocked criticism of China's human rights record.[50]

There are practical and political advantages as well. These annual gatherings allow Chinese officials to efficiently lavish high-level attention on smaller economies. And when China comes to town, its summits are less board meetings than auditions. The seventeen countries compete for the attention of the one. China uses variations of this model elsewhere, positioning itself at the center of summits in Africa and Latin America.

But China has yet to offer deep multilateralism at scale. Its closest attempt, the Asian Infrastructure Investment Bank (AIIB), has attracted broad participation and adopted rules similar to those of the World Bank. But having lent only $12 billion at the end of 2019, the AIIB is easily overshadowed by Beijing's bilateral lending mechanisms.[51] China Development Bank, which is the world's largest development-finance institution, pledged to lend $250 billion to BRI partners over a five-year period.[52]

The limits of China's bilateral approach are evident in the MOUs that Beijing has pushed so many countries to sign. Chinese officials make a point of claiming that the BRI will be tailored to promote local development goals, but the MOUs use boilerplate, nonbinding language. Occasionally, a mention is made to "link" or "align" the BRI with a partner's development plan, but how that will happen is not spelled out.

The value of these documents is purely symbolic, though increasingly not as China intended. Chinese state media make a habit of touting how many cooperation documents have been signed with countries and international organizations. But participation is no guarantee of investment, and the longer the list of BRI cooperation documents grows, the less signing them means. More than any port or high-speed railway, it is perhaps the MOU that best captures what the BRI is—and is not.

For all the lip service paid to openness, China's checkbook disproportionately favors the five non-EU governments, where investment rules are less transparent and open. Collectively, the five non-EU economies (Albania, Bosnia and Herzegovina, North Macedonia, Montenegro, and Serbia) have a GDP that is roughly one-sixteenth of the eleven EU economies. Yet in 2016 and 2017, they attracted roughly half of announced Chinese investment across the sixteen economies in transport infrastructure, energy, real estate, and mergers-and-acquisitions deals.[53] Citing these outsized investments, some European officials worry that China is creeping through a "Balkan back door."

China's promises for investment must be taken with a grain, if not a mountain, of salt. For each project that has started, there are countless others that remain aspirational. During Xi's visit to the Czech Republic in 2016, for example, he proposed building canals linking the Danube, Oder, and Elbe Rivers. If completed, they would allow ships to travel from the Baltic and North Seas to the Black Sea. The idea was not China's, nor was it new, having been proposed in various forms for hundreds of years. But its sheer scale seemed a natural fit for China's ambitions and the insatiable appetite of Chinese construction companies. After some initial fanfare, however, little has occurred.

"The Secular Struggle"

On the train to Budapest, I was startled by a voice, the first I had heard in hours. "Passport," a uniformed woman said, standing in the doorway of my cabin with one hand out. In her other hand was a small box. As my documents were stamped, I looked out the window and realized I had been expecting the physical landscape to change. But identical fields stretched on. Some borders have natural physical divides: a river, a mountain, or the sea. Others, like the one between Serbia and Hungary, feel entirely arbitrary. But they have consequences for the people caught between them. The average salary in Serbia is 40 percent lower than in Hungary.[54]

Other than a brief change of staff and the appearance of customs officers, the stop on the Serbian-Hungarian border was remarkably similar to all the other stops. At each stop, a railway official emerged from a building with a small notebook, judiciously noted the presence of the train, and exchanged some quick banter with the conductor. At the border, the entire process took less than fifteen minutes, helped by the fact that there were few passports to stamp. We continued onward, and finally, after twenty-four stops and nine hours, the train rolled into Budapest.

For China's state-owned construction firms, the EU remains much more difficult to enter. The biggest obstacles are EU funding and rules. To compete for EU projects, China must drop its preferred approach of offering loans that require using Chinese firms and compete more directly for contracts. Chinese firms are struggling but learning, and with time, they will surely get better at meeting EU environmental safeguards and other rules. But the availability of EU funding for infrastructure, as well as private investment, means that China's loans are not as attractive. Compared to developing and emerging markets, where China's BRI is most active, China has a higher bar to clear and less leverage for negotiating in the EU.

That bar could get even higher. Chinese investments are receiving greater scrutiny, particularly those related to technology and critical infrastructure.[55] Along with stricter foreign investment reviews, EU states are considering industrial policies that would support their firms against China's large and heavily subsidized state-owned enterprises.[56] Calls for conditioning China's access to the EU market on reciprocal access to the Chinese market are growing louder as well.

The thorn at the center of this debate is whether Europe must become more like China in order to compete with it. If the EU does nothing, it risks defeat on what many European officials believe is an uneven playing field. If it overreacts, the urge to protect European companies could come at the expense of their competitiveness.

The EU is still struggling to find the right balance. To compete with China's railway companies, French and German leaders supported merging their state railway companies, Alstom and Siemens. In February 2019, however, the deal was stopped by antitrust authorities in Brussels on the grounds that it would raise costs for consumers and reduce competition. The process for evaluating mergers looks only at the EU market. "There is no prospect of Chinese entry in the European market in the foreseeable future," explained Margrethe Vestager, the EU commissioner in charge of competition policy.[57]

That future is not so difficult to imagine, however, and the global view looks different. China's state-owned firms benefit from scale as well as generous state subsidies, and they are using the BRI to learn how to deliver projects outside China. It is sobering to note that even if the merger were approved, China's largest railway company, CRRC Corporation Limited, would still have annual sales totaling more than twice that of a combined Siemens and Alstom.[58] European business interests, particularly in France and Germany, are pressing for policies that would make mergers easier.[59]

It is ultimately a question about how to compete. Free-market advocates still see more danger in domestic protection than in China's expanding global footprint. In the Siemens and Alstom case, for example, the worst outcome would be an EU railway champion that atrophies because it is overly protected. In that scenario, a weak EU champion would become a liability and could even become a target for Chinese acquisition. Even for the EU, turning inward is not a viable long-term strategy, since more than three-quarters of the global economy is outside it.

The EU is not marching in lockstep, of course, and never has. At least ten EU members, primarily in central and eastern Europe, had signed BRI MOUs by mid-2019.[60] When Xi Jinping visited Rome in April 2019, the Italian government rolled out the red carpet, literally, and signed onto the BRI. The decision provoked public criticism from the U.S. government, but it was another nonbinding document, more politically symbolic than commercially meaningful. By pulling in a new Italian government that was more favorable to Beijing than its predecessors, the deal demonstrated China's ability to take advantage of political windows of opportunity. After Rome, however, Xi continued on to France, which did not sign an MOU but did announce $45 billion in deals, sixteen times more than Italy had done.[61] Inadvertently, Xi's trip also signaled how little value the MOU carries.

Even "neutral" Switzerland has signed onto the BRI. At the second Belt and Road Forum in April 2019, Switzerland, which is not an EU member but participates in the EU's single market, signed a document to facilitate cooperation in third markets. China's main interest is attracting more private investment to its projects. Of course, the MOU does nothing to reduce the risks that investors face in foreign markets. For all the headlines that these documents have generated, they remain neither necessary nor sufficient for doing business with China.

But the EU's debate is less about ends than means, signaling a major shift in its stance toward China.[62] For years, the EU's engagement with China was based on the hope that China would liberalize its economy and open up. As recently as 2016, for example, the EU's main China strategy document took a relatively cautious position, noting, "China's increased weight and a renewed emphasis on 'going global' mean that it is seeking a bigger role and exerting greater influence on an evolving system of global governance."[63] Three years later, it called China a "strategic competitor" and "an economic competitor in pursuit of technological leadership and a systemic rival promoting alternative models of governance."[64]

These are modest steps, more rhetorical than transformational; but they reflect a growing consensus among policy makers, and their direction is clear. As the EU ramps up investment screening and considers new industrial policies, it has launched its own connectivity initiative aimed at competing with the BRI in its backyard. It has also refused to grant China market-economy status at the WTO. "Maybe we have overestimated Russia and underestimated China," Johannes Hahn, the EU commissioner formerly responsible for accession, said in March 2019.[65] If more Europeans agree, elevating China as the primary threat, the shift in perceptions could be transformative, not only for the EU's relations with China but also for the EU itself.

That shift has not yet occurred in the broader public mind. Roughly the same percentage of people in France and Germany were concerned about China's and Russia's power and influence, according to a 2018 poll.[66] Other EU members surveyed, including the United Kingdom, Italy, Spain, Hungary, and Poland, had higher percentages concerned about Russia. More people in Germany and France viewed U.S. power and influence as threatening than viewed either China or Russia that way. The more U.S. and European perceptions diverge, the more difficult it will be to fashion a united response to China.[67]

Of course, the BRI is just one dimension of Chinese power and influence. In the short term, European views of China are likely to be shaped more by events within China. Beijing's use of surveillance technology, its persecution of ethnic minorities, and its treatment of Western firms are among the top areas of European concern. But through the BRI, some of these challenges will move closer to the EU. In early 2019, for example, Belgrade announced plans to install one thousand surveillance cameras through a partnership with the Chinese tech giant Huawei. As Chinese construction firms learn to navigate the EU market, the friction created by competition with Western firms will intensify.

China's divisive push into the EU's neighborhood could eventually help unite it. After all, the Soviet Union helped bring the EU into existence. Before that, threats came from the Ottoman Empire during the sixteenth century and the Mongol empire during the thirteenth century. Halford Mackinder, the British geographer, argued that European civilization itself is a reaction to threats from the East. "European civilization is, in a very real sense, the outcome of the secular struggle against Asiatic invasion," he wrote in 1904.[68] Sometimes external enemies divided and ruled; other times Europe unified and resisted.

The BRI in its current form presents a different threat. The invaders are not massing at the EU's borders with horses or tanks but strolling into European capitals with briefcases in hand. Yet China's influence, and its use of economic tools for political aims, has already caught the attention of European leaders. Even as they debate whether to become more like China in their responses, a consensus has emerged that China is not going to become more like the EU. There is a growing sense of urgency, but the threat China presents is not yet viewed as existential. To truly unite Europe, China's BRI will have to stretch closer and become more menacing in European minds.

PART III

To the Sea

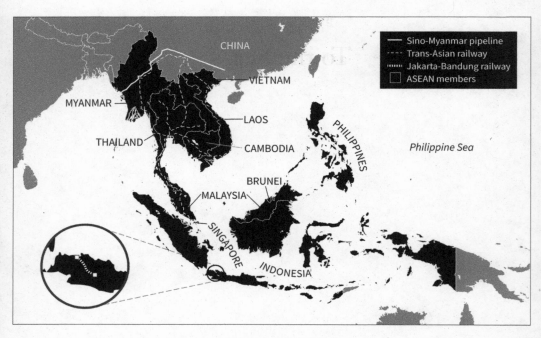

Southeast Asia

Center for Strategic and International Studies, Reconnecting Asia Project; United Nations Economic and Social Commission for Asia and the Pacific

CHAPTER SIX

The Weak Are Powerful

Southeast Asia

"THE POWERFUL WILL TAKE what they will, the weak will yield what they must," Malaysia's Prime Minister Mahathir Mohamad reflected in July 2018, paraphrasing the Greek historian Thucydides to summarize the challenge that China presents. "They are more powerful, and we cannot fight against them. How do we benefit from their wealth and their power?"[1] It is a question that many developing countries are grappling with, none more urgently than those in Southeast Asia. Cleverly, it also hides the power that smaller countries wield when they court China and its competitors, playing them off each other.

As a geographic construct, Southeast Asia was first defined by outsiders. Howard Malcom, a reverend from Boston, Massachusetts, is often recognized as being the first to use the term in his book *Travels in South-Eastern Asia*, published in 1839. The concept was cemented during World War II, when Franklin Roosevelt and Winston Churchill created the South East Asia Command. British and U.S. government agencies further debated and revised their definitions of the region, its membership and boundaries, but the basic idea stuck.[2]

Following the war and decolonization, the region defined itself. A landmark development was the creation of the Association for

Southeast Asian Nations (ASEAN) in 1967 by Indonesia, Malaysia, Singapore, Thailand, and the Philippines. Five more countries have since joined, and the remaining country in the region, East Timor, is an observer. Originally aiming to offset communist insurgencies in the region, ASEAN gradually developed an economic focus.

Squint your eyes, and ASEAN looks like a whale's tale. Thailand is the spine of mainland Southeast Asia, its second largest economy and the gatekeeper for overland connections between the South China Sea in the east and the Bay of Bengal in the west. It is surrounded by Cambodia, Laos, and Myanmar, three fast-growing economies whose fates are increasingly bound with China. In the maritime space, Indonesia is the region's powerhouse, responsible for roughly two-fifths of ASEAN's collective population and a third of its GDP.[3]

For countries on the outside looking in, the region's pull is irresistible. If ASEAN was a single economy, it would have been the fifth largest in the world in 2018.[4] It is an exporting juggernaut, home to some of the fastest-growing middle-income populations, which are becoming burgeoning markets of their own. Even those countries not looking to do business with ASEAN can hardly avoid it. Sitting among Asia's largest economies, it hosts the second-busiest shipping lane in the world, the Malacca Strait, through which nearly one hundred thousand vessels—carrying a quarter of global traded goods—pass every year.[5]

The contest to access and influence ASEAN is multifaceted, but the strongest tug-of-war is between China and Japan. China is playing a north-south game, reaching down from Yunnan, the southern province that Owen Lattimore, an American scholar of China, once called the "pivot" of Southeast Asia.[6] China's proximity is a blessing and a curse. Along with ports, it can build overland infrastructure—fiber-optic cables, pipelines, railways, and roads—expanding its supply chains southward. As Chinese wages climb, the prospect of relocating its manufacturing activities to Vietnam, where wages are lower, becomes more attractive.

But China's size and increasingly strident behavior have created unease in the region. Chinese officials have taken an expansive view of China's territorial claims in the South China Sea, resisting attempts to negotiate territorial disputes multilaterally and disregarding rulings by international tribunals. In 2010, during an annual ASEAN security forum, China's foreign minister, Yang Jiechi, stormed out after Secretary of State Hillary Clinton challenged China's claims. He returned with an aggressive message for the ASEAN countries: "China is a big country and other countries are small countries, and that's just a fact."[7]

China's actions in the South China Sea have been even more alarming than its words. Where the facts on the ground have not suited its position, China has changed the ground. Between 2013 and 2017, Chinese dredgers added thirty-two hundred acres to land features in the Spratly Islands, nearly the equivalent of the Los Angeles International Airport.[8] International condemnation has grown louder as China has outfitted artificial islands with runways and deployed antiship and antiaircraft missiles. But these "salami-slicing" tactics have been effective because no single change seems dramatic enough to warrant a sufficient response.

Japan is playing an east-west game. It is approaching from the sea; but with deep experience in Southeast Asia, Japan is the incumbent, and China is the newcomer. Much of the region's infrastructure already reflects the interests of Japanese firms, whose supply chains depend on maritime connections. Japan cannot match the global scale of China's BRI, but it is intensely focused on Southeast Asia, where it is outspending China in several countries and going toe-to-toe with it in others.

Japan's east-west preferences can be seen in its support for several "economic corridors," which connect major cities with transport infrastructure. It is backing a "Southern Economic Corridor" that hops across major cities in four countries: Ho Chi Minh City (Vietnam), Phnom Penn (Cambodia), Bangkok (Thailand), and Dawei (Myanmar). To the north, an "East-West Economic Corridor" runs from the port of Danang in central Vietnam, through Laos and Thailand, to the port of Mawlamyine in Myanmar. It is also developing ports in Malaysia, Indonesia, Brunei, and the Philippines.[9] What these efforts have in common is a desire to funnel more commerce to the coastlines.

Japan also benefits from a reputation for delivering reliable products, and it has made quality a focus of its efforts. In 2015, Prime Minister Shinzo Abe launched the "Partnership for Quality

Infrastructure," a not-so-subtle way of contrasting Japanese infrastructure with Chinese infrastructure. Backed by $200 billion, it
aims to persuade countries to pay more up front for projects that
cost less over their lifetime. Japan has also pushed hard for the
world's leading economies, including China, to endorse "quality infrastructure" principles. Safety, sustainability, and reliability are
among the goals mentioned. These principles stem not only from a
desire to compete with China but also from Japan's own experience
in the region. In the 1970s and 1980s, it made many of the same
mistakes that China has been making during the BRI's initial years.

Japan has another advantage that China does not: allies. No
country has been more successful than Japan in shaping recent
U.S. government policy for the region. Abe got off to an early start
in November 2016, when he strode into Trump Tower with a gold-
plated golf club, a gift for the president-elect. The charm offensive
has continued with over forty conversations. Many more meetings
between lower-level officials have hammered out overlapping policies. In 2016, Abe unveiled his "Free and Open Indo-Pacific" strategy, and the following year, the Trump administration announced
its "Free and Open Indo-Pacific" strategy.

But while the Japanese and U.S. bumper stickers are nearly
identical, Japan has taken a more diplomatic approach to China's
BRI. Japanese officials have underscored the region's need for infrastructure and put forward criteria for the type of "quality infrastructure" they support. That engagement, however, should not be
confused with endorsement. Naturally, many Chinese projects do
not meet those criteria. Japan also supports cooperation among
Japanese and Chinese companies working in third countries. These
arrangements provide Japan with a window into China's approach
and a seat at the table. Abe has even softened his sales pitch, refer-
ring to the "Free and Open Indo-Pacific" as a vision rather than a
strategy, after some ASEAN countries claimed it was too divisive.[10]

Critically, the countries at the center of this competition are far
from pawns. The savviest among them have turned a contest
among outside powers into a buffet of options for themselves.
They do this directly, through open competitions for megaprojects. When Indonesia called for bids for a high-speed railway in
2015, for example, it was as if Sotheby's put the *Mona Lisa* on the

auction block. They do it indirectly, by traveling to capitals and announcing deals, courting better offers from larger powers, who fear being cut out of some of the world's fastest-growing markets. In 2016, all four of the region's new leaders traveled to China and Japan, and all had infrastructure at the top of their wish lists.[11]

The result is not a simple dichotomy between the powerful and the powerless. Although China's shadow is growing, Japan is fighting to retain an edge in markets where it has invested heavily for decades. The United States, for its part, is invested commercially and has a network of security partners, including the Philippines and Thailand as treaty allies and Indonesia, Malaysia, Singapore, and Vietnam as enhanced security partners. India's rise will be felt more acutely in the coming years. Deals are constantly being made, relationships adjusted and recalibrated. Thucydides would be intrigued by the flurry of action but also lost. In Southeast Asia, the powerful pay what they must, and the weak take what they can.

"Look East"

No one has played the game longer than Mahathir, whose first term as Malaysia's prime minster spanned twenty-two years. A doctor by training, he is an infamously blunt speaker whose anti-Western and anti-Semitic remarks have generated a mountain of controversy.[12] To the world's surprise, in May 2018, he was back in the job at the age of ninety-two, riding a wave of public anger to a surprise victory. On the campaign trail, he made borrowing from China a major issue, warning that Malaysia was selling its sovereignty. As other opposition leaders in South and Southeast Asia watched Mahathir win, they realized he was onto something.

Mahathir's tactics worked so well not because he changed but because much remained the same. There was plenty in his two decades in office that prepared him for the challenge. "I have always been fascinated by the metamorphosis of bare land into housing estates, industrial estates, highways, bridges and other structures," Mahathir writes in his memoirs.[13] Indeed, he was behind Malaysia's most iconic projects: the Penang Bridge, the KL Towers, the North-South Highway, and even a Formula One race track. Many of these grand projects were carried out under the banner of privatization and industrialization, but Mahathir believed they also had psychological benefits, putting Malaysia on par with other countries. If details of the projects were disputed, Mahathir accused critics of being against Malaysia's development.[14]

To bring about that transformation, Mahathir embraced Japan, which was the global economy's rising star. From the ashes of World War II, Japan regained its industrial capacity and was so successful by the 1980s that some observers predicted it would overtake the United States. Two decades earlier, Mahathir's first visit to Tokyo shaped his thinking about what Malaysia might achieve. He and his wife, Siti Hasmah, stood outside the Tokyo train station and watched the trains arrive and depart. "It was an endless stream and it was really quite breathtaking for I had never seen anything like it," Mahathir recalled. "That scene of the Tokyo Station in 1961 implanted itself in my mind, never to be forgotten. For Malaya to have a similarly impressive railway was a dream."[15]

In 1981, six months after taking office, Mahathir launched the "Look East" policy. He viewed Japan as a source of inspiration and, smartly, as a source of investment. The policy included sending Malaysians to study and train in Japan and Korea. Mahathir explained that the goal was not to copy Japan in every way, not to become Japanese, but to borrow from the management practices, industrial policies, and work ethic that fueled Japan's booming exports. His overtures appealed to Japanese policy makers, who were beginning to push harder at the World Bank and other Western-dominated institutions for recognition of their approach to development, in which the state played a larger and more activist role.

Japan was emerging as a leading foreign-aid provider and would become the world's largest donor by the end of the decade.[16] Its investments were heavily focused on infrastructure in Asia, and the aggregate statistics are astounding. By the late 1980s, Japanese aid was 15–20 percent of the budget expenditures of every country in Southeast Asia.[17] At one point, 60 percent of Indonesia's loans from Japan were being used to service debt owed to Japan.[18] In the early 1990s, nearly two-thirds of Japanese aid went to Asia, and in some years, roughly 40 percent of its bilateral aid went toward infrastructure.[19] During the same period, the United States provided less than a sixth as much to Asia, and less than 4 percent of U.S. bilateral aid went toward infrastructure.

Tokyo used foreign aid as a runway for Japanese firms to relocate their manufacturing capabilities. During the 1980s, overcapacity grew, and the yen strengthened, squeezing the exporting potential of Japanese firms. As Japan's vice minister of finance said in 1991, "Japan will increasingly use its aid . . . as seed money to attract Japanese manufacturers or other industrial concerns with an attractive investment environment."[20] Japanese officials wanted to avoid the "hollowing out" they witnessed in the United States, where the departure of U.S. manufacturing to economies with lower production costs had taken a toll on American communities.[21]

Maintaining control, however, required keeping a tight grip on technology. By moving production into Southeast Asia, Japanese companies risked having their knowledge and methods copied and reproduced, essentially empowering their future competitors. To protect their edge, Japanese firms in Southeast Asia often kept Japanese management in top positions. They trained local staff to operate machinery and equipment, but the more fundamental knowledge behind those processes was kept in Japan. They shared the "how" but not the "why," as the scholars Walter Hatch and Kozo Yamamura observed.[22]

As Japan pushed deeper into Southeast Asia, criticism began to mount that its foreign aid mainly benefited Japanese firms. Compared to other leading donors, Japan was giving away less through grants and relying more on tougher loan terms. Japan's low-interest loans became more expensive for recipients in the 1980s as the yen strengthened. These loans were often "tied," meaning they required the recipient to use Japanese firms. When Japan moved to untie more of its aid, it initially only allowed developing countries to bid against Japanese firms, protecting its companies from international competition. After the policy change, Japanese firms still won over two-thirds of all procurement.[23]

Japan also had informal avenues for influencing project outcomes. Japan's aid process required requests from recipients, for whom Japanese firms eagerly recommended projects and helped draft proposals.[24] Design consultants were often Japanese and used specifications that, intentionally or not, favored Japanese firms.

Bribes were sometimes chalked up as part of the cost of doing business. When President Ferdinand Marcos of the Philippines left office in 1986 and fled to Hawaii, his papers exposed a system of corruption implicating over fifty Japanese companies.[25] The revelation made waves in Japan, where the Japanese parliament was dubbed the "Marcos Diet," strengthening calls for reform that led to Japan's first official aid charter in 1992.[26]

Importantly, Japan stood to benefit even if it did not construct the projects. From the perspective of the recipient country, better infrastructure was critical but far from the only item that would benefit from foreign assistance. There were also pressing needs for education and health services, for example. This focus on infrastructure benefited Japanese contractors and, over the longer term, encouraged more Japanese firms to set up production facilities.[27] Infrastructure was not merely an end but a means for developing regional supply chains that reflected Japanese interests.

Mahathir took issue with these practices. In 1984, he asked an audience of Japanese government and corporate representatives, "Is mighty Japan earnest and sincere enough in developing her economic, political and social relationships with a developing Malaysia?" He continued, "Where you have shown enlightened self-interest, I congratulate you. But I do believe that something has to be done to improve the pattern of economic relations between our two countries. That pattern conforms in many regards to the classic pattern of economic colonialism. It is a pattern that cannot but generate tensions in the years ahead."[28] It was a potent line of attack that he would dust off and redirect toward China more than three decades later.

Mahathir realized that technology transfer would not happen voluntarily, and he was using the bully pulpit to improve Malaysia's bargaining position. As he told the audience in 1984, "We cannot and will not remain merely as hewers of wood and drawers of water. . . . We also have to ensure a better picture with regard to the transfer of technology, the use of local materials, equal partnership and participation with regard to consultants, sub-contractors and professionals. We must not forget manpower training and development."[29] These basic concerns about who benefits from large-scale projects are bubbling up along China's BRI, in Southeast Asia and beyond.

"Predatory" Economics

Many of the criticisms leveled at China in recent years—overem-phasizing infrastructure, favoring its own companies, using com-mercial loans that dangerously increase the debts of smaller economies, restricting technology transfers—were made against Japan during the 1980s. In the United States, criticism of Japan's foreign-aid practices overlapped with concerns about its trade poli-cies. In April 1986, the U.S. Congress passed a "sense of Congress" resolution that called out "predatory" aid practices, a term that for-mer U.S. Secretary of State Rex Tillerson, Vice President Mike Pence, and other Trump-administration officials have used to de-scribe Chinese lending.[30]

Official Japanese government plans for industrializing Asia only exacerbated these fears. In 1987, Japan's Ministry of International Trade and Industry (MITI) released its New Asian Industries De-velopment Plan, which envisioned turning Asian states into special-ized exporters of various products. As Bernard Wysocki Jr., the *Wall Street Journal*'s Tokyo bureau chief, summarized the plan, "First, Japanese loans, mostly of government money, build up roads, bridges and such. Second, the Japanese government sends technical experts. Third, Japanese loans filter down to industry within the Asian country, to finance joint ventures and other business alliances. Fourth, Japan opens its doors to imports from these offshore facto-ries."[31] It was, in short, a plan for integrating Asia around Japan.

Like Chinese officials' homages to the ancient Silk Road, Japa-nese officials used colorful metaphors to make the plan and their economic aims in the region appear innocuous. The flying geese theory, which emerged in the 1930s and regained popularity in the 1960s, was a favorite. Its supporters claimed that Japan was like the lead goose in a flying formation, breaking the wind for Asia's less developed economies. They benefited from Japan's advances on the leading edge of technology, the theory speculated, because Japan was shedding industries to the countries behind it. One MITI doc-ument called for Japan serving as the region's "brains."[32] Some of this salesmanship backfired. What these images all had in common was that Japan would be in charge, at the center of things, at the top of a hierarchy.

Memories of the decades leading to World War II still lingered, stoking suspicion about Japan's ultimate aims. To some observers, Japan's aims sounded like a new incarnation of the Greater East Asia Co-Prosperity Sphere, a concept that Japanese imperialists used to justify military action during the 1930s.[33] "What Japan was unable to do with military force 50 years ago, it is achieving today through its money, diplomacy and technical skill," Wysocki suggested.[34] "Government officials and business executives all over the region fear that, before too long, their economies will be smothered in Japan's embrace," Hatch and Yamamura warned in 1996.[35]

In retrospect, fears about Japan's aid and infrastructure activities were overblown. For all the fanfare the New AID Plan received, it mainly reflected the view of a single Japanese government agency rather than the entire Japanese government. As Robert Orr, a Japan scholar and businessman who later became the U.S. ambassador to the Asian Development Bank, wrote, "The notion that Japan has hegemonic intentions in its overseas economic aid program derives from the assumption that a consensus exists within the government and the private sector on the use of aid to this end." In reality, he pointed out, "there exists no consensus on objectives," and this "causes confusion over Japanese intentions among aid recipients and donors alike."[36] Rather than strategically directing the might of Japan Inc. toward specific objectives set by the state, the "new" plan reaffirmed in broad terms what many Japanese multinational corporations were already doing.

Even if such a consensus had existed, Japan would have struggled to carry it out. In Indonesia during 1987, for example, Japan had twenty-six professionals overseeing more than $700 million in aid.[37] Around the same time, Japan had roughly one-third as many aid professionals as the United States, which was providing less aid.[38] The New AID Plan, and the metaphors used to illustrate Japan's activities more broadly, made Japanese actions appear more coordinated in theory than they were on the ground. The Japanese government was not an all-powerful puppet master but several competing participants and, more often than acknowledged, an observer.

Of course, there are major differences between Japan's experience in Southeast Asia during the 1980s and China's BRI.[39] Japan was more developed and richer in per capita terms. Japan is a democracy, most obviously, while China is not. Chinese contractors are more insulated from public pressure, able to endure corruption scandals abroad. Japan was, and remains, an ally of the United States. As early as 1980, U.S. and Japanese officials agreed to cooperate on aid projects.[40] Even while Japan was being criticized for "predatory" economic practices, it had much-closer diplomatic relations with the United States.

Yet during the 1980s, supporting China's rise was one issue the United States and Japan could agree on. Viewing China as a bulwark against the Soviet Union, U.S. policy makers authorized the sale of military equipment to China. They also encouraged Japan to increase its foreign aid to China. Eager to access China's large and growing market, Japan was happy to oblige. Japanese aid to China began in 1979, driven in part by a desire to encourage economic reforms announced by Deng Xiaoping, and climbed quickly. The floodgates had been opened, and by 1983, China was Japan's top aid recipient.

In many ways, Japan Inc. helped create China Inc. During the 1980s and 1990s, Japan provided roughly $24 billion in aid to China, much of which was used for infrastructure projects. A Japanese-government survey in 1998 found that a third of China's total electrified railway network was constructed using Japanese loans.[41] In 2000, more than 60 percent of all China's bilateral aid was from Japan.[42] As China's defense budget grew, enthusiasm began to wane among Japanese officials, who also complained that Chinese officials were not adequately publicizing Japan's generosity within China.

China's smaller neighbors were nervous much earlier. When Mahathir met with U.S. Secretary of State George Shultz in 1984, he warned about the threat that a stronger China would present. "A prosperous China, a more economically advanced China, would be equally a militarily strong China, which could then revert to the policies of hegemony, which from a historical perspective in this part of the world has always been found to be a serious concern," Mahathir's spokesman said after the meeting, summarizing his message to Shultz.[43] After returning to office in 2018, Mahathir downplayed the threat. "I have never felt any fear of China . . . they never conquered us," he said.[44]

More than any other country, Japan shaped China's view of foreign-aid practices. Many of Japan's early infrastructure deals in

China were repaid with oil, a model that China was subsequently criticized for using in developing countries. "China saw all of these tactics as beneficial for China's development," as Deborah Brautigam, an expert on Chinese aid, explains. "Japan and the West could use their modern technologies to exploit natural resources that Chinese technology could not yet unlock. China could pay for this investment later, with the resources that were uncovered. The subsidies and aid used by the West and Japan to wrap their naked hunger for China's markets meant that China was getting a discount on finance the country needed for its modernization."[45]

Chinese officials closely studied Japan's practices. There was genuine interest within China to understand Japan's economic practices in general, of which foreign aid was a distinct feature. The official history of Japan's MITI was translated faster in China than anywhere else.[46] In addition to providing loans for large projects, Japan also provided technical assistance, training thousands of Chinese officials. The Japan International Cooperation Agency had accepted more than fifteen thousand Chinese trainees by 2004. Training Chinese administrators made it more likely that future officials would favor Japanese companies by adopting processes and standards set in Tokyo.

This self-conscious modeling extended to the highest levels. When China's Vice Premier Zhu Rongji visited Japan in 1994, he made it a point to praise Japan's economic policies and success in gradually opening up. In Tokyo, Zhu told Japan's Foreign Minister Tsutomu Hata that with growing Sino-Japanese economic relations, "mutual dependency will increase and that is why we need more investment and technology transfer from Japan."[47] Later that year, China announced the creation of its own Export-Import Bank, the China Development Bank, and an agricultural bank, all based on Japan's experience. Within a decade, China would become the world's largest export creditor.[48]

The Pan-Asian Dream

In 1995, Mahathir revived a plan for a "pan-Asian" railway network. Versions of the idea have existed since the early 1900s, when British and French colonialists built some of the region's first tracks and began drafting plans for more extensive networks.[49] The concept resurfaced in an even more ambitious form in 1960, when a regional planning body at the United Nations proposed highway and railway networks connecting the region. The UN "trans-Asian" railway, if completed, would entail roughly 118,000 kilometers of railway, nearly enough to circle the Earth three times.

But Southeast Asia has been the gap in these sweeping proposals. As of 2017, ASEAN nations were responsible for nearly 40 percent of the trans-Asian railway's missing links.[50] When technical consultants for the UN studied the region's infrastructure in the 1990s, they noted that narrow, one-meter track gauge was often accompanied by light track, small trains, and slow speeds.[51] That made the system poorly equipped for handling standard-sized containers and larger volumes of cargo. Although one-meter gauge is common throughout mainland Southeast Asia, China and Indonesia use different gauges, posing challenges for transshipments by land and sea.

Since Mahathir reenergized the plan, ASEAN has focused on creating three main routes stretching from Kunming, the capital of China's Yunnan province, to Bangkok, Thailand. The eastern route would pass through Vietnam and Cambodia, the middle route through Laos, and the western route through Myanmar. At Bangkok, the routes are intended to converge and continue south, passing through Kuala Lumpur, Malaysia, and terminating in Singapore.

In addition to these three main routes, countries have proposed a dizzying number of supporting railways in the region. Indonesia alone has planned over thirty-two hundred kilometers of railway.[52] James Clark, a freelance writer who runs a travel agency, has pieced together these proposals in a subway-style map that he updates each year. Reflecting the pan-Asian railway's enduring appeal, these maps are entrancing and make the exotic familiar. Infrastructure takes center stage, and Southeast Asia looks as accessible as Manhattan. For an instant, it is easy to forget all that stands in the way. Build the railways, these images whisper, and integration will follow.[53]

Of course, even if the entire network became whole overnight, a prospect that could cost $75 billion, differences in track gauges and procedures at borders would still constrain greater connectivity.[54] "It's a question for all the train investments because they just talk about building the lines and that is it," explains Ruth

Banomyong, head of the Transport Department at Bangkok's Thammasat Business School. "They don't talk about the actual modality of managing a system that is supposed to go across borders. You probably need a new agreement for international rail transport for the region."[55]

Depictions of the pan-Asian railway can be deceptive in a second sense: they presume there is sufficient demand for these services to exist. Putting aside intrepid travelers and railway aficionados, most people traveling from Kunming to Singapore would still prefer to fly, which will remain cheaper and faster. Likewise, cargo shuttled between the two destinations would be cheaper if transported first to the coast and then by boat to Singapore. Most studies have found that a pan-Asian rail system would complement maritime shipping rather than compete with it.

The pan-Asian railway is more potent politically than commercially. It is something to strive toward, in bits and pieces, that will complement existing trade networks. It is something for politicians to invoke in the name of regional solidarity, integration, and development. As Mahathir explained during a visit to Kazakhstan in 1996, "In East Asia we are seriously studying a railway system linking Southeast Asia with China. It will be the logical step to link this system eventually with the railway system in Central Asia passing via and through Kazakhstan. This will give many land-bound Central Asian Nations access to the sea."[56]

During the same trip, Mahathir's comments foreshadowed what would become China's BRI: "Kazakhstan is indeed located in a strategic position in Euro-Asia between China, an important neighbour, which is in the process of becoming an important economic power and the Russian Federation in the north, and to the West the whole of the European Continent. Since trade involves transportation of peoples and goods, we see Kazakhstan providing an important road and rail link between East Asia, Russia and Europe."[57] Of course, seventeen years later, Xi would announce the BRI's overland dimension during a visit to Kazakhstan.

But even before the BRI was announced, Chinese officials were talking up their role in supporting the pan-Asian railway. In 2006, one official predicted that the eastern route would be complete in 2010.[58] A year later, at the tenth ASEAN summit, China's Premier

Wen Jiabao cited the pan-Asian railway in his speech, and Chinese state media predicted completion of all three routes by 2015.[59] Despite missing these deadlines, China has made the pan-Asian railway an even more central part of its regional engagement. From time to time, new officials rekindle the effort. The idea of a pan-Asian line remains powerful, diminished only for those who can recall the undelivered promises of earlier efforts.

"Old-Fashioned Incompetence"

Under the BRI banner, China has made the effort its own. In 2016, China's ambassador to ASEAN stated that BRI projects would "promote the construction of the pan-Asian railway, increasing connectivity and the exchange of goods and people."[60] As China touts the importance of rail connectivity, it is also financing dozens of power plants, roads, and several ports across Southeast Asia. But it is the railways that best capture the scale of China's infrastructure ambitions and the limits of its power.

Can China achieve what the United Nations was unable to achieve multilaterally and what ASEAN has been unable to achieve regionally? It brings mountains of money to the table, and its bilateral deal making offers more flexible terms. But the same basic challenges that have limited the pan-Asian railway's expansion, the political challenge of coordinating the routes and the financial challenge of paying for them, remain.

Limits to China's power are already evident. As China pushes south, it faces less resistance in the region's smaller economies than among the larger economies. In 2009, following the financial crisis, China announced a large aid package to Southeast Asia. Much of this aid targeted infrastructure projects and required recipients to use Chinese contractors, effectively serving as an extension of China's own $500 billion domestic stimulus package.[61] Chinese offers are difficult to refuse, but Southeast Asian countries are not without options. Although many deals are made, few are truly ever done, leaving room for renegotiation in the future.

It was during this period that China began negotiations to build a railway from its border to Vientiane, the capital of Laos. Among Chinese railways in the region, the China-Laos railway has the dual distinction of being the furthest along and the furthest behind. Stretching some four hundred kilometers, the railway is estimated to cost $5.9 billion, more than a third of Laos's GDP. China has provided financing for 70 percent of the project, and Laos's 30 percent contribution will cover payments to its citizens for relocation. But the agreement's ink had barely dried in 2011 when a dispute about lending terms arose. Studies examining the project's environmental and social impacts had not been completed.[62] It would take another six years for the sides to reach an agreement.

The project is technically challenging as well. Of the pan-Asian railway's missing links, some of the most difficult stretches run through Laos. Filled with mountains and rivers, the landlocked nation is a hiker's dream and a railway engineer's nightmare. The route includes 72 tunnels and 170 bridges, covering more than 60 percent of its total length.[63] To make way for the railway, the Lao government has relocated over 4,400 families, and it will be on the hook for relocation costs that could reach $300 million.[64] Many families are still waiting for compensation.

China has aggressively marketed the project as a "win-win" benefiting the people of Laos as well as its own companies, but the deal seems slanted toward the latter. "Without a formal job, Bounmy once struggled to make a living," a YouTube video produced by New China TV, a state media outlet, says. "Things changed when Power Construction Corp. of China came to build the China-Laos railway."[65] Bounmy, a Lao mother, has found work as a kitchen assistant, the video explains. It does not explain whom she is assisting or serving, but the odds make it easy to guess. China is bringing twenty thousand to fifty thousand of its own workers for the project, as compared to seven thousand local workers from within Laos.

The basic economic case for the railway is weak. It is designed to handle both cargo and passenger trains, but Laos has little of either. Much of Laos's limited manufacturing is concentrated in Savannakhet Province, where the railway will not run.[66] With incomes among the lowest in the world, few Laotians will buy tickets for the train. It would be safer financially, and smarter practically, to scrap the railway and invest a fraction of its multibillion-dollar price tag in better roads.[67] All of this suggests a project molded more in China's short-term interests than in Laos's long-term interest.

Laos has not been willing to walk away from the project, but it has renegotiated slightly better terms.[68] Citing debt risks, Laos convinced China to increase the size of its stake and waive its requirement for a government guarantee. After learning that China offered Thailand a 2 percent interest rate for its railway loan, Laos bargained for similar terms, down from 3 percent. China ended up with less land alongside the railway, which could be developed for retail and tourism. The experience demonstrates that even when China is dealing bilaterally with a much-smaller economy, it cannot dictate terms or expect its partners to ignore other deals.

Rather than Southeast Asia marching to China's tune, Beijing is being forced to dance as it auditions for new projects, especially in the region's largest economies. When Indonesia's President Joko Widodo, popularly called Jokowi, took office in 2015, his first two foreign visits were Tokyo and Beijing. Having made infrastructure a signature issue on the campaign trail, Jokowi was eager to attract the foreign investment needed for a major building spree. Indonesia's infrastructure gap is $1.5 trillion a year, by far the largest in the region.[69] The trips were successful and smartly timed. Jokowi bagged investment promises and sparked a competition for future projects.

No project in the region has generated as much competition as Indonesia's Jakarta-Bandung high-speed railway. Jokowi discussed it with Abe and Xi during his visits to their capitals, and while he left Tokyo with an expression of interest, Jokowi extracted even more from Beijing. Among the deals he signed in Beijing was an agreement to start feasibility studies for the railway between Indonesia's capital and its fourth-largest city. China also agreed to create a $50 billion joint loan facility, of which it would provide the lion's share.[70]

A month later, Tokyo responded with an offer of its own to build the railway. It would provide a loan for 74 percent of the project costs with a very low interest rate and long repayment and grace periods. Japan's *shinkansen*, or bullet-train, technology was already used in China, Taiwan, and the United Kingdom, and Japanese diplomats like to remind foreign audiences that the trains' safety record is unparalleled.

Chinese firms had built more kilometers of high-speed railway than anyone else in the world, but their experience abroad was still limited. They were building a slower, medium-speed railway in Kenya, and they had participated in different phases of high-speed rail projects in Russia and Thailand. The Jakarta-Bandung railway would be China's first high-speed rail project for which it took the lead role throughout the process.[71]

That might be why Beijing was willing to offer two things that Tokyo did not. First, even though China's loan rates were higher, it was not requiring the Indonesian government to make a direct contribution to the project or provide a state guarantee. That was attractive to Jokowi's bottom line, which would allow him to pursue more projects in the short term rather than lock up a large chunk of government funding for the railway project. Second, Beijing was willing to commit to a shorter timeline. It promised that construction would be completed in 2018 and the project would begin operating in 2019. Not coincidentally, that was just in time for Jokowi's reelection.

When Jokowi went with China's offer, he triggered a regional reaction. He insisted that the project was not part of China's BRI and, as a consolation prize, offered Japan a metro project in Jakarta. But Japanese officials felt they needed to sharpen their toolkit. Abe responded by rolling out the "Partnership for Quality Infrastructure" in September 2015, and the following year, Japan increased its foreign aid for the first time in seventeen years. Along with additional funding for infrastructure and several new investment vehicles, the Japanese government expedited its lending procedures and loosened some borrowing requirements. To compete, Tokyo recognized that it needed to become faster and more flexible.[72]

Despite the fierce competition leading up to the project's announcement, progress has been slow. What Jokowi intended as a reelection boost became a liability on the campaign trail during 2019. His challenger promised to review the railway deal and accused Jokowi of favoring China.[73] Jokowi prevailed, but the project has crept along. "It's not geopolitics or politics or policy or ideology. It's just good, old-fashioned mismanagement and incompetence," Thomas Lembong, Indonesia's state investment chief, said in 2019.[74]

So far, the railway's biggest impact has been outside Indonesia. China's offer to Indonesia reset expectations in other Southeast Asian capitals. In Bangkok, Thai officials have pressed their Chinese counterparts to improve their terms for a high-speed line between Bangkok and Nong Khai, a city of fifty thousand on the border with Laos. The proposed route misses most of Thailand's population centers, and an existing narrow-gauge railway that runs from Bangkok to the Laos border is being expanded.[75] The new Chinese line is expensive, duplicative, and commercially uncertain, even if the China-Laos railway is successfully completed.

The project's fate remains uncertain, but it is more compelling as a bargaining chip than as a commercial endeavor. Killing the Bangkok–Nong Khai high-speed railway makes economic sense. The project does not address an urgent need or even a foreseeable one. It is an unnecessary luxury, grafted awkwardly onto a railway system with clearer and more pressing needs. Getting rid of it would allow Thai officials to concentrate on other priorities and could even push Chinese officials toward supporting more viable projects.

But in political terms, it is better for Thailand that the high-speed rail project dies a slow death. By keeping Chinese and Japanese officials engaged, Thailand is able to extract better offers from both sides for future projects. As Indonesia's Finance Minister Sri Mulyani Indrawati said in 2017, "This is a good competition. You do not want to build infrastructure, high quality but [that the] people cannot afford and [the] country cannot afford. ... With the combination of pressure which is coming from China, [and] many other players, that creates a competition that will reduce the cost."[76] Hedging helps protect each country's independence, and it is good for business.

Playing this game requires an ability to attract competing offers and bargain effectively. It is risky, given the strong incentives for green-lighting questionable projects and the large price tags that come with high-speed rail projects. Missteps can be measured in the billions of dollars, not a trivial amount even for the region's largest economies. The stakes are even higher for smaller economies.

Missing Billions

Malaysia's experience reveals the dangers of overindulging at the region's infrastructure buffet. Najib Razak, who served as prime minister from 2009 to 2018, aggressively courted Chinese investment. By 2015, China was providing about half of all foreign construction in Malaysia, but Najib was eager to deepen ties.[77] When he visited Beijing in 2016, he announced a package of deals reportedly worth

$47 billion, including the East Coast Rail Line, Melaka Gateway, and a steel plant in Sarawak.[78]

Najib even published an op-ed in *China Daily*, a state-owned outlet. He tried to showcase a growing partnership between Malaysia and China, but his effusiveness hinted at desperation. In the piece, Najib takes a swipe at the West, noting that "former colonial powers" should not "lecture countries they once exploited on how to conduct their own internal affairs today." He praises Xi and calls the BRI "visionary." He mentions a port project under way at Melaka and a "futuristic underground metropolis" that would be developed in Kuala Lumpur.[79] Both projects promised large infusions of cash, and Najib was running out of money.

Privately, Najib was struggling to contain one of the largest corruption scandals in recent history.[80] He had used a state-owned investment fund, 1MDB, to siphon off public funds. The cash was intended to keep his patronage network happy and his political future bright, but it was also a family affair. Najib's wife received $30 million in jewelry, his son started a movie production company, and the family bought multimillion-dollar properties in Los Angeles, New York, and London. The fund's problems first came to light in 2015, when the *Wall Street Journal* reported that $700 million was directed into Najib's personal bank accounts.[81] Najib denied any wrongdoing, and the Malaysian attorney general, whom he appointed, issued a statement clearing him of any association with the accounts.

But 1MDB's financial distress was real, and Najib's associates were scrambling for new investments that could be diverted to help avoid further scrutiny. Naturally, large infrastructure projects were an attractive target. Transactions related to the fund are still being investigated, but reporting and a former aid's testimony allege that Najib wanted to inflate the cost of two pipelines and a railway, the East Coast Rail Link, and divert Chinese investments to help bail out 1MDB.[82] The $20 billion contract for the railway was awarded to China Communications Construction Company (CCCC), which the World Bank blacklisted in 2009 for fraud.

The East Coast Rail Link was intended to connect to Bandar Malaysia, the "futuristic underground metropolis" that Najib had promoted during his 2016 visit to Beijing. A joint venture between Malaysia's Iskandar Waterfront Holdings and state-owned China

Railway Engineering Corporation had purchased a 60 percent stake in the Bandar Malaysia project from 1MDB. The plan was to turn the site into a global business district, complete with retail stores, restaurants, and other attractions.[83]

Najib was scheduled to visit the site in early May 2017, but hours before his visit, the deal fell apart.[84] The Malaysian government blamed the joint venture, which it claimed had missed payment deadlines. The failed project was another easy target for Najib's critics. "The new season of the blockbuster 1MDB political drama thriller could not have kicked off on a more suspenseful note," wrote Tony Pua, a member of Malaysia's parliament and spokesperson for one of the main opposition parties.[85]

A week later, Najib lashed out in an opinion piece timed to coincide with the Belt and Road Forum in Beijing. "It may seem ridiculous to readers in China or other visitors at the forum, but there are some opposition politicians in my country who say we are selling our sovereignty by agreeing to such projects," he wrote in the *South China Morning Post*. "But I make no apologies for wanting to build world-class infrastructure for Malaysia that will, with local ownership being preserved, open up huge swathes of our country, bringing more trade and opportunity to our people, thousands of new jobs, improved living standards and prosperity."[86]

Najib viewed China's BRI as a lifeline, but it became a noose around his neck. Mahathir frequently criticized the government's handling of 1MDB and called for greater transparency around foreign investment. He did not hesitate to invoke the specter of colonialism. "We cannot be proud of a magnificently developed Malaysia, occupied and owned by foreigners," he wrote on his personal blog, making an argument that was a recurring theme in his posts, which were read by millions.[87] If elected, he promised to review all foreign deals.

"Big Trains"

Mahathir's surprise victory in May 2018 slowed China's BRI but did not derail it. After taking office, he suspended the East Coast Rail Link and pipeline. Despite only 13 percent of the pipeline construction being completed, 90 percent of the total project funds had been transferred, apparently following a calendar system that did not take into account actual progress, or lack thereof.[88] Najib faces a string of charges and the prospect of spending the rest of his life in prison.

If anyone understood what it was like for Najib to watch these projects being reevaluated, it was Mahathir. In his memoirs, Mahathir describes his shock that a railway project was being canceled after he left office in 2003: "The claim was that there was no more money to carry on with this track upgrade after my profligate ways." When the government canceled a hydroelectric project, he recalls, "I began hearing accusations that I had spent all the Government's money on megaprojects which the country apparently did not need." And when a bridge to Singapore was canceled, he writes, "I was flabbergasted. By allowing Singaporeans to dictate terms, the current administration had effectively undermined the sovereignty of our country."[89]

But even while Mahathir was taking a closer look at the BRI, he was still dreaming about Malaysia's development possibilities. During a press conference on his first day back in office, Mahathir pointed to how ships have grown dramatically over the past half century, especially following the invention of standard containers. He wondered whether something similar could happen with railway transport. Already, he had a partner in mind: "I suggested to Xi Jinping in a personal letter to him, that we should have big trains, and China has the technology to build big trains, which can carry goods from China to Europe, and will also make Central Asia— Kazakhstan and Uzbekistan, and all that, more accessible," he said.[90]

It soon became clear that Mahathir's opposition to the BRI was purely tactical. In April 2019, Malaysia and China announced a new deal for the East Coast Rail Link.[91] The $20 billion price tag was cut by nearly a third, local labor participation was increased, and Malaysia shifted some of the operational risk to China. Four days later, Mahathir announced that the Bandar Malaysia project would move forward as a joint venture between the original contractors.[92] Both announcements were missing key details. The total cost of the Bandar project was not announced. The loan terms for the East Coast Rail Link were still being negotiated with China's Export-Import Bank.

But with the second Belt and Road Forum later that month, both sides were eager to declare victory. Malaysia had become a prime example of backlash building against the BRI, and Chinese officials were eager to push back against that narrative. Mahathir was eager to announce development projects and take credit for securing better deals.

The official explanation of Mahathir's about-face made it sound as if he had an epiphany at the forum. "The Prime Minister ... had initially thought that the [BRI] was China's attempt to dominate Southeast Asia as the trade passage for the project includes the South China Sea and the Straits of Melaka," a Malaysian government press release explained. "However, during the forum, Dr. Mahathir said he saw that the initiative was a cooperative effort to develop participating countries via infrastructure development and funding from banks."[93]

Mahathir did not invent this game, nor will it end with his time in office. The cycle of opposition, negotiation, and deal making will continue in Southeast Asia and beyond. Candidates rail against China when it helps their case for office. After they take office, however, their options for undoing existing projects are limited, as are their options for attracting new foreign investment. They are as eager as their predecessors were to announce deals, but they need to look tough and keep their promises for scrutinizing past deals. So they threaten to cancel projects, China comes to the negotiating table, and the incentives on both sides encourage salvaging deals and saving face.

These dynamics make the BRI politically resilient at the expense of its longer-term economic performance. Canceling bad projects is difficult but essential. Sunk costs can be a powerful, and dangerously misleading, justification for spending even more. It is why management experts call megaprojects "Vietnams"—easy to begin and difficult and expensive to stop.[94] Chinese projects are even harder to kill because the BRI is Xi's signature foreign-policy initiative. Especially large projects like Malaysia's East Coast Rail Link take on symbolic importance, and cancellation comes with a higher reputational cost. Keeping too many projects from the grave could come back to haunt China and its partners.

The cycle also feeds off the competition among outside powers, which recipient countries play off each other to their advantage. Speaking at the second Belt and Road Forum, Mahathir proclaimed, "Yes, the Belt and Road idea is great."[95] His praise was a gift to Xi, who sat smiling in the front row. It was also a calling card for China's competitors.

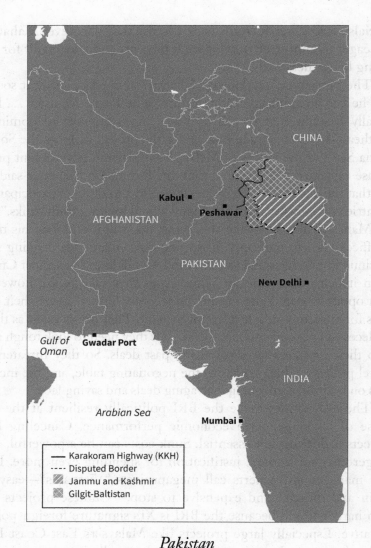

Pakistan

Center for Strategic and International Studies, Reconnecting Asia Project

CHAPTER SEVEN

The Black Hole

Pakistan

THE CHINA-PAKISTAN ECONOMIC CORRIDOR (CPEC) stands out among the BRI's broad brushstrokes. Stretching from the Karakorum mountains to the Arabian Sea, it is where China's overland and maritime ambitions meet.[1] Of the BRI's six corridors, it contains the largest portfolio of promised Chinese investments and some of its most controversial projects. Xi Jinping has put his personal stamp on CPEC, traveling to Pakistan in April 2015 to cement the two countries' "all-weather strategic cooperative partnership" and sign a host of agreements. "If One Belt One Road is like a symphony involving and benefitting every country, then construction of the China-Pakistan Economic Corridor is the sweet melody of the symphony's first movement," Wang Yi, China's foreign minister, said around the same time.[2]

But CPEC has produced more discord than harmony, turning China's boldest move through the BRI into its greatest test. In Pakistan, China is betting it can succeed where the United States and the international community have failed for decades. Since Pakistan's independence in 1948, its cunning leaders and booming population have caught the world's attention and pulled in outside partners. The chief among them, the United States, has provided Pakistan over $80

billion in assistance, with relatively little to show for it.[3] Generations
of U.S. diplomats have come, gone, and returned to confront remarkably similar problems. If neighboring Afghanistan is the graveyard of empires, Pakistan is the black hole of foreign assistance.

CPEC, like the grand development efforts that preceded it, has
already promised more than it can deliver. Despite being a "corridor," connectivity is its weakest dimension. Roads, telecommunications, and other connectivity projects make up a small portion of
the overall effort. An even smaller portion includes projects that
span China and Pakistan. Its best-known projects are not new, and
economics is not their strong suit. Gwadar Port, for example, was
conceived in the 1950s, was finally started in 2001, and will struggle to compete with existing shipping hubs. The Karakoram Highway, which traverses the rugged Pakistan-China border, was first
completed in 1978, and after it is upgraded and expanded as part of
CPEC, it will still be closed every winter due to heavy snowfall.
"All-weather" might work as a metaphor for China-Pakistan relations, but taken literally, it will be a stretch for CPEC.

Rather than connecting China, CPEC is better understood as
an attempt to develop Pakistan. Most of its announced funding re-
lates to energy projects within Pakistan, and if accompanied by necessary reforms, their success could be transformative. Pakistan's top
leaders have almost uniformly cast CPEC as the solution to many
of their country's economic woes, from solving energy shortages to
boosting manufacturing and exports. Nawaz Sharif called CPEC a
"new era of development . . . opening up new trade and investment
linkages."[4] Shahid Khaqan Abbasi called it a "game changer."[5] Even
Imran Khan, a CPEC skeptic prior to his election in 2018, has
since declared it a "top priority."[6] International financial institutions
have praised the effort's promise as well. The International Monetary Fund (IMF) expects CPEC will "promote growth and job creation" and "facilitate regional integration."[7] The World Bank says it
has "enormous potential for Pakistan."[8]

China's aims extend beyond economics.[9] In June 2017, the
Pakistani newspaper *Dawn* reported details from a leaked long-
term-planning document that revealed how deep China hopes to
reach into Pakistani society. Among the activities envisioned for
CPEC through 2030, Chinese firms would lease thousands of acres

of farmland. Using Chinese technology, Pakistan would roll out surveillance systems in its cities. CPEC, the document said, was a "cultural transmission carrier." Fiber-optic cables would carry Chinese content to more Pakistanis. Chinese tourists would benefit from a visa-free program, while a reciprocal arrangement for Pakistani tourists visiting China was not mentioned. The transmission was largely one-way.[10]

CPEC is both an instrument of Chinese power and a test of it. As Robert Kaplan has written, "Nothing since independence in 1947 has the potential to help stabilize Pakistan—calming its frontier insurgencies—than the completion of this project, and nothing would do more to firm up China's domination of its own steppeland periphery."[11] With Pakistan stabilized, Chinese power would be liberated to reach deeper into Afghanistan, to the Arabian Sea, and closer to India's borders. Bringing stability to a country wracked by political turmoil and crippling debt would reveal an incredibly sophisticated ability to wield power. Success would demonstrate that Beijing can do what Washington could not.

Failure would suggest that Chinese officials misjudged their abilities and could signal a broader overreach in their designs for the BRI. Pakistan is the only BRI corridor involving only one country, and the others will require even-greater coordination to successfully complete. Public opinion within Pakistan about China is also extremely positive, often among the highest in the world.[12] Having made CPEC the BRI's flagship effort, Chinese officials would suffer the reputational consequences of failure. They may regret choosing Pakistan as the BRI's proving grounds. Its history is littered with best-laid plans.

"We Need Everything"

That Pakistan still exists is a major achievement. At independence, it was split between West Pakistan and East Pakistan, the latter of which became Bangladesh. It was "widely considered an economic monstrosity," reflected Gustav Papanek, an economist and early adviser to Pakistan's government.[13] Pakistan inherited roads and railways, but these were designed as part of a larger entity that was now fragmented. India sat between Pakistan's two wings and, even more importantly, retained most of the human capital. Pakistan had few civil servants, few industrialists, and few universities to train them.

Pakistan's government needed help, and it found a willing partner in the United States. During his inaugural speech in 1949, U.S. President Harry Truman announced a global program of technical assistance. "We must embark on a bold new program for making the benefits of our scientific advances and industrial progress available for the improvement and growth of underdeveloped areas," he said.[14] As the fourth of his "major courses of action" for foreign policy, it became known as the Point IV program. A planning group was established in the State Department later that year to operationalize the idea and to propose a budget. Congress agreed and approved the program the following year.

For all the talk of goodwill, the communist threat was the primary catalyst for greater U.S. involvement. In 1954, the United States and Pakistan signed a Mutual Defense Agreement. The same year, the United States led the creation of the Southeast Asia Collective Defense Treaty, or Manila Pact. U.S. Secretary of State John Foster Dulles strongly supported Pakistan's membership, despite the geographic incongruity.[15] The following year, Pakistan joined the Central Treaty Organization (CENTO), or Baghdad Pact, which included Turkey, Iraq, Iran, and the United Kingdom. With the exception of the United Kingdom and the United States, Pakistan was the only country in both treaties.

Pakistan's leaders had successfully moved their country from relative obscurity in U.S. foreign policy to the center of its efforts to counter communism. "Asia will have at least one big country dedicated to Western principles of economic development," *Businessweek* wrote of Pakistan's development policies in 1956. "And this could make a big difference in the increasingly fierce East-West struggle for the allegiance of the world's underdeveloped countries."[16] Pakistan's willingness to band with the United States and publicly criticize Communist China paid dividends. U.S. assistance to Pakistan climbed through the 1950s and included greater access to U.S. military equipment.

As U.S. resources poured in, Pakistan's government struggled to use them effectively. "When I went to Pakistan, I had the $60 million to spend and no plan, no program, nothing," recalled John

Bell, who oversaw U.S. foreign assistance in Pakistan during 1955–1957. "I remember asking the Secretary of the Pakistan Economic Ministry, Said Hassan, to give me his ideas of what priorities they had. . . . 'Oh,' he said, 'I've got a long list of projects. Take any one you like.' . . . No details, just names. I said, you must have some priorities in your own mind, don't you? 'Oh,' he said, 'No we need everything, we need everything.' "[17] That was true, of course, but Pakistan was not going to get everything. It needed a plan for prioritizing and coordinating projects.

The Harvard Development Advisory Group, which consisted mainly of Western economists, was instrumental in creating Pakistan's planning capacity. Supported by the Ford Foundation, the group arrived in Pakistan in 1954 with three goals: help Pakistan prepare a long-term development plan; advise the government on decisions impacting tax and fiscal policy, foreign trade, and other major economic issues; and train Pakistani officials to fill these two functions. Accomplishing all of this, the advisers initially estimated, would take about eighteen months. The project ended up running for more than a decade.

The advisers underestimated the challenges they would face and overestimated their own abilities. Asked to describe the characteristics of a successful adviser, one veteran of the program recommended, "Brains, tact, flexibility, and patience . . . coupled with firmness, good judgement, an intuitive ability to 'size up' people and situations, a sense of humor, integrity, essential modesty, high resistance to frustration."[18] Another adviser later boasted, "A new type of human being has come into existence. He is the foreign advisor, the expert, the specialist—call him what you will—who has replaced the colonial service officer as the representative of the richer countries . . . in the poorer one."[19]

As pioneers, however, the first advisers had little practical experience on which to draw. Almost none had any experience in Asia, let alone specific knowledge of Pakistan. Few had any experience with national economic planning. During their early years in Pakistan, the advisers were essentially students, learning as they were ostensibly teaching Pakistan's civil servants.

The field of economics itself was underdeveloped. Basic assumptions about how and why nations grow were based mostly on the experience of Western economies and would be tested and revised in the coming decades. "We were all Keynesians from our training as economists in the late 30s, and the concept of using government as an engine of economic change and progress was commonplace among us," recalled David Bell, who was the program's first field director in Pakistan.[20] The economists were confident that this Keynesian toolkit was universal—portable across cultures and geographies and unburdened by history.

They discovered that Pakistan was a laboratory where facts were elusive. With the exception of population data, many key indicators in Pakistan were difficult or impossible to collect. Most projects were proposed for their financial implications without taking into account how they would be built or maintained.[21] "Key decisions had to be based more on guesses ... than on verifiable fact," David Bell recalled. "[Many] proposals which came to the Board were little more than idle speculation or wishful thinking. Accordingly, the Board ... had to ... [turn] vague schemes into reasonably feasible proposals and [to create] proposals where none were submitted."[22]

Some guesses created facts. Pakistan's investment rate, for example, could help U.S. officials calibrate how much aid was needed to generate economic growth just above Pakistan's population growth, so per capita income would increase. In this basic calculus, it did not matter how the aid was spent. "That was the Bible," recalled Papanek.[23] Due to a shortage of data, Pakistan's rate of investment was essentially unknown in the early and mid-1950s. But U.S. and Pakistani officials needed something to plan around, and they became desperate for even a rough estimate.

When President Eisenhower sent H. J. Heinz II, the third-generation CEO of the eponymous food company, to lead a special mission to assess U.S. aid to Pakistan in 1954, the pressure for numbers became impossible to resist. After several unsuccessful requests, a member of the Heinz mission cornered Papanek at a cocktail party and demanded an estimate. "The rate of investment is probably between 16 and 20 percent, but we don't know," Papanek submitted. Two days later, one of Papanek's Pakistani colleagues approached him excitedly: "Thank God, we finally know the rate of investment. ... The Heinz mission has said it is 18 percent," Papanek recalls the colleague saying. "My own number had come back to me as the truth."[24]

Through trial and error, the Harvard advisers helped produce Pakistan's first five-year plan in 1955. Like U.S. military "trainers" who end up fighting alongside foreign forces, the advisers were also participants during this first process. There was simply too much to do and too few qualified Pakistani staff. "There are few very competent experienced older people, in or out of the government, and those that do exist cannot, in many cases, be separated from their present positions to work with the Planning Board," Edward Mason, who directed the Harvard Advisory Group from 1954 to 1962, lamented.[25] With pressure to produce the document, the advisers wrote large parts of the plan and had little time to train their Pakistani counterparts.[26]

The plan was completed late, two years into the period it covered, and its recommendations were politically unfeasible. The Pakistani government was preoccupied with debates about regional autonomy, the electoral system, and foreign policy. Among other things, the plan recommended large-scale land reforms, which would have challenged the country's wealthiest families. Running hundreds of pages, the document was technical, and little effort was made to communicate its contents to the 80 percent of Pakistan's population that was illiterate.[27] Nor did Pakistan's president, Iskander Mirza, formally endorse the plan.[28]

But the exercise was still useful in two respects. The first was that Pakistan's government was becoming familiar with the planning process. Although it lacked the capacity to plan independently, going through the process was a significant step forward. "Pakistan is no longer a land of the blind, where the one-eyed advisor is king. More Pakistanis are now competent," declared a Ford Foundation review of the advisory program.[29]

More immediately, the plan also helped secure additional U.S. assistance, even while U.S. officials were becoming more aware of the challenges ahead. As John Bell, who oversaw U.S. assistance in Pakistan, recalled, "We went back to Washington with [the five-year plan] and said IF (about six ifs all of which were no way certain): no flood, no famine, no war, no disaster of any kind and political stability, all these different things, we've got about a 50-50 chance of making this work if you put in about $200 million a year for at least five years."[30]

As U.S. aid increased, examples of mismanagement began to multiply. In 1957, a few months after arriving as the U.S. ambassador to Pakistan, James Langley sent a dire cable to Washington: "In Pakistan we have an unruly horse by the tail and are confronted by the dilemma of trying to tame it before we can let go safely. ... I fear that our past generosity in helping out our friends has too often permitted them to avoid 'grasping the nettle' and facing their problems with the required spirit of urgency and determination." Langley endorsed reviewing U.S. aid to eliminate "secondary or marginal projects."[31]

Dennis Kux stumbled across one of those marginal projects. Kux, an economic officer with the U.S. State Department, was first stationed in Pakistan from 1957 to 1960. During a research trip some two hundred miles north of Karachi, his Pakistani hosts were eager to show him what U.S. generosity had given them. "Oh, you are from the American Embassy. You must see our aid project. We have a wonderful science laboratory," they insisted. When Kux walked into the science facility, there was plenty of equipment, but he noticed that none of it was plugged in. "Well, there is a little problem," his hosts explained. "We don't have any electricity." Apparently, no one in the aid process had bothered to check, or they had optimistically assumed power was on the way.[32]

Wasteful and embarrassing, these projects were still just a drop in the growing bucket of U.S. assistance, which was justified more on strategic merits rather than on economic impact. Understanding this, Pakistan's leaders never missed an opportunity to invoke the threat of communism. In 1961, General Ayub Khan, who had taken power three years earlier in a coup, visited the United States. "We are pressing against you today as friends, and if we make good I think you will in some fashion get it back, in many ways you will get it back," he told a joint session of the U.S. Congress. "If we do not make good and if, heaven forbid, we go under communism, then we shall still press against you but not as friends."[33]

By the early 1960s, U.S. aid to Pakistan was exceeding $400 million a year. At its height during the first half of that decade, U.S. aid was more than half of Pakistan's foreign aid, covering half of

Pakistan's imports and one-third of its development budget.[34] Along with funds from the World Bank, a major donor to Pakistan and India, foreign lending allowed the Pakistani government to spend more on its military when those resources would have been better saved and invested in economic activities.

Pakistan was making progress, though, and the second five-year plan, covering 1960–1965, was more successful. Khan's government put a greater focus on economic development and gave more authority to the central planning staff. Between 1960 and 1965, Western Pakistan nearly averaged 6 percent growth, inspiring talk of an "economic miracle."[35] "By 1965, Pakistan had the machinery to rationally examine and execute quite sophisticated economic policies. If it wanted to engage in considerable planning, it had the means to do so without making many more mistakes than would be inherent in the task or inevitable in most governments," Papanek later wrote.[36]

Pakistan had developed a planning capacity, but it still lacked the capacity to execute those plans. "The obstacles, the obstacles," John Bell recalled decades later. "The biggest problem, human resources and institutions. Not money. Money you need, yes. But, it's not much use without human resources and institutions and you can't shift them from factories or plants to recipient country. They have to be grown, trained, cultivated and then motivated to want to do it. That was the first time it really dawned on me that the success of [the Marshall Plan] was due to the Europeans and that third world nations did not have the requirements needed to achieve development so rapidly. Development is not recovery!"[37]

Pakistan's first war with India, in September 1965, pushed it away from the United States and toward China. As fighting raged across the line of control in the Kashmir valley, the United States remained neutral and suspended aid despite its defense agreements with Pakistan.[38] The same year, China made its first loan to Pakistan, roughly $60 million to import coal, cement, iron, steel, and electrical equipment.[39] It was a small amount but symbolically important. While China could not replace U.S. aid, the loan made an important impact on Pakistani officials, who were feeling betrayed by the United States. "People in Pakistan were becoming disillusioned [with the United States]; a relationship which had been built up after a great deal of hard work during the fifties was ceasing to command respect," Khan later wrote.[40]

"Thoughtless Urgency"

During this period of growing disillusionment, Pakistan and China embarked on building the Karakorum Highway, or KKH, which more than any other project has become a symbol of their lasting bond. Cutting through some of the world's highest mountains, it is a physical connection put down at great human cost, including the deaths of hundreds of Pakistani and Chinese workers.[41] Decades later, the project remerged at the center of CPEC, but the desire to view the highway as a symbol has obscured the project's troubled beginnings and modest impact.

There are two versions of the highway's origin story, according to Muhammad Khalid, a former brigadier general in the Pakistan Army Corps of Engineers turned historian. In one telling, China's Premier Zhou Enlai met with Pakistan's ambassador to China, General N. A. M. Raza, and offered to provide military hardware. But there was a catch. "We can give you anything you want, but you have to arrange the transportation yourself," Zhou Enlai reportedly said. "Our navy cannot ship these because of the American intervention; we do not have the transport aircraft; and we have no road communication between the two countries." When a second Pakistani delegation visited Beijing after the war with India and thanked Zhou for China's support, he replied, "If we had a road link with Pakistan, don't you think we would have been of greater help to you?"[42]

In the second version, Pakistani officials proposed the idea. After midnight, Zhou surprised his Pakistani guests by dropping by for an unscheduled meeting. When the conversation turned to China's trade with the Middle East, Pakistan's minister for commerce, who was also the defense adviser, pointed out that the nearest outlet for Chinese trade with the Middle East was Karachi, not the port of Shanghai. The key to increasing China's trade, he claimed, was to reopen "an ancient trade route . . . lost to modern times, not only for trade but for strategic purposes as well." Zhou sent for a map, and after a glimpse of the route, he allegedly asked, "When can our engineers meet?"[43]

What is clear is that from the beginning, the highway's commercial importance was secondary to strategic concerns. A Pakistani government memo summarizing a conversation with Khan in May 1966 notes, "The President was pleased to remark that in order of priority the first urgency of the highway was strategic and one of the immediate significance. The second objective was economic and commercial importance of the highway, i.e. the opening up of an inaccessible region and the establishment of a land route to the adjourning country. The second was a long-term objective, as of necessity, the full utilization would be over a period of time."[44] Critically, the route ran through Pakistani-controlled Kashmir. Its construction would bind those remote areas closer to Pakistan, Khan reasoned, and over time erode India's competing claims to the territory.

For China, the KKH offered a new supply line out of a shrinking, and increasingly menacing, neighborhood. Chinese officials were already responding to perceived threats by land and by sea. In 1964, they began a large investment program to move factories into southern and western China. The goal was to create an industrial base away from China's urban centers that could serve as a reserve in the event of war.[45] At the time, the United States was escalating its operations in Vietnam, and the Soviet Union was making inroads with Mongolia, where it stationed troops in 1966. Reflecting these priorities, Chinese officials insisted on building the KKH through Khunjerab Pass rather than Mintika Pass, which was closer to Soviet territory.[46]

The original plan was that each country would build the road within the territory it controlled. The Pakistan Army Corps of Engineers set up a dedicated unit, the Frontier Works Organization, to take the lead within Pakistan. Although the road was an open secret, in planning documents, Pakistan referred to the Chinese as "friends" to avoid antagonizing the United States.[47] China agreed to provide Pakistan with construction equipment. At the time, Pakistani engineers were familiar with U.S. equipment, which was more durable. The Chinese, recognizing the shortcomings of their own equipment, not only agreed to Pakistan's list of requested items but doubled it. The initial estimate assumed the project could be completed in five years.[48]

Afraid to disappoint Khan, the Pakistani Army's engineer in chief agreed to the unrealistic timetable. Without having assembled, let alone trained, a workforce and without having conducted a detailed survey of the route, he agreed to begin the project in a matter of months. "Thoughtless urgency would become a particular feature of this mega project, and perhaps for all future ones," writes Khalid. "Any presidential order, or for that matter any higher command dictates, would rarely be questioned by the Corps' top brass regardless of the serious technical, financial, and administrative problems, time constraints or frictions of terrain, and weather."[49]

When Pakistan's route surveyors reached the Chinese border during the summer of 1966, a surprise was waiting for them. "The rugged mountains with steep slopes, the gushing rivers and glaciers suddenly vanished, as we drove across and saw thousands of Chinese working on the road," remembers a Pakistani officer who was among the survey team. "They had, in fact, completed their side of the road before we commenced ours."[50] The Pakistani survey team had no geological experience but needed to make decisions about constructing the highest road in the world. They were asked to complete the survey, which covered over 250 kilometers, in six weeks. In the north, Pakistan's soldiers were effectively foreigners in their own country.

The chaos continued a few weeks later, when Pakistan's main construction force began arriving at Khunjerab Pass. As a Pakistani officer recalled, "An hour after reaching Khunjerab, the ignorant new arrivals started feeling giddy and sleepy, which they first regarded as normal fatigue due to hectic travelling. . . . Some people fell unconscious while conversing. Upon gaining consciousness the following day, some were still vomiting."[51] No one had warned the Pakistani soldiers about altitude sickness before sending them up to the sixteen-thousand-foot pass or advised them about the harsh climate. They discovered that their bulldozers were too cold to start in the morning and that other equipment did not work at all. It was a preview of the dangers that would plague Pakistan's road workers, who were given precious little and told to move mountains.

After these false starts, Chinese officials did not have to offer twice to start building roads within Pakistan. While Pakistani officials were grateful for China's assistance, they worried that the Chinese laborers could spread communism, especially in the remote areas where they would be working. But their countermeasures were haphazard at best. Pakistan ordered intelligence agents to camp near the Chinese workers, but they did not speak Chinese. Incredibly, Pakistan did not bother to establish a system for monitoring Chinese workers arriving and departing at the border. Official figures estimated that roughly eight thousand Chinese workers entered Pakistan to work on the KKH, but the actual figure is probably closer to twenty thousand.[52]

During the KKH's first decade of construction, the Chinese workers won their hosts' respect. They moved fast, using enormous amounts of explosives to cut through the mountains. It was dangerous work, and their techniques took a human and environmental toll. Workers perished in landslides, and the explosions destabilized the mountains for years. In June 1978, when General Muhammad Zia ul-Haq and China's Vice Premier Geng Biao held a ceremony at Thakot Bridge, both sides paid tribute to these sacrifices.[53] "The Karakoram Highway today heralds the dawn of a new era of Pak-China relations," General Zia proclaimed.[54]

The road was technically operational, but it would not open to normal traffic until 1986. Even after that, it would remain limited by seasonal weather and plagued by landslides. And as the years passed, the shortcuts taken began to show as the road deteriorated. A landslide in 2010 blocked a river, creating a lake and flooding a section of the KKH. Until new tunnels opened in 2015, vehicles had to be ferried across the lake in handmade boats.[55] By April 2016, there was enough need for repair that the two sides felt justified in holding a ground-breaking ceremony in the same place. Rather than opening the road, they would celebrate its reconstruction as part of CPEC. "Pakistan is poised for an economic takeoff," Prime Minister Sharif assured the audience.[56]

"A White Elephant"

In 1958, Pakistan had purchased Gwadar, an enclave previously controlled by Oman that is roughly 120 kilometers from Iran. It became part of Baluchistan, Pakistan's largest and least populated province. It needed development, and Pakistan's president, Zulfikar Ali Bhutto, had an idea.

"We want a port in Baluchistan," Bhutto told Nixon during a visit to the United States in September 1973. Bhutto knew the United States had paid for military access in the past. In the late 1950s, the United States used facilities near Peshawar to monitor Soviet communications and launch U-2 flights, until Francis Gary Powers, a retired U.S. Air Force officer working for the CIA, was shot down and captured in 1960. President Bhutto now hoped the U.S. Navy would be interested in Pakistan's access to the Arabian Sea.

Like Khan before him, Bhutto hinted that in the absence of U.S. support, the Soviet Union would fill the void. "The Iranians are building a port at [Chabahar]. We need one on our coast. The Soviets are deeply interested in this coast and they have offered us to help with oil exploration, geological survey and that kind of thing. We would rather have a U.S. presence."[57] Bhutto later joked to the U.S. ambassador in Pakistan that he became so focused on this issue during his conversation with Nixon that he "literally left this problem" at the White House, forgetting to bring his papers with him after the meeting.[58]

Nixon diplomatically feigned interest in Bhutto's idea. "The port proposal that you made intrigued me," he told Bhutto. But Nixon was noncommittal. "We cannot say anything definitive on this today," he said. "We have not checked with the Navy. Dr. Kissinger will look into this."[59]

In fact, Kissinger had already looked into it and, echoing the advice of his National Security Council staff, recommended avoiding the project. "A new U.S. presence of this nature would antagonize the Soviets, the Indians, the Afghans, and perhaps others without contributing to U.S. interests either in the Persian Gulf or in South Asia," he wrote in a pre-meeting memo for Nixon. "The key point, however, is that this would probably cost some hundreds of millions of dollars, and the political impact of the project will depend in part on its not being a white elephant."[60]

In addition to recognizing the project's shaky commercial prospects, Kissinger and his staff understood that Gwadar Port was chiefly a political project. "Bhutto's main motive in seeking a Baluchistan port is probably to help him bring more commerce and jobs and win more support in that backward, sparsely populated, chronically unstable, opposition-dominated province," the memo noted.[61] Seeking those political payoffs, Bhutto's successors rekindled the idea decades later, eventually turning Gwadar Port into one of CPEC's most controversial projects. In response, India is expanding the competing port in Chabahar, Iran.

With little interest on the U.S. side, the Gwadar proposal was eventually lost in the larger vortex of U.S.-Pakistani relations, a drama that has been admirably explained by other scholars.[62] High points in the relationship have mainly coincided with U.S. security priorities during the Cold War, the proxy war against the Soviet Union in Afghanistan, and after the 9/11 terrorist attacks. All have come crashing down, with each declaration of partnership eventually giving way to disagreement and ultimately disappointment. As Husain Haqqani, a former ambassador of Pakistan to the United States, has written, "The relationship between the United States and Pakistan is a tale of exaggerated expectations, broken promises, and disastrous misunderstandings."[63]

"The New Silk Road"

While that entire tale cannot be told in passing, its most recent chapter set the stage for deeper relations between Pakistan and China and the emergence of CPEC. The war in Afghanistan again made cooperation with Pakistan essential, and the United States doled out assistance to improve relations. In 2004, the United States designated Pakistan a major non-NATO ally, giving it greater access to U.S. military equipment and training. A few months later, the 9/11 Commission recommended a "comprehensive effort that extends from military aid to support for better education, so long as Pakistan's leaders remain willing to make difficult choices of their own."[64] Support for Pakistan remained a bipartisan cause, and in 2009, the U.S. Congress passed a bill, sponsored by John Kerry and Richard Lugar, providing $7.5 billion in nonmilitary aid to Pakistan over five years.[65]

The U.S. aid package to Pakistan made infrastructure its top priority, allocating $3.5 billion for "high visibility, high impact" projects.[66] These projects were intended to help address Pakistan's development challenges while improving public perceptions of the United States. "Many Pakistanis talk nostalgically about the days when U.S. assistance efforts were more noticeable, technology-based, and longer-term," a U.S. State Department report, required by the legislation, explained.[67] After largely abandoning the business of delivering large infrastructure projects in the 1960s and 1970s, the U.S. government was getting back into the game.

The United States even introduced a vision for regional connectivity: the New Silk Road. Planners at the U.S. Department of Defense's Central Command (CENTCOM) picked up the idea from S. Frederick Starr, a scholar on Russian and Eurasian affairs who long advocated building transport links across the Eurasian supercontinent.[68] General David Petraeus, then CENTCOM commander, was intrigued and encouraged his staff to pursue it. But the idea struggled to gain traction with the U.S. State Department and Ambassador Richard Holbrooke, the U.S. special representative for Afghanistan and Pakistan.

After Holbrooke's death, CENTCOM's New Silk Road advocates caught the ear of Ambassador Marc Grossman, Holbrooke's successor. Eager to define an economic effort that complemented the military and diplomatic surges under way, Secretary of State Hillary Clinton forged ahead with the idea. "Let's work together to create a new Silk Road," she declared in Chennai, India, on July 20, 2011. "Not a single thoroughfare like its namesake, but an international web and network of economic and transit connections. That means building more rail lines, highways, energy infrastructure, like the proposed pipeline to run from Turkmenistan, through Afghanistan, through Pakistan into India."[69]

Afghanistan's President Hamid Karzai embraced the idea, even calling for his country to become "the Asian Roundabout" in the New Silk Road, but it barely registered in Pakistan.[70] In January 2011, Raymond Davis, working as a contractor for the U.S. Central Intelligence Agency in Lahore, had killed two men, who he thought were robbers. On May 2 of that year, U.S. Special Forces raided a compound in Abbottabad and killed Osama bin Laden. Announcing the New Silk Road in India did little to improve its reception in Pakistan, where policy makers tend to view U.S.-India efforts as coming at their expense.

As the U.S. government's focus shifted toward limiting its foot-print in the region, the New Silk Road fell among its priorities. Without strong support for additional resources, it was mainly a repackaging of existing efforts.[71] A few months after announcing the effort, Clinton cushioned expectations, telling a meeting of thirty foreign ministers in New York, "This isn't about grand infra-structure projects—it's about promoting sustainable cross-border economic activity."[72] U.S. assistance to Pakistan peaked in 2010, the year prior, and declined in the following years.[73] By January 2015, when President Obama visited India, the New Silk Road did not merit a mention in his remarks.[74]

On the ground, U.S.-funded projects in Pakistan ran into fa-miliar challenges.[75] USAID emphasized hiring local workers, as it does around the world, while adhering to both local and U.S. gov-ernment regulations. Both goals are admirable. Local employment benefits Pakistani workers. Requiring that work meet not only local regulations but also U.S. regulations ensures that higher-quality projects are delivered. But meeting U.S. regulations with foreign workers, who are not familiar with those regulations, takes longer. And U.S. officials, like their predecessors in Pakistan, felt that time was in short supply.

The U.S. funding surge was too little to meet Pakistan's needs and too much to manage effectively. Unlike the Chinese invest-ment that would follow, U.S. assistance was poured into supporting smaller projects and social infrastructure such as schools. Lacking the funds to deliver the big-ticket industrial projects that have be-come CPEC's hallmark, U.S. assistance was also used to help iden-tify and prepare projects that could attract other sources of investment. But many Pakistani elites viewed USAID activities with suspicion, and trust did not increase along with U.S. funds.[76]

The surge in funding exceeded the U.S. government's ability to effectively manage the assistance, especially given that U.S. agencies had competing priorities. The State Department supported spend-ing faster to achieve political objectives in service of the U.S. war ef-fort in Afghanistan. USAID was more focused on longer-term development objectives.[77] Some U.S. staffers took shortcuts during project procurement, declining to obtain independent cost esti-mates before making contract awards. Still, a pipeline of unspent funds built up. An audit by the USAID inspector general, an internal watchdog, found that only 15 percent of projects fully met their intended goals.[78]

U.S. officials were criticized if they pushed projects forward quickly and criticized if they proceeded with caution. In one example of speed, they helped complete the Satpara Dam, in Gilgit Baltistan, only to discover that the project was unsustainable. Tax revenue from the energy produced only covered salaries for dam workers and not maintenance costs. For decades, officials from the World Bank and Asian Development Bank had been calling for energy-tariff reforms, pointing out that power generation had become a fixation at the expense of transmission and taxation. To make matters worse, the Gilgit Baltistan government did not have the expertise to run the dam, and locals diverted streams to other power sources, leaving the dam operating at less than 40 percent capacity.[79] It became a high-visibility, low-impact project.

When U.S. officials exercised greater caution, they risked being overtaken by events. In July 2013, after three years of lobbying by the government of Pakistan, the U.S. approved a feasibility study for the Diamer-Bhasha Dam, also located in Gilgit Baltistan. The study was intended to give international investors greater confidence to invest in the project, which at $12–14 billion, was nearly twice the entire U.S. aid budget for Pakistan. Several concerns about the project stem from its location: disputed territory, with high seismic activity, settled by thirty thousand people who would need to be relocated.[80]

By the time the feasibility study was approved, China was rising among Pakistan's donors and investors. In 2014, China announced $12 billion in official financing, three-fifths of which was on commercial terms.[81] The announcement of CPEC in May 2013, during a visit by Li Keqiang to Pakistan, came as U.S. aid was dropping. Just as China seized the opportunity in 1965 to offer its assistance when the United States was reevaluating its ties with Pakistan, it was stepping forward again.

But this time, China had much more to offer. Although the initial MOU for CPEC was light on details, agreements signed in 2014 and 2015 began to suggest that CPEC could reach $46 billion. During Xi's visit to Pakistan in April 2015, the two sides signed fifty-one MOUs. Prime Minister Nawaz Sharif assured the Chinese that he "would extend all possible facilitation" as projects broke ground.[82] Expectations were sky high. CPEC, some Pakistani observers believed, was China's "Marshall Plan."

In 2016, Pakistani officials sent USAID a letter asking it to stop the feasibility study for the Diamer-Bhasha Dam.[83] The following year, Pakistan and China signed an MOU to finance the project with three other dams as part of a $50 billion package. With that announcement, CPEC swelled to a mythical $100 billion.

But the Diamer-Bhasha Dam, like other parts of CPEC, has not materialized. Six months after announcing the $50 billion MOU, Pakistan's Water and Power Development Authority (WAPDA) withdrew its request for Chinese financing. "Chinese conditions for financing the Diamer-Bhasha Dam were not doable and against our interests," Muzammil Hussain, WAPDA's chairman, explained.[84] Whether that was a negotiating tactic for better terms or an honest refusal, the project's future remains uncertain. It is also possible that China structured an offer to Pakistan that it knew would be rejected. In 2018, Pakistan's top judge started a crowd-funding campaign for the dam, and a handful of celebrities, including the R&B singer Akon, have encouraged Pakistanis to donate.[85] As of early 2020, they had raised less than 1 percent of the estimated cost.[86]

"Please Build a Naval Base"

CPEC has slowly come down to Earth. In October 2018, Pakistan declared that it would seek a bailout from the IMF, which has provided $27 billion in financial assistance to Pakistan over the past six decades.[87] Facing criticism about unsustainable debt in other BRI-participating countries, especially Sri Lanka, Chinese officials have been eager to make CPEC appear safer by releasing more sober estimates. At the end of 2018, the Chinese government claimed that twenty-two projects were completed or under way, totaling $19 billion. The largest category was energy, totaling almost $13 billion, two-thirds of which was for coal power plants.[88]

Both sides set out to manage Pakistan's debt risks, but long-term planning is no match for short-term political incentives.[89] The CPEC long-term plan, according to *Dawn*'s reporting, recommended securing financial guarantees from Pakistan and noted that Pakistan's economy could only absorb $2 billion a year in direct investment, $1 billion in preferential loans, and $1.5 billion in commercial loans.[90] But when Sharif pushed for a $21 billion package of power projects before facing reelection in 2018, he was willing to give generous guarantees, reportedly as high as 34 percent in investment returns for some power plants.[91] Those deals could squeeze Pakistan further in the coming years.

Gwadar Port continues to inch ahead. The project was briefly reenergized in 1997, when Sharif formed a task force that endorsed developing the port. But the following year, Pakistan held its first public test of nuclear weapons, triggering international sanctions and limiting outside investment for the port. During President Pervez Musharraf's 2001 visit to Beijing, marking the fiftieth anniversary of Chinese-Pakistan relations, he signed an agreement to develop the port. The first phase of construction was completed in 2005, a year ahead of schedule, but due to security concerns, an opening ceremony was not held until 2007.[92] When the port received its first commercial shipment in 2008, the ship was carrying too much wheat for the port to handle and needed to offload onto another vessel before docking.[93]

Official ceremonies have continued to outpace the port's actual performance. In 2015, with Sharif back in office, a second phase of construction was announced as part of CPEC. Both sides were eager to declare victory, and in November 2016, Sharif hosted a ceremony that strained even the politician's imagination for ribbon cutting. "This idea was conceived only two years ago, and this day marks the breaking of the dawn of a new era," he told reporters. The ceremony was timed to coincide with the arrival of a convoy that had left Kashgar nearly two weeks earlier and traveled along the KKH. "The newly-constructed roads in Balochistan have opened up new areas that were inaccessible and deprived of development . . . and have brought peace to a volatile region," Sharif claimed.[94]

Peace and prosperity have yet to dock at Gwadar. Little of anything has arrived. The port received its first container ship in October 2018, and it is equipped with only three berths for unloading cargo, hardly enough to make Gwadar the "next Dubai," as its boosters have claimed.[95] It is still largely disconnected from the rest of the country and has struggled to provide basic services, including reliable potable water and electricity. If large cargo ships suddenly began arriving, the port and its weak infrastructure reaching inland would not be able to handle them.

The port's local benefits are questionable. If and when the port becomes profitable, China will receive the lion's share of profits, 91 percent, and Pakistan's federal government will receive 9 percent, leaving nothing for Baluchistan's provincial government. Locals have expressed concerns about being excluded from construction jobs, forced relocation, fishing communities losing access to the water, and increased security checkpoints and surveillance.[96] These concerns feed into a larger criticism that CPEC's benefits run one-way.[97]

Baluchistan remains risky, especially for those who are working on CPEC projects. In September 2016, two months before Sharif's declarations of peace, a spokesman for Pakistan's Frontier Works Organization, the same group that was created to build the KKH, announced that militants had killed forty-four Pakistani workers since 2014. In November 2018, militants attacked the Chinese consulate in Karachi. The Baluchistan Liberation Army, which took responsibility for the attack, accused China of exploiting Pakistan's resources.[98]

China has leaned on Pakistan to improve security. In 2004, following attacks on Chinese workers at the Gomal Zam Dam, in northern Pakistan, China put the project on hold.[99] But the attention around CPEC has made it more difficult to pause projects or to send Chinese troops without attracting undue attention. At China's urging, Pakistan created an army division of fifteen thousand troops to secure projects. Chinese firms also employ private security contractors, taking advantage of a gray area in Pakistan's legal regime, where joint ventures between Pakistani and foreign security firms have thrived.[100]

Security risks, coupled with Gwadar's weak commercial performance, have fueled speculation that the port will become a Chinese naval facility.[101] "We have asked our Chinese brothers to please build a naval base at Gwadar," Chaudhary Ahmed Mukhtar, Pakistan's defense minister, told the *Financial Times* in 2011.[102] Chinese and Pakistani officials have since denied that possibility.[103]

China does not need a standing naval presence at Gwadar, and it might settle for the ability to access the port. Indeed, the terms that Pakistan offered the United States decades ago provide one option. In 1972, Pakistan's defense minister, acting on Bhutto's direction, noted that Pakistan did not want large numbers of U.S. military personnel stationed at the port but that the United States might find it valuable to have access to facilities as needed.[104]

China and Pakistan's most ambitious connectivity projects, a pipeline and railway, remain pipe dreams. The pipeline would be among the longest and highest in the world, stretching from Gwadar, across the Karakorum mountains, to Kashgar in western China.[105] Pumping oil from sea level to fifteen thousand feet, across a distance of more than three thousand kilometers, would require powerful pumps, extra heating, and special insulation. Construction is estimated at $10 billion, which even appears conservative when compared to other high-rising pipelines.[106] After construction, operations would add roughly eight dollars to the cost of each barrel pumped.[107]

The pipeline's strategic value does not appear commensurate with its high price tag.[108] Some observers have suggested that it could help reduce China's reliance on oil shipped through the Strait of Malacca. But if the project's main purpose is to provide an alternative oil supply in the event that the Strait of Malacca was closed, it would still remain vulnerable to sabotage from the ground or aerial bombing. It would be even easier to blockade or disable Gwadar Port than the Strait of Malacca. The prospect of a Strait of Malacca closure and conflict, presumably between the United States and China, now seems remote, but the pipeline would remain vulnerable to attacks from Baluch militants in the meantime.

The railway could allow commerce to continue overland all year, but it would come at an astronomical cost. Extending Pakistan's railway network north to Khunjerab would require building an estimated two hundred kilometers of tunnel and seventy bridges. Building south to Gwadar would require upgrading an existing line, for which feasibility studies have only begun.[109] Altogether, the two extensions are estimated to cost $16 billion, and each will take at least five years to build.[110] Officially, the southern component is slated to begin construction in 2025, and the northern component will begin in 2030, close enough to allow officials to speak about the project with a straight face and far enough away to allow them to comfortably delay it.[111]

While the railway and pipeline have not moved forward, the Chinese telecom giant Huawei has laid a fiber-optic cable across the Khunjerab Pass. At $44 million, it is less expensive and more practical.[112] Huawei representatives point out that it will allow Pakistanis to access Chinese content more quickly, and by avoiding undersea cables, the route makes espionage from neighboring countries other than China more difficult.[113] Unlike the proposed pipeline, the fiber-optic cable is less vulnerable to attack and cheaper to repair. Unlike the proposed railway, it cannot carry people. It offers the type of connectivity that is most comfortable to both governments.

"Higher than the Himalayas"

Slowly, CPEC is beginning to echo Haqqani's summary of U.S.-Pakistani relations. Expectations have been nothing if not exaggerated. Promises have been broken, as only a fraction of CPEC's projects have materialized. Prime Minister Imran Khan, who assumed office in 2018, has put most of CPEC's remaining projects on hold. "Perhaps we can stretch CPEC out over another five years or so," Abdul Razak Dawood, Khan's commerce and industry adviser, said in September 2018.[114] Khan's administration has blamed the previous government for negotiating bad deals that benefit Chinese companies at the expense of Pakistani companies. But it is hard to escape the unstated implication that China took advantage of Pakistan's weakness.

China's list of grievances is growing as well. Chinese firms have complained about corruption within the initiative, delays in procurement and licensing processes, and failures by Pakistan to make payments on time.[115] Pakistani businesses have pressed their provincial governments to delay the creation of special economic zones, which the Chinese government is eager to set up. In 2017, China signaled its displeasure with Pakistan's stewardship of CPEC by temporarily halting funding for multiple projects.[116]

So far, China and Pakistan have avoided dangerous misunderstandings. Even as expectations are not met, new promises are made that allow officials on both sides to maintain optimism. Pakistan has few alternatives, and with nearly two-thirds of its population below the age of thirty, its demographic clock is ticking. Without tangible results, enthusiasm for Chinese investment and tolerance for Chinese workers could turn into resentment.

China faces many of the same challenges that plagued U.S. efforts in Pakistan, but its interests are more direct and enduring. U.S. involvement in Pakistan has never really been first and foremost about Pakistan but about some larger battle in which Pakistan's cooperation was needed. For China, CPEC is more direct. It lives there and does not enjoy the United States' geography of splendid isolation. Even if China wanted to, it cannot leave entirely.

The balance of power is in China's favor, but in the struggle to define CPEC on the ground, Pakistan has more experience. During the twentieth century, China was never as heavily involved with foreign development as the United States was during its high points. Pakistan has been working with, and against, outside partners since it became independent. Its leaders are adept at attracting outside support without bending too much to outside pressure, for better or, quite often, for worse. In the basic contest between development and independence, they have favored the latter at the expense of the former. They have resisted change, often to protect the interests of elites. On its home turf, Pakistan has a long streak of winning without winning.

CPEC has been advertised as a "game changer," but it has allowed old games to continue. The tragedy is that the policies to develop Pakistan have been known for some time. Despite decades of advice and billions of dollars in assistance from international donors, for example, Pakistan has been unable to fix its energy sector. Distortions to the sector, caused by bad policies, cost 6.5 percent of the country's GDP each year.[117] Khan's election signals more continuity than change. His coalition was backed by Pakistan's army, which is the strongest defender of the status quo.[118]

The parallels with Pakistan's early days are even personal. In October 2018, Khan's minister of power, Omar Ayub Khan, traveled to Suzhou, China, for a Belt and Road conference. "One of the most important countries in the One Belt One Road Project is Pakistan. The Karakoram Highway that connects Pakistan and

China is one of the pivots of CPEC," he told the conference.[119] He did not mention that his grandfather, General Ayub Khan, presided over the chaotic construction of the KKH. Like General Khan, who pressed the U.S. Congress for support in 1961 before turning to China, he was there to reassure his foreign sponsors and, of course, to ask for more investment.

China, for its part, has been repeating the mistakes of the powers that came before it. It has failed to make its investments contingent on difficult reforms. Rather than encouraging Pakistan to set stricter priorities, it has been willing to pick from expansive wish lists of projects. China's approach to projects in Pakistan has been based far too much on its own experience. Like the Western economists who advised Pakistan, Chinese officials have overestimated their abilities. Chinese officials have been surprised when projects in Pakistan have been halted for reasons that would not stop projects in China.[120] These mistakes are all the more remarkable because China has chosen to make CPEC the BRI's flagship.

China has entered a contest from which it will be even more difficult to withdraw. Proximity is an asset when things are going well, but it makes cutting losses in Pakistan more difficult. China's lighter engagement in the past allowed it to maintain a steadier course in its relations with Pakistan, inspiring officials to declare that their friendship "is higher than the Himalayas and deeper than the deepest sea in the world, and sweeter than honey."[121] But with deeper engagement comes greater turbulence, and that saying also carries a warning. Honey is sweet, but like spending on megaprojects, it provides a temporary boost that soon wears off. Mountains are high, and oceans are deep; but like large amounts of debt, they are dangerous.

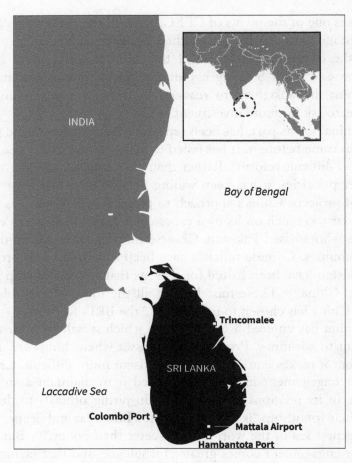

Sri Lanka

Center for Strategic and International Studies, Reconnecting Asia Project

CHAPTER EIGHT

Game of Loans

Sri Lanka

Overlooking Sri Lanka's southern coast, Hambantota's Martello Tower is a monument to a violent past and a witness to a struggle still unfolding. Round and stout, at only twenty-five feet tall the tower gets its height from the quiet hill on which it is perched. It was built by British soldiers in the early 1800s, a tactical outpost and statement of their intentions to stay. Their arrival brought an end to the Kandy Kingdom, which had ruled the area for nearly four centuries. In the 1990s, four decades after the British left, the tower was rebuilt, incongruously, as part of a fisheries museum. Inside, light leaks through the gun holes that British soldiers once peered out of and streams down from the ceiling, where a hatch opens to the roof.

There are two views from the top of the tower. Look south, into the Indian Ocean, and hulking ships move smoothly and slowly. Each plots its own course, but all are locked in the same larger dance. Tankers filled with oil are heading east toward China. Massive container ships, their decks stacked and colored with Lego-like precision, carry goods toward Europe. The largest of them are more than half a football field wide and longer than the Empire State Building is tall. Altogether, some sixty thousand ships pass by each year. The mantra for real estate is generally true for ports: location, location, location. Hambantota is a mere ten nautical miles away from one of the world's busiest shipping lanes.

Look west, down the coastline, and gigantic state-of-the art shipping cranes, each costing $30 million, rise above a Chinese owned and operated port. Until construction started in 2008, the area was mostly jungle. Wild elephants still roam nearby, coming out of their protected areas and into contact with humans as new construction shrinks their habitat. Sri Lanka has some of the world's best natural harbors, but curiously, this port was carved out of the coast. A logistics and industrial zone with refueling services, cargo transshipment, and ship repair was unveiled in 2017 with promises that it would create one hundred thousand jobs.[1] Such prosperity would transform Hambantota, a fishing town of sixty thousand people.

The problem is that these two images—the world's busiest shipping lanes and Sri Lanka's gamble to tap into them—remain miles apart. In 2017, the port handled less than 1 percent of Sri Lanka's total traffic. To create activity, shipments of cars are diverted from Colombo, Sri Lanka's capital and the home of its busiest port, which is thriving and has plans to expand further in the coming years. When Hambantota's modest cargo is unloaded, much of it is driven north toward Colombo and other urban areas, where most Sri Lankans live. It is a classic example of poorly targeted government intervention, increasing inefficiency rather than addressing its root causes.

Rather than fueling local development, Hambantota Port has become the poster child for the dangers of Chinese lending. The port was never intended to be Chinese owned and operated, but it was Chinese financed and built, adding to Sri Lanka's crippling debt. U.S. officials have seized on the example to illustrate the perils of borrowing from China. As U.S. Vice President Mike Pence said in October 2018, "China uses so-called 'debt diplomacy' to expand its influence. . . . Just ask Sri Lanka, which took on massive debt to let Chinese state companies build a port of questionable commercial value."[2]

As a former speechwriter, I can appreciate the chest-thumping appeal of those lines, particularly for an American audience. But as an analyst, thinking about how they sound to a global audience, I wish that someone had cut them. Sri Lanka's complexities have been turned into a cheap spy novel, reframed as a simple zero-sum competition between outside powers rather than a messy, and mostly domestic, human drama.

The Merchant of Hambantota

Behind Hambantota Port is a tale of reckless ambition that Shakespeare would recognize. In the opening scene of *The Merchant of Venice*, Bassanio, an ambitious and spendthrift nobleman, is broke and desperate to secure a loan for his courtship of Portia, a rich heiress. "How much I have disabled mine estate / By something showing a more swelling port / Than my faint means would grant continuance," he says. Even more than the nautical similarities, it is the relationship between Bassanio's drive and dangerous debt that Hambantota evokes. Bassanio is driven less by love than by ego, and Portia is his shortcut to the top of society. His friend Antonio, a wealthy merchant, agrees to guarantee the loan. The deal comes with a famous condition: if Antonio cannot repay the loan, the lender may take a pound of his flesh.

In Sri Lanka's case, the ambitious nobleman was Mahinda Rajapaksa, and the ending was not as kind to the people of Sri Lanka, who continue to pay for his unchecked drive. Rajapaksa was born to a well-known political family in Hambantota, and his father served in the Sri Lankan parliament for nearly two decades. When the elder Rajapaksa died in 1967, it fell to Mahinda to carry on the family tradition. In 1970, at only twenty-four years old, he campaigned for his father's seat in parliament and won, becoming the youngest member of parliament in Sri Lanka's history. He served for seven years before losing his seat and joining a law practice in Tangalle, a large fishing town in Hambantota District. In 1983, he married Shiranthi Wickramasinghe, a former beauty queen whose connections would help his quest for higher office.

No one can accuse Rajapaksa of forgetting where he came from because he never misses an opportunity to remind everyone. Draped over traditional white garb, his trademark maroon shawl is supposedly inspired by his uncle, who as a public attorney for Hambantota wore a brown shawl that represented finger millet, a local crop. Rajapaksa has cast himself as a savior of Sri Lankan farmers.[3] It is a savvy move for a politician with a rural base, and somehow, the act continued even while his wealth grew in the public eye. He loves jewelry and has been called "Lord of the Rings" for wearing up to eight rings at once.

Rajapaksa reentered politics in 1989, winning a seat in parliament and later serving as minister of labor and minister of fisheries. As a cabinet member, he funneled state money to pet projects, including turning Hambantota's Martello Tower into a fisheries museum. He also promised to bring big ships to Hambantota.[4] In 2002, Rajapaksa became leader of the main opposition party, a challenger in waiting for the nation's highest office.

Later that year, the ruling coalition government, led by Chandrika Kumaratunga and Ranil Wickremesinghe, unveiled a sweeping development plan. Released in December 2002, "Regaining Sri Lanka" has clues for the chaos that would later unfold.[5] It reads more like a wish list than a coherent plan or strategy. One part of the document notes that developing Hambantota Port is a "longer-term" priority, while another says it is a "medium-term" priority. Part of the confusion might have stemmed from the fact that the port had not been studied yet in any great detail.

Feasibility studies are essential for planning large projects, but they are a mix of art and science, allowing for honest mistakes as well as manipulation. Reasonable people can disagree about which assumptions to use and how to interpret results. Less objectively, these studies can be massaged to support a preferred course of action, and the sponsor always has the option of seeking a different study. "Regaining Sri Lanka" noted that SNC Lavalin, a Canadian engineering firm, would complete a feasibility study for the port.

Evaluating projects that are intended to develop rural areas is especially hazardous. Like Khorgos Gateway and Gwadar Port, examined in Chapters 3 and 7, Hambantota was conceived as a game-changing engine for growth. The appeal of bringing economic opportunities to disadvantaged areas is so powerful that it can mask related costs. A new port in an underdeveloped area often needs better local and national roads, power generation and distribution, and water services. Many of these expenses are not captured in the cost of the port itself and normally would be viewed as disadvantages when comparing sites for the port. But when rural development is a primary goal, these challenges become justifications for the project.

Initially, the Sri Lankan government made the right call. In 2003, a government-appointed task force reviewed and ultimately rejected the SNC study, faulting it for ignoring the port's potential impact on Colombo Port.[6] A natural trade hub for centuries, Colombo's port was developed under British rule and then modernized to accommodate shipping containers in the 1970s. In 2016, it was ranked among the top twenty-five busiest ports in the world.[7] It has the capacity to handle even more cargo, and if that runs out, it has space and plans to expand.[8] The biggest threat to the success of Hambantota Port has always come from within Sri Lanka.

Ideas for megaprojects come and go, but they rarely die. Before the Suez Canal became a reality, it was dreamt up, studied, and abandoned by a succession of leaders from Egypt's pharaohs to Napoleon. Proposals for an extensive U.S. highway system emerged in the early 1800s, but it took the threat of the Soviet Union for Eisenhower to sell the U.S. Congress on supporting it. Projects can resurface with a new urgency when technology opens new possibilities, when greater financial resources emerge, or because domestic politics demand it. Every big project needs a strong political patron, and in 2003, Hambantota Port did not have enough support. The idea was studied and declined but not buried.

When Rajapaksa ran for the presidency in 2005, he capitalized on two disasters, one natural and one manmade. A tsunami in December 2004 killed more than thirty-five thousand Sri Lankans, including many in Rajapaksa's base of support. In the north, the country was mired in a civil war between Tamil Tigers and the Sri Lanka government. On election day, Rajapaksa emerged from a polling booth and made two promises. First, he would "bring about an honourable peace" to Sri Lanka.[9] Second, he would "build a new Sri Lanka."[10] When the votes were tallied, Rajapaksa narrowly won, capturing just over half the vote. After decades of climbing, Hambantota's man had reached the top.

"Helping Hambantota"

As president, Rajapaksa was as generous to his family and friends as he was merciless to his enemies and adversaries. He appointed fifty-two cabinet ministers, setting a world record for the largest cabinet.[11] Among those were three of his five brothers, giving the Rajapaksa family control over 80 percent of the national budget.[12] As defense secretary, his brother Gotabaya oversaw a military campaign to end the Tamil conflict. More than one hundred thousand people died, including forty thousand Tamil civilians killed by government forces, according to the UN.[13] Rajapaksa was a villain in the eyes of the minority Tamils but a hero to many Sinhalese citizens, who make up three-quarters of the population.[14]

While conflict raged in the north, Rajapaksa wasted little time building, especially in the south. An investigation by a journalist, Sonali Samarasinghe, alleged that Rajapaksa and his aides embezzled $1 million from international donations designated for the tsunami relief efforts by moving funds into a private account labeled "Helping Hambantota."[15] The government launched an investigation, but the Supreme Court ordered an end to it, a decision that the chief justice publicly regretted.[16] Samarasinghe and her husband, Lasantha Wickrematunge, endured harassment from the government until 2009, when Lasantha was killed, forcing her to leave the country.[17]

Rajapaksa continued to help Hambantota by helping himself. Hambantota Port is the best known of his projects, but its handover to Chinese owners would not have occurred without the pursuit of other dubious projects at the same time. Each new project added to Sri Lanka's growing debt, and many did not produce enough economic activity to cover the loans. The worst of these big-ticket projects had three things in common: they used Chinese financing, Chinese contractors, and Rajapaksa's name. Years later, they have a fourth thing in common: they are barely used.

Enough people believed these projects could succeed, or were willing to say so, before they failed. In 2006, the Danish consulting firm Ramboll completed a second feasibility study on Hambantota Port. It took a relatively optimistic view of the port's potential, basing traffic projections on Sri Lanka's future growth and overflow from existing ports at Colombo, Galle, and Trincomalee.[18] By 2040, it estimated, the port would handle nearly six and a half times as many containers as the Port of Colombo did in 2006.[19]

Even with the optimistic assessment, Rajapaksa struggled to find the money to pay for the port. India, Sri Lanka's largest trading partner at the time, declined to finance it. The Asian Development Bank (ADB) declined. That left China, which was willing not only to finance the project but to pursue an even more ambitious version of it. Early plans for Hambantota focused on offering fuel services, but under Rajapaksa, it was scaled up to include other activities, many of them already carried out at Colombo. This duplication would have been difficult for Chinese authorities to miss, let alone Sri Lankan authorities, given that they were also helping to expand Colombo and later began operating one of its container terminals.

During a tour of Colombo Port, I noticed subtler signs of Chinese influence as well. The port's equipment tells a story of China's rise in manufacturing and maritime commerce. The oldest cranes were European made. There was some Japanese and South Korean equipment. But the newest machinery was almost entirely Chinese, and the shipping containers were dominated by Chinese firms. Nearly two-thirds of the world's top fifty ports have received Chinese investment.[20]

Adjacent to the port, Sri Lanka is developing Port City, a financial center on reclaimed land that will eventually be as large as central London, nearly doubling the size of Colombo. Proposals for expansion date back to 2004, but the grand plan that emerged has China's fingerprints all over it. In 2011, the China Communications Construction Company (CCCC) proposed the project and offered to invest $1.4 billion in financing.[21] It will lease two-fifths of the new land for ninety-nine years. The blueprints look like a Dubai-inspired magic trick, creating a mini-metropolis out of nothing. Dredging machines run at all hours, sucking up sand from the ocean floor and coughing it out. Cubic foot by cubic foot of sand, an island is slowly emerging and expanding. It could be a vision taking shape or a bubble expanding toward explosion.

Port City reflects the perils of unsolicited proposals. Most international donors craft their offers in response to proposals from recipient countries. Public solicitations can result in more offers, stiffer competition, and ultimately better deals for recipients. But for Port City, and several other projects in Sri Lanka, Chinese companies and officials effectively made the proposal. In these cases, China sets the table for discussions and greatly simplifies the process by offering the proposal, financing, and a contractor ready to get started. In the most egregious instances, Chinese firms even complete the feasibility study for the project they were proposing, effectively approving their own work and providing another opportunity to inflate costs.

From a purely commercial perspective, the best option for improving the trade competitiveness of Sri Lanka's ports would have been a modest expansion of the Port of Colombo while improving operations there and at other existing ports. But Rajapaksa had bigger ambitions. He wanted to bring economic opportunities to his rural base of support and, in doing so, cement his own legacy.

The temptation to build transformative projects is universal. Politicians understand that technical and management improvements do not generate the same excitement as ribbon-cutting ceremonies. The scale is further tipped toward building new facilities, rather than upgrading existing ones, because of the lag between project announcement and completion. Successful projects can take years to complete and even longer before they become profitable. Officials who reap the political benefits of starting new projects are rarely around to be held accountable for their long performance.[22]

Colombo's Lotus Tower is another Chinese megaproject with questionable utility. At $100 million, it is South Asia's second-tallest building and, true to its name, looks like a metallic green stem and red flower. Pitched as a telecommunications hub, it can house up to 120 telecom companies.[23] Yet there are only 115 licensed telecommunications operators and radio and television broadcasters in all of Sri Lanka.[24] Even if the tower attracts tourists, it seems destined to join the list of vanity projects that have dangerously increased Sri Lanka's debt.

To be sure, Chinese financing in Sri Lanka during Rajapaksa's two terms was not entirely wasteful. Thanks in part to Chinese-built roads, I was able to drive a counterclockwise miniloop of the island over three days, touching the southern and western coasts before returning to Colombo. When highways gave way to rural roads, often when traveling from the coasts into the island, it felt like two different countries. Outside the cities, the coastal highways were smooth, fast, and comparatively safe. Inland, on the rural roads, there was deceleration, vibration, and chaos as trucks and tricars, three-wheeled motor carts, dodged potholes and each other. Near rural town centers, the sides of the roads were bustling with people on the move, children playing, and tiny shops. The roads are where life happens, and everyone seemed inches away from collision.

But Chinese loans have dangers of their own. In Sri Lanka, China was lending at relatively high rates, for comparatively short periods, and encouraging refinancing and additional borrowing. The first phase of the Hambantota Port project was a $307 million loan at 6.3 percent interest. Unlike these commercial rates, multi-lateral development banks typically offer loans at rates closer to 2 or 3 percent and sometimes even closer to zero. China gave Sri Lanka fifteen years to pay back the first Hambantota loan, while the ADB had provided a twenty-five-year loan for the Port of Colombo. As delays began to mount, the additional time would have been helpful. And of course, Chinese officials were happy to help Rajapaksa borrow extra and refinance at a higher rate.

Speed is China's strongest appeal and its greatest risk. Chinese loans, while often requiring the partner to use Chinese contractors, are often not as stringent in their requirements for safeguards and reforms. In 2011, Sri Lanka's official external financing strategy singled out the differences between Chinese loans, noting, "Loan processing time for these loans is very short, conditions required to be completed for obtaining these loans are much fewer compared with the other lending agencies."[25] The officials writing that report should have acknowledged the risks that came with a faster loan process, but in the moment, all they saw was upside.

All That Glistens

China was not the preferred lender but often Sri Lanka's last or only resort. There were no competing offers for Hambantota's port, suggesting that other potential lenders did not see rewards commensurate with the project's risks. Sri Lankan officials should have interpreted that lack of interest as an important warning. Instead, with the project having been judged too risky by international lenders for a loan with a lower rate, they pushed ahead with loans at higher rates.

Rajapaksa was so eager to build that some feasibility studies became a box-checking exercise rather than a tool for risk mitigation.

The most glaring example is a thirty-minute drive from Hambantota Port. Out of the jungle, past signs warning drivers about wild
elephants, a $210 million airport emerges. China Export-Import
Bank provided a concessional loan, and China Harbour Engineering Company, the same company behind Hambantota Port, built
the facility. The government reportedly spent less than $6,000 on
the feasibility study for the airport, ignoring previous work that examined options for a second international airport. At the time, Rajapaksa's cousin Prasanna Wickramasuriya was chairman of the state
agency that operated the airports.[26]

The Mattala Rajapaksa International Airport was intended to become a gateway for tourists but has become a destination itself since
opening in 2013.[27] For less than a dollar, people can visit the airport's
main hall, where a large Buddha statue greets visitors. At the airport's
peak, a handful of airlines used it, including a new state-owned airline called Mihin, the diminutive form of Mahinda. For a brief
period of time, it was possible to buy tickets using currency with Rajapaksa's image on it to fly Mihin to Rajapaksa Airport.[28] After landing
in Mattala, you could go to the Rajapaksa port, the Rajapaksa cricket
stadium, or the Rajapaksa National Tele-Cinema Park.

As it turned out, not many people wanted to do any of those
things. Mihin ceased operations in 2016, and without sufficient demand, even Sri Lanka's largest national airline stopped operations at
Mattala. In 2017, the airport averaged seven passengers a day, and in
2018, the last commercial airline, FlyDubai, announced it was canceling its service. Except for the occasional emergency landing, and a
skeleton staff to perform essential tasks, the facility then sat unused.

While skimping on the airport feasibility study, Rajapaksa
spent nearly $800,000 of public money for an opening ceremony
for Hambantota Port, on November 18, 2010. It was his sixty-fifth
birthday and the last day of his first term in office. Rajapaksa must
have consulted his personal astrologer, Sumanadasa Abeygunawardena, who was trusted to select auspicious dates and times for state
events. As Rajapaksa rose, so did Abeygunawardena. His horoscope
text-message service expanded thanks to a deal with the state telecom company, and Rajapaksa appointed him to Sri Lanka's National Savings Bank board despite his complete lack of banking
experience.[29]

The Hambantota Port opening was an opportunity to celebrate with friends and, naturally, to reward loyalty. The Sri Lankan actor Jackson Anthony emceed the event and collected a $179,000 fee, ostensibly for helping to organize it. Anthony was another good friend, having claimed in 2011 that Rajapaksa was "related to Lord Buddha."[30] More than $80,000 was spent on dancers. "Five years ago ... I promised the nation that I would bring an honourable peace to this country and also to build a new Sri Lanka. I am glad to state that I was able to fulfill both these promises within five years, even before the end of my term," Rajapaksa told his audience.[31] After his speech, Rajapaksa released water into the port.

The show hid the fact that the port was not yet functional. A sensationalist press release from the lead Chinese construction firm, China Harbour Engineering Company (CHEC), recounted, "The crowds immediately became excited and many employees of CHEC having participated in the port construction were so excited that they couldn't hold their tears." It claimed that CHEC "smoothly managed to make the port accessible by ships four months before the date required by the Owner."[32] In reality, a large rock was obstructing the entrance to the port and still needed to be removed. Rather than risk delaying the opening, CHEC had prematurely flooded the port. It charged $40 million over the next year to remove the rock.[33]

As Rajapaksa partied, Sri Lanka's economy was developing a hangover. Doubts about his investments began to mount as their promised benefits—jobs, rural development, and transformative growth—failed to materialize. His response was to borrow more. In 2012, he secured an additional $757 million loan from China's Export-Import Bank to further expand Hambantota Port, which was barely attracting traffic. By 2015, Rajapaksa had tripled Sri Lanka's debt, and roughly 95 percent of Sri Lanka's government revenue was going toward servicing it.

Rajapaksa's spending became a prime target for the opposition party, led by his own health minister, Maithripala Sirisena, who left Rajapaksa's cabinet to challenge him in the 2015 election. Accusing Rajapaksa of accumulating debts that "generations of our children and grandchildren would be unable to completely finish paying off," Sirisena made Sri Lanka's debt a centerpiece of his campaign and promised in his campaign platform to "expose to the country the true state of state loans," take "urgent steps to lighten the state debt burden," and "re-assess all mega projects undertaken recently."[34] In a surprise upset, he unseated Rajapaksa in January 2015.

Sirisena's administration reexamined some deals and temporarily halted the second phase of construction at Hambantota's port. Although well intentioned, this also delayed any revenue the port could generate, effectively making it even more difficult to service the loans.

But the new government's options were limited, and it learned how large projects, once started, are difficult to kill. Even if cancellation makes economic sense, political and legal barriers stand in the way. Politically, it is always easier to give, announcing a new project, than to cancel and take away. India and some Western partners were willing to provide technical support, but even in aggregate, they could not match China's financial largess. The administration discovered that existing contracts were difficult to terminate, and many included clauses requiring any disputes to be resolved in Chinese courts. Even despite an election mandate for change, Sirisena had little room to maneuver.

With Sri Lanka unable to repay its debt, its pound of flesh came due. In July 2017, Chinese and Sri Lankan officials agreed to a concession that granted China Merchants a controlling stake in Hambantota Port and a ninety-nine-year lease for $1.12 billion.[35] The agreement sparked protests in Hambantota and accusations of neocolonialism. The project would not be as disappointing if its scope was not stretched and its supposed benefits were not spectacularly exaggerated.[36] The windfall of one hundred thousand jobs has not materialized, and in November 2017, over four hundred port employees were let go.[37] In December, on the day of the handover, Sri Lankans gathered in front of the port's main gate to protest. Using an aerial picture of the port, rather than the people on the ground, Xinhua, China's official news agency, tweeted triumphantly, "Another milestone along path of #BeltandRoad."[38]

"Debt Diplomacy"

When I visited Hambantota a month after the handover, the signs of China's growing influence were hard to miss.[39] As the sun rose one Saturday morning, groups of Chinese workers in half-zipped blue jumpsuits made their way to the port. One of the few vessels anchored at the port was affiliated with China Shipping. The port's headquarters, a triangular thirteen-story wedge built by a Chinese contractor, juts out of the flat green landscape like it was copied and pasted from a hotel resort catalogue. Nearby, seventy or so Sri Lankans staged a quiet protest. A small group stood behind a booth with signs that asked, "Authorities, what do we get, our job or death?" Most of the protesters were across the street, sitting at tables underneath the shade of trees. A few days earlier, the port's employees' union announced that former workers were starting a hunger strike.

Exactly how the Hambantota agreement came together remains a matter of some speculation, a result of the lack of transparency around it and other financing agreements. Sri Lanka's parliament approved the revised Hambantota Port deal, but the text has not been made public, allowing suspicions to fester. The Sirisena administration claims that Chinese officials insisted on a Chinese firm taking a controlling stake in the port.[40] After leaving office, Rajapaksa claimed that Chinese firms were never intended to have a controlling ownership stake and operational control of the entire port but should have operated an individual terminal, as they do in Colombo.

As Hambantota's story has been told and retold, it has become Exhibit A for a growing case against China's "debt diplomacy," the term of art for loading up small economies with loans to extract strategic concessions.[41]

Without a doubt, lending risks along the BRI are high.[42] In 2018, Christine Lagarde, then managing director of the International Monetary Fund, warned in a speech that "the first challenge is ensuring that Belt and Road only travels where it is needed."[43] She mentioned the risk of debt increases but stopped short of saying that China was using this leverage. In truth, the IMF wields the same basic power. Its loans are issued with requirements that recipient states undertake specific reforms.

The case against Chinese officials' malpractice is strong. They had the means, motive, and opportunity. China was not Sri Lanka's leading creditor, but it was willing to accept payment terms that more responsible lenders would not. At the time of the Hambantota deal, China only held 10 percent of Sri Lanka's foreign debt. In comparison, the World Bank held 11 percent, Japan held 12 percent, and the ADB held 14 percent.[44] Not all lenders behaved the same, however. For example, the ADB has three major financing guidelines: it seldom takes an equity stake larger than 25 percent of total share capital, it will seldom be the largest single investor in an enterprise, and it will not assume responsibility for managing an enterprise. In the case of Hambantota Port, China took an 80 percent share, became the largest investor, and assumed responsibility for managing the enterprise.[45]

China's motive is allegedly strategic, and Beijing's behavior leaves cause for concern. During 2014, two Chinese submarines and a warship docked at Colombo, Sri Lanka's capital, setting off alarms about China's expanding military footprint. In recent years, Chinese officials and defense experts have started to speak more openly about using Chinese-funded ports in the Indian Ocean with questionable commercial merits, including Gwadar Port in Pakistan, for peacekeeping and disaster-relief operations.[46]

But the port is not yet a Chinese naval facility, and Sri Lankan officials have tried to calm fears that it will become one. "Sri Lanka headed by President Maithripala Sirisena does not enter into military alliances with any country or make our bases available to foreign countries," Prime Minister Ranil Wickremesinghe promised in August 2017.[47] Early the following year, Sri Lanka's highest-ranking military officer said, "There had been this widespread claim about the port being earmarked to be used as a military base. . . . No action, whatsoever will be taken in our harbor or in our waters that jeopardizes India's security concerns."[48] In mid-2018, Sri Lanka announced that it was moving the southern command of its navy to Hambantota, underscoring its intent to control the port. Since then, U.S. Navy and Japanese Maritime Self-Defense Force ships have made port calls to Hambantota.[49]

In military terms, Hambantota could be useful for Beijing, but it is not a game changer. The port's operations are still overseen by Sri Lankan authorities, and any visiting military vessels need their approval.[50] That could change in the future, of course, and a country heavily indebted to China will be less likely to refuse requests to host Chinese military vessels. If China did gain unfettered access, the port's location is a double-edged sword. It is located close to a major shipping lane, which is strategically valuable, but dangerously close to one of China's major competitors, India, whose military is moments away.

Without a doubt, China's irresponsibility helped create Hambantota Port. Sri Lanka's overall debt levels were unsustainable, and it was looking for relief. China contributed significantly to that problem because of the speed at which it lent. Between 2008 and 2017, the beginning of its renegotiations over Hambantota Port, China lent $8 billion as other lenders were calling for caution.[51] Chinese officials claim that other foreign creditors deserve their share of the blame. But pointing to shares of foreign debt is like saying debt is debt, regardless of where it comes from and how it is used. That would be true if China adhered to the same standards and safeguards as Western lenders do. It did not and should bear more responsibility.

Ironically, the debt-diplomacy narrative is actually too generous to China. Foreign-policy experts occasionally see strategy where it does not exist, viewing their competitor's actions as more coordinated than they are in reality. The trope is that China is masterfully planning for decades, if not centuries, while Western politicians are struggling to survive tomorrow and next week. Too often, China's governance style is viewed as a strength, the assumption being that its authoritarian government has lasting and superior control while democratic governments are thrown out every few years.

Behind the Hambantota fiasco is not a unitary China but a host of interest groups, each with its own parochial interests, most of which have nothing to do with long-term objectives in general and military aims in particular. In planning for a range of scenarios, Chinese officials must have considered the possibility that Sri Lanka would not be able to pay back its loans, but it is not clear that taking over Hambantota Port was their primary objective.

It is more likely that Hambantota is the result of an absence of strategy among both Chinese and Sri Lankan officials. Eager to support Xi's signature vision, Chinese officials approved loans for projects without adequate due diligence. Chinese firms were eager to build the projects and would get paid regardless of their commercial viability. Sri Lankan officials took the loans without coordinating projects under a coherent development plan. They reaped the immediate political, and in some cases financial, benefits of building new projects. Everyone took something for themselves, eagerly and without much care for the longer-term repercussions. It was chaotic, not strategic.

Getting the story right matters. Preventing the next Hambantota could require greater, not less, oversight and coordination of Chinese lending. China has so far refused to join the world's other major official creditors, which belong to the Paris Club and agree to cap their lending rates, share information, and coordinate debt relief. China is an observer and must be persuaded to become a member, so it is required to play by the same rules or, at the very least, to raise its lending standards.

The debt-diplomacy narrative also ignores the costs China incurs for troubled projects. The unstated, and inaccurate, assumption is that China wins even when its projects fail. The reality is that China will face financial and reputational costs as its projects fail. Hambantota, a fishing village, has become a global lighthouse, warning against getting too close to China. In taking the port, China tarnished its own major foreign-policy vision and will struggle to remove the stain.

It is difficult to imagine China changing its behavior, however, without incurring further losses. It derives a comparative advantage in staying outside the Paris Club, able to pursue a wider range of actions and make offers that other major lenders cannot. Likewise, it gains speed from not adhering to the same risk-assessment processes as the World Bank, ADB, and other multilateral development banks. But China also assumes greater risk, as history cautions. The world's major creditors did not bind themselves out of philanthropy but out of self-interest, after suffering the reputational and financial consequences of going it alone. China may have to repeat more of their mistakes before adopting more of their solutions.

Critically, the debt-diplomacy narrative, and China's rebuttal to it, minimizes Sri Lanka's agency, which is where responsibility and solutions ultimately lie. Fixating on the port's commercial failure and military value misses the mechanism that made it all possible: politics. There are interest groups that want to build projects, regardless of their commercial or strategic value, especially politicians looking to give back to their home bases of support. By far the largest share of Sri Lanka's foreign debt is bond issuances and term loans, which are sold in auctions run by the state.[52] In 2018, Sri Lanka's auditor general even admitted that he could not say with certainty how much public debt the country owed.[53] If there was a debt trap, Sri Lanka's leaders laid it and walked into it.

"Grave Responsibilities"

The next test for Sri Lanka could be on its east coast. In July 2018, the government unveiled a master plan for turning the city of Trincomalee into an "eastern gateway" by 2050. On its face, it is an ambitious proposal that seeks to leverage Sri Lanka's geography and tap into regional economic trends. Trincomalee has one of the world's largest naturally protected harbors. By 2050, the Bay of Bengal region, which includes India, Sri Lanka, Bangladesh, and Myanmar, is expected to have nearly three billion people.

Tucked into the plan are some red flags. It includes a $1 billion port project that would take several years to complete.[54] It would have two container terminals with additional capacity that Sri Lanka does not urgently need. It also proposes a $65 million airport that would be able to handle one million passengers a year.[55] The problem is that Trincomalee already has a domestic airport that it wants to expand.

The political incentives are clearer than these economic projections. The proposal does not adequately take into account other developments in Sri Lanka, just as Hambantota Port was pursued without enough attention to the Port of Colombo. The plan is also too forward looking. When projections are stretched into decades, it is tempting to believe that an investment will pay off handsomely. It is sobering how many of those projections become outdated after five years.

The challenge for China's competitors in Sri Lanka is to avoid throwing good money after bad. Indian and Japanese officials have expressed interest in developing Trincomalee's port, which media already describe as a "counter" to Chinese influence. Japan has already made several investments to improve the existing airport.

India has considered turning the Mattala Rajapaksa International Airport into a flight school. Given the airport's track record of incidents, including bird strikes and elephants attacking workers, it would be an unusually challenging proving ground for new pilots. Privately, Indian officials suggest that owning and operating the airport could serve as a deterrent, helping to check Chinese naval activities at Hambantota. India could even land military aircraft during training exercises, with the permission of Sri Lanka's government, to reinforce that message.

But India's interest in this failed project sends an odd signal. It is responding to military concerns around a commercially dubious project by potentially militarizing it. The prospect of turning around a failing project is tempting, and if it works, India could play the hero, rescuing its southern neighbor from a Chinese-built boondoggle. But if it fails, India risks assuming some of the reputational damage that China would otherwise suffer. India's bailout might also contribute to a sort of moral hazard, providing future Sri Lankan officials with a false sense of security to pursue more risky projects. Rather than India playing China's game and having its reputation dragged into the mud, it might be better served by focusing on economic fundamentals.

For China, Sri Lanka's 2015 election was a leading indicator of trouble to come. During 2018, opposition candidates harnessed criticism of the BRI in Malaysia and Pakistan, as Chapters 6 and 7 recounted, as well as in the Maldives. All three governments, heavy supporters of the BRI, were replaced. After Mohamed Ibrahim Solih took office in the Maldives, he discovered that the country's debt to China was twice as high as expected.[56] This backlash is the natural result of a cycle of too much lending without adequate transparency and oversight. It was happening even in a global economy that was performing well, softening and concealing the extent of the BRI's risky lending. As those conditions deteriorate, more problems will surely come to the surface.

Whether the BRI brand becomes toxic will depend not only on how China reacts but also on whether recipient countries are willing and able to exercise greater oversight and discipline over their project decisions. Sri Lanka's experience suggests that will be difficult, demonstrating that it is not enough to warn against embarking on risky projects. When leaders weigh the short-term incentives of starting projects against the long-term risks of debt and subpar performance, the former often wins out. Better financing alternatives could limit recipient countries' exposure to high interest rates and project terms that create dangerous dependencies. Capacity-building measures could help train governments to evaluate projects and negotiate terms.

But no source of alternative financing will solve the fundamental challenge of walking away from unviable projects, from declining to build the next Mattala airports and Hambantota ports. Better financing alternatives cannot and should not be made available for all proposed projects. Some projects simply should not be pursued. That responsibility falls to government officials and, in democracies, the citizens who elect them. As Sri Lanka's first prime minster, D. S. Senanayake, told the nation upon its independence, "Freedom carries with it grave responsibilities."[57]

Rajapaksa's ambition is undiminished. In 2018, Sirisena fired Ranil Wickremesinghe and replaced him with Rajapaksa as prime minister, throwing Sri Lanka into a constitutional crisis after the new government was unable to form a majority and parliament was dissolved. After Sri Lanka's Supreme Court intervened, Rajapaksa was forced to step down. He was prime minister for less than two months, but that was long enough to sign two deals worth more than $50 million with Chinese firms for port upgrades.[58] "We will bring the forces opposed to the country down to their knees by organizing the people," Rajapaksa said defiantly in his resignation speech.[59] It was a setback for a political climber who had only moved up throughout his career, from member of parliament to fisheries minister, opposition leader, and prime minister.

But Rajapaksa has always found opportunity in chaos, and after Sri Lanka's Easter Sunday bombings in 2019, the political winds turned again in his favor. Rajapaksa rushed to remind Sri Lankans of his strongman credentials, claiming, "the Easter Sunday attacks would have never taken place under our government."[60] Although Mahinda was ineligible to run for a third presidential term, his brother Gotabaya, the former defense secretary, ran and won in November 2019. Naturally, Gotabaya appointed Mahinda as prime minister. Sri Lanka's financial future may be cloudy, but the forecast for Mahinda Rajapaksa and his family is improving.

Rajapaksa's legacy will be felt in Sri Lanka for decades to come. The true cost of his personal ambition has yet to be tallied. The

government plans to resume flights at Mattala Airport and restart
other projects in Hambantota.[61] It is impossible to go far in Hambantota without seeing something that elevates Rajapaksa at the
country's expense. In addition to the port, airport, and cricket stadium, there are smaller signs as well. When you climb down from
Hambantota's Martello Tower, the colonial fort that Rajapaksa
turned into a national fisheries museum, there is a plaque and picture of him, smiling, at the bottom of the ladder.

PART IV
Danger Ahead

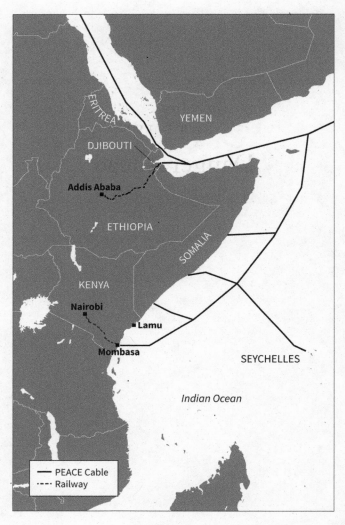

East Africa

Center for Strategic and International Studies, Reconnecting Asia Project; TeleGeography

CHAPTER NINE

War and PEACE

East Africa

"THEY WILL SHOOT IF we go closer," my guide said, pointing toward China's first military base on foreign soil, while his other hand gripped the fishing boat's throttle. Old trawlers were anchored between us and the cluster of sand-colored buildings on shore, forming a rusty partial blockade that obstructed a closer approach and suggested there was nothing new to see. Under a nuclear sun, we bobbed up and down with the waves. It was eerily quiet along the coast of Djibouti, where commercial and military moves mix as easily as the Red Sea and the Indian Ocean.

Djibouti is a riddle that only geography can answer. It is deprived and small, and yet it commands the attention of the world's most powerful countries. Its greatest natural endowment is salt, a supply that is believed to be limitless but is barely exported. It is roughly the size of New Jersey and has less than a million citizens, hardly a blip on Africa's booming demographic landscape. Its ethnic divisions are old, its national identity still cohering. Its neighbors—Eritrea to the west, Somalia and self-declared Somaliland to the east, and Yemen to the north—all had greater economic advantages and have fared worse.

Their turmoil has been Djibouti's opportunity. It is a landing point of relative stability amid turmoil, a desert that sells access to the ocean. "Here, beggars do not ask for money; they ask for water," a French naval strategist once wrote.[1] The same logic applies to great powers, which have come begging for access to Djibouti's coastline. Roughly 20 percent of global trade travels through the Gulf of Aden and past Djibouti's doorstep. On the Horn of Africa's coastline, Djibouti is king. It hosts five foreign military bases, the most of any country in the world, and military rents make up almost a fifth of its GDP.[2]

You cannot be a real country without a beer and an airline, to steal a line from the American musician Frank Zappa, but it helps to have a military base in Djibouti. The United States sent troops to Djibouti in 2002, as part of its response to the 9/11 attacks, and never left. U.S. facilities have expanded to include nearly five hundred acres at Camp Lemonnier, which became part of U.S. Africa Command in 2008. Japan established its first long-term overseas base in Djibouti in 2009 and, after China's arrival in 2017, announced that it would upgrade the facility and station at least one Japanese personnel for every ten Chinese military personnel.[3] France and Italy have bases, too. Not to be left out, Russia and Saudi Arabia have expressed interest in setting up bases.

One of Djibouti's greatest assets is beneath the waves. It is a major landing point for underseas fiber-optic cables and a critical stop on China's "digital silk road." Globally, there are about 380 active underseas cables, which carry the vast majority of international data. Data from cell phones, for example, is sent to a tower and then onward across terrestrial and submarine cables. These cables will only become more important with the arrival of 5G and other services that will increase the speed and volume of data that is transferred. Using the cloud, despite its name, often requires data to travel under the ocean.[4]

Western policy makers were slow to grasp the challenge that China's dominance in global telecommunications could present. More recently, they have mainly focused on security risks at home. But as Western capitals debate whether to allow Chinese technology into their next-generation wireless networks, Chinese firms are rapidly connecting the world's next-generation markets. Half of the world's population growth through 2050 is expected in Africa, which is also home to the fastest-growing internet market.⁵ With generous financing, artificially low costs, and a knack for connecting rural areas, Chinese tech firms are positioning themselves to grow even if their Western presence withers.

China has set ambitious industrial targets for winning global market shares in high-tech sectors, and using the BRI as a primary avenue, it is marching toward them. In 2008, Chinese companies were involved with just a handful of cables, almost exclusively in China, Taiwan, and Hong Kong. A decade later, Huawei Marine, an offshoot of the Chinese tech giant Huawei, was involved with ninety submarine cables around the world. Under Made in China 2025, Xi Jinping's signature policy for taking the commanding heights of high-tech manufacturing, Beijing aims to capture 60 percent of the global market for fiber-optic cables. Of all the BRI's dimensions, its digital connections may ultimately prove the most consequential.

Beijing's commercial and strategic motives in global communications are difficult to untangle, as one flagship project illustrates. Beginning with its name, the Pakistan and East Africa Connecting Europe, or PEACE, cable seems relatively benign. The underseas cable was originally named the Pakistan and East Africa Express but was rebranded after the addition of France as a landing point. It is slated to become the shortest route for high-speed internet traffic between Asia and Africa when it becomes operational in late 2020. The company behind the project estimates that it will pull in annual profits of $130 million.⁶

The project could also pay strategic dividends. A century and a half ago, British dominance of global telegraph networks was initially driven by commercial motives, as Chapter 2 recounted. British firms dominated the market with their innovative materials and cable-laying techniques and had a leading role in setting global standards. At the close of the nineteenth century, the British government began developing a smaller system of cables touching only Britain and its possessions. These cables were useful in peacetime for espionage, and when World War I erupted, the British were better prepared than anyone to maintain communications among their forces while monitoring and disrupting enemy communications.

The cable's developer, Hengtong Group, is China's largest producer of fiber-optic cables and a darling of the People's Liberation Army (PLA).[7] The Chinese government has praised Hengtong as a model of "civil-military integration" for developing military-grade cable technology.[8] The PLA gave it an innovation award in 2015, and the following year, they formed a partnership to research underseas cables.[9] A separate company was formed to oversee the PEACE cable, common practice in an industry that often relies on forming consortia-style partnerships for each project. Its chief operating officer spent nearly two decades as an employee of Hengtong Group, including as deputy general manager of the subsidiary that partnered with the PLA.[10] Further strengthening these ties, in late 2019, Hengtong announced plans to acquire Huawei Marine.

In the spring of 2019, I set out to visit three of the PEACE cable's proposed stops in East Africa. It will stretch from Gwadar, Pakistan, which could become a Chinese naval facility, as Chapter 7 described, to Djibouti, home to China's first military base. Ethiopia, which is landlocked and connects to underseas cables landing in Djibouti, will access the cable as well. It will also land in Mombasa, Kenya, home to a major port that Kenya's auditor general has warned China could take if Kenya defaults on its loans.[11] In all three countries, China's high-tech footprint is expanding along with the other signature BRI projects.

"China's Strength Will Always Support You"

In East Africa, China is following in the footsteps of European powers, which competed during the late nineteenth and early twentieth centuries for territory in what is sometimes called the "scramble for Africa." It was really the partition of Africa, and infrastructure was a favored tool for carving up territory. The Europeans arrived on Africa's coasts and established ports as toeholds. Then they pushed inland, building railways and laying telegraph wires, redrawing Africa's political map as they went. In 1870, only a tenth of Africa was under European control. But by the 1890s, France, Italy, Belgium, Portugal, Germany, and Britain were all pursuing railway projects in Africa as part of their colonial enterprises.[12] By 1914, only a tenth of Africa was not under Europe's notional control.

France was the first to plant its flag at modern-day Djibouti, and its interest was initially modest. Looking to establish a coaling station for ships heading to Madagascar and Indochina, French officials negotiated treaties with the Afars and Issas (a Somali subclan), Djibouti's two main ethnic groups. But France's interest grew as Europe's competition for control intensified, and as the continent was being carved up, these measures seemed too temporary. In 1894, France declared the area French Somaliland, an answer to British Somaliland, which occupied a competing slice of coastline to the east.

More than a century later, in 2017, China established a base for antipiracy, peacekeeping, and relief operations. Over a million Chinese citizens live in Africa, according to Chinese state media, although the real number could be higher.[13] China has also sent troops to South Sudan for UN peacekeeping operations. Counterintuitively, the presence of foreign militaries in Djibouti was a major selling point for Beijing. After all, how could they criticize China for joining them? But proximity has also created challenges, as Chinese troops learn how to operate in a foreign country.

China's highest-grossing film, *Wolf Warrior 2*, is a window, or perhaps a fun-house mirror, into nationalist views of Africa and foreign competition. Playing up stereotypes, the plot focuses on a rescue mission in a war-torn and disease-ridden African country. The film's hero, a retired elite Chinese soldier named Leng Feng, kicks and shoots his way through hundreds of enemies, Rambo style. Leng is also a man of the people. At one point, standing outside a Chinese embassy, he disarms an African militia simply by reminding them, "China and Africa are friends."

The film builds toward a fight between its hero, Leng, and its villain, Big Daddy, an American mercenary played by Frank Grillo. "People like you will always be inferior to people like me. Get used to it," Big Daddy tells Leng with a knife at his throat. But Leng gains the upper hand at the last moment, kills Big Daddy, and gets the last word. "That's fucking history," Leng says. Before the credits roll, the film delivers a message: "To citizens of China: When you find yourself in danger in a foreign country, never give up hope. China's strength will always support you."

Wolf Warrior 2 is not playing out on Djibouti's streets, but Chinese forces have been aggressive. U.S. officials have accused China of attempting to gain access to Camp Lemonnier, using drones to interfere with U.S. aircraft, and using military-grade lasers from their base to distract U.S. pilots, two of whom sustained eye injuries.[14] The Soviet Union was accused of similar tactics during the Cold War.[15] Officially, China's base housed 250 troops in 2018, but its footprint, including extensive underground facilities, could easily accommodate greater numbers.[16]

Local fishermen have learned to keep their distance. "Last month, a drone flew above our boat, and its speakers said in Somali, 'Go away, Go away, Go away,' " one told me. A Chinese patrol boat had recently apprehended his friend and held him until the Djiboutian Coast Guard arrived. The Coast Guard did not bother to question the Chinese. "Our country takes their money, and [the Chinese] do whatever they want," the fisherman said, his arms extended outward with palms up, hanging helplessly in the air. If the base signals China's increased assertiveness under Xi, the behavior of its troops suggests inexperience and insecurity.

"It Scared the Death Out of Us"

Chinese officials may believe they have an insurance policy. Djibouti's debt to China was 70 percent of its GDP in late 2019, and its borrowing has inspired warnings that it could become the "next Hambantota," a reference to the Sri Lankan port discussed in Chapter 8.[17] In Djibouti, the port that worries U.S. officials the most is the Doraleh Container Terminal, a star performer that has already ignited an international legal battle.

During my visit, the terminal was humming with activity, oblivious to the fact that its fate was being debated in courtrooms in London and Hong Kong. In 2006, the Dubai-based DP World, the same group that helps manage the Khorgos Gateway facility discussed in Chapter 3, signed a twenty-five-year concession agreement to develop the container terminal. During that period, the deal also gave DP World exclusive rights to all container-handling facilities in Djibouti. The arrangement worked well initially, establishing one of the most efficient ports in Africa.[18]

The dispute is captured on a two-mile stretch of Djibouti's coastline. Sitting between China's military base and the Doraleh

Container Terminal is another port, the Doraleh Multipurpose Port. In 2012, Djibouti struck a deal with China Merchants, a Chinese state-owned enterprise, to develop a multipurpose port and free-trade zone.[19] A red pipeline runs from an oil terminal on shore to a dock, and large cranes hang over a second dock. From the water, the facility nearly blends together with China's base.

DP World objected to this deal, which undercut its exclusivity arrangement. In February 2018, following a protracted dispute, Djibouti unilaterally terminated its contract with DP World. A storm of accusations and litigation ensued, putting Djibouti on the defensive. In April 2019, a London tribunal ordered Djibouti to pay DP World over $500 million for breaching the contract. DP World is also seeking relief from a court in Hong Kong, where China Merchants is listed.[20]

By demonstrating the container terminal's value, DP World may have become a victim of its own success. If the Djiboutian government intended to make that success its own, its actions have been self-defeating, alarming current and potential foreign investors. "It scared the death out of us," one foreign investor with business operations in Djibouti told me.[21]

Djibouti's competitive edge as a point of stability will not last forever, and it aspires to become more than the Horn of Africa's gun rack. Its leaders believe they have a window, perhaps a decade or two, during which Djibouti could turn its current edge over its waterfront neighbors into a longer-lasting advantage. Ethiopia's rise is the opportunity, while the stabilization of neighboring ports will present new challengers. Like so many other port cities, Djibouti is trying to become the next Hong Kong, Singapore, or Dubai. Lacking natural resources, it has turned to other countries for investment and, increasingly, toward China's checkbook.

The nightmare scenario for U.S. officials is that China ends up controlling the Doraleh Container Terminal. John Bolton, then U.S. national security advisor, played up the stakes in a December 2018 speech unveiling the Trump administration's new policy toward Africa: "Should this occur, the balance of power in the Horn of Africa—astride major arteries of maritime trade between Europe, the Middle East, and South Asia—would shift in favor of China. And, our U.S. military personnel at Camp Lemonnier, could face even further challenges in their efforts to protect the American people."[22] Bolton's warning—that if the port falls into Chinese hands, so will the region—makes even the domino theory seem modest.

To be sure, the port is valuable, much more so than Sri Lanka's Hambantota. About 90 percent of Ethiopia's trade passes through Djibouti.[23] As a result, its operations impact not only U.S. personnel in Djibouti but also the U.S. embassy in Ethiopia and the U.S. mission to the African Union, both based in Addis Ababa, Ethiopia's capital. But the United States has other options for shifting its supply chains, including ports at Berbera, Somaliland.[24] If Eritrea continues to normalize its foreign relations, its ports at Assab and Massawa may become more viable options in the future as well. Making these adjustments will not be cheap or convenient, but the entire Horn of Africa does not hang in the balance.

Fixating on Djibouti's ports might miss the bigger prize. The Djiboutian government has invested heavily in positioning Djibouti as an emerging communications hub and would be hard-pressed to part with control of Djibouti Telecom, its state-owned telecommunications company. The company runs Djibouti's cellular and internet networks as well as two undersea cable landing stations, where eleven international and regional fiber-optic cables converge and more are planned in the future.[25] If China has a wish list of strategic assets, telecommunications should be near the top.

The United States is not alone in worrying about China's intentions. Even despite Ethiopia's growing loans from China, Ethiopian officials are not eager to allow any foreign power to control the container terminal. Ethiopia has even more leverage than the United States or China. It could threaten to divert trade to Somaliland or Eritrea, and it also has deep ties with the Djiboutian leadership. Djiboutian officials claim that the container terminal is so profitable that they would not hand it over to anyone. Of course, debt can make people, and countries, part with prized possessions. But if the United States wants to keep the port out of Chinese hands, it has international partners with common interests.

But Bolton's remarks, delivered at a conservative think tank in Washington, DC, whistled past his international audience. "We want something more to show for Americans' hard-earned taxpayer dollars," he explained. "Under our new Africa strategy, we will target U.S. funding toward key countries and particular strategic objectives. All U.S. aid on the continent will advance U.S. interests, and help African nations move toward self-reliance." Bizarrely, Bolton sounded like he was promoting the very approach to aid that U.S. officials have criticized China for pursuing, one that puts the donor's strategic interests ahead of the recipient's economic interests. Bolton attacked the recipients of U.S. aid: "From now on, the United States will not tolerate this longstanding pattern of aid without effect, assistance without accountability, and relief without reform."[26] What he offered, however, was a soliloquy without solutions. "America First" does not resonate well in Africa, especially when China is singing a sweeter tune.

"One by One, I Will Teach You"

China is already overshadowing France's historic ties in Djibouti. In 1917, France completed Djibouti's first railway, which tied Djibouti's fate with Ethiopia, and cemented the location of their capitals, Djibouti City and Addis Ababa. The first passenger trains took sixty hours to travel across the route's thirty-two stations, and freight services took twice as long.[27] The railway was disrupted by Italy's occupation of Ethiopia from 1935 to 1941, during which Italian engineers built a road from Addis Ababa to Assab, a port city on modern-day Eritrea's coast. Its tracks were damaged during World War II, and the closure of the Suez Canal in 1956 choked activity through the ports.[28]

Having survived all of that, the railway eventually succumbed to something dull but deadly: routine maintenance. In the 1970s, after Djibouti became independent and Ethiopia's government was replaced by a military coup, both sides neglected repairs, and the railway began falling apart. The full original line has not functioned since 2004. In Djibouti, the French railway station has been reclaimed by locals, who have moved in and set up ramshackle dwellings. Decrepit trains, emblazoned with silver "Alstom" badges of France's largest railway manufacturer, sit rusting in the old railway yard.

France also views China's growing foothold with suspicion. "I wouldn't want a new generation of international investments to encroach on our historical partners' sovereignty or weaken their economies," France's President Emmanuel Macron said during a visit to Djibouti in March 2019.[29] As recently as the mid-1980s, spending by French military personnel and nationals made up a quarter of Djibouti's GDP.[30] Three decades later, France's foreign direct-investment in Djibouti does not even register in most estimates, and Macron did not announce any new commitments.[31] French influence can still be seen on street signs and on restaurant menus, but like the old train station, it no longer glimmers.

Three flags flew above Djibouti's new train station when it opened in 2018. The project is a joint venture between Djibouti and Ethiopia, the countries it connects, but China's colors were front and center as well. China provided $3.3 billion in loans, built the railway, and will operate it until 2023.[32] The new railway was built to do essentially what the old line did. It carries passengers and freight and mostly runs parallel to the old line. The passenger line is single tracked, so it goes in one direction on odd-numbered days of the month and runs the other way on even-numbered days.

Riding the new train was like watching a chameleon change color. Empty of passengers, it began as a Chinese train with brown walls, red seats, and a dull gray floor. When it was time to board, elderly women wearing brightly colored dresses, shawls, and head wraps jolted into action. Passengers rushed their designated wagon, carrying suitcases and large plastic bags. A Chinese train official, dressed in a black three-piece suit, red tie, and black conductor's hat, stood at the door to the train, trying to turn the wave into a river. When people began pushing, he extended his arm outward, blocking the entrance. "One by one, I will teach you," he repeated in English. "One by one, I will teach you." Boarding a train in China, of course, is rarely orderly.

Inside, Chinese staff asked everyone to place their bags on the overhead racks. An hour into the ride, passengers were reaching for their plastic bags and pulling out large bundles of khat, a plant that provides a strong buzz. Tables between seats facing each other became mini production lines, as people broke the stems off their branches and assembled smaller bundles of green leaves. With each snap, branches were discarded onto the ground. Tables turned green, and the floor turned brown. A hum filled the train as people chewed leaves, talked, and worked on their bundles.

Shortly after opening, the new railway literally ran into trouble. Local herders were filing claims after the train hit their goats, camels, and other livestock. In one incident, fifteen camels were plowed down. The railway company offered payments to the aggrieved herder, but it paid too generously, offering terms that were twice the market price. This incentivized more animal casualties, which was unfortunate but not unexpected.[33] A century earlier, France confronted the same challenge. It doled out payments until discovering that herders were grazing their oldest and sickest livestock near the tracks.[34]

"Nations Must Advance or They Must Fall"

The French railway helped to cement Ethiopia's capital, Addis Ababa, by forging communications links. The railway's technicians installed Ethiopia's first telephone line, between Addis Ababa and Harar, a trading hub to the north, in 1897. A decade later, its first international telegraph line was built from Dire Dawa to Djibouti. More telephone lines began to radiate outward from Addis Ababa into the Ethiopian countryside. By 1930, over 170 towns were part of a telephone network that stretched 4,350 miles.[35] Like the Chinese fiber-optic cables that would follow in the twenty-first century, these new connections strengthened the Ethiopian government, which benefited from foreign funding and centralized access to information.

Ethiopia has been more successful than its neighbors in courting great powers while protecting its independence. During the partition of Africa, Ethiopia was the only country to avoid European colonization. Its rugged terrain, containing many of Africa's tallest mountains, frustrated European attempts to push inward from the coast. Ethiopia's diplomacy and military were even more decisive. After securing arms shipments from Russia, Ethiopia routed Italy's invading forces at the Battle of Adwa in 1896. The victory blew a hole in narratives about the inevitability of European rule in Africa.[36] Shortly after, Ethiopia's ruler, King Menelik II, signed treaties with France and Britain, further securing Ethiopia's independence.

Ethiopia's Achilles' heel is access to the sea, which it lost during the partition of Africa and regained when it formed a federation with Eritrea in 1952. But that access was lost again in 1993, when Eritrea became independent, and Ethiopia's trade has suffered as a result. The labor costs of making a T-shirt in Ethiopia are one-third the costs of China, but after logistics expenses are added, they sell for the same price. With a surplus of inexpensive labor and energy, Ethiopia could become an export powerhouse in the coming decades.[37]

King Menelik II also looked beyond Europe for inspiration and assistance. "He has heard of Japan, and in his own way is trying to emulate that striking example," reported Robert Skinner, who led the first U.S. mission to Ethiopia in 1903. "The new railroad, the new highways, the bridges, the telephones—all these things he probably cares very little for in themselves, but he realizes that nations must advance or they must fall." Skinner believed the United States was outside the great-power fray. "America was the first country to establish diplomatic relations for the avowed purpose of protecting and extending commerce, and without a political issue of any character to discuss," he wrote. For the European powers, by contrast, "the matter of frontiers, balance of power, and kindred questions, are so far in the foreground that the ultimate commercial ambition is entirely overshadowed."[38]

But little U.S. assistance flowed to Ethiopia until the United States was competing with the Soviet Union during the Cold War. Italian forces had built roughly seven thousand kilometers of roads, which Ethiopia struggled to maintain. Galvanized by President Truman's Point IV program, the United States trained Ethiopian engineers, geographers, and other technical experts and guaranteed loans for rebuilding its roads.[39] In return for U.S. economic and political support, Ethiopia allowed the United States to continue using Kagnew Station, a listening post that the U.S. Army had established in Asmara during World War II.[40]

A rift opened between the United States and Ethiopia in 1974, when a military coup replaced Emperor Haile Selassie and installed the Derg, a military junta that embraced Marxist-Leninism and ruled with an iron first.[41] The Soviet Union threw its support from Somalia to Ethiopia, and the United States threw its support from Ethiopia to Somalia. During this period, Ethiopia's development plans were eclipsed by security priorities. Eritrean rebels demanded independence, and a civil war raged in the north for nearly three decades. While Ethiopia's citizens starved and the railway to

Djibouti deteriorated, the country amassed the largest army in sub-Saharan Africa. In return for military assistance, Ethiopia provided access to its airfield and coastline, allowing Soviet forces to establish a naval facility and listening post.[42] These arrangements fell away by 1991, when Ethiopia's government collapsed.

Ethiopia has enjoyed a special status among China's partners since 1996, when China's President Jiang Zemin visited six African countries and delivered a speech at the African Union headquarters in Addis Ababa.[43] Jiang, who later encouraged Chinese firms to "go out," also helped create the Forum on China-Africa Cooperation (FOCAC).[44] China hosted the first forum in 2000, and Ethiopia was selected to host the second forum in 2003. While playing host may seem trivial, these forums have become major venues for Chinese investments, which increased from $5 billion at the 2006 forum to $60 billion in 2015 and 2018.[45] Countries jockeying for investment shower Beijing with praise. In 2018, the Ghanaian president said the gathering left him "inspired by [China's] model, and [Ghana is] trying to replicate it."[46]

China's push into Africa has been closely tied to resources. In the early days of Chinese development assistance, Beijing offered African countries "resource-credit swaps," loans for access to natural resources. As the scholar Deborah Brautigam writes, African countries' payment methods matched their natural endowments: "Angola would use oil; Congo would use minerals; Senegal, peanut oil; and Ghana, cocoa, to repay their loans."[47]

But China's immediate attraction to Ethiopia has more to do with politics and prestige. Ethiopia does not produce the raw materials that China has sourced from other African countries, but its history makes it a powerful symbol of African independence and pan-Africanism. It also hosts several regional institutions, including the African Union headquarters and the United Nations Economic Commission for Africa.

China's engagement in Ethiopia may also preview its longer-term ambitions for the continent.[48] As the journalist Howard French writes, "When most people think about China's relationship with Africa they reduce it to a single proposition: securing access to natural resources, of which Africa is the world's greatest storehouse. . . . But there is a more farsighted motive, one overlooked in almost all the speculation about China's ambitions in Africa: to cultivate, or perhaps even create, future markets for China's export-oriented industries, markets that could one day pick up the slack from the aging consumers and debt-ridden economies of the West and of Japan."[49] With the second-largest population in Africa, a strong growth outlook, and improving investment environment, Ethiopia is an increasingly desirable market.[50]

Chinese officials also see a kindred spirit. As China's ambassador to Ethiopia, Tan Jian, said, "Both are age-old civilizations. Yet the sad truth is that we are 'developing countries.' But we are catching up."[51] Ethiopia traces its history to biblical times, and like China, its rise is also a return to the past. Ethiopia abandoned its experiment with communism, but the state retains a strong hand in its economy.[52] Both governments take pride in deviating from Western policy prescriptions. Responding to criticism from the World Bank and IMF, Ethiopia's Prime Minister Meles Zenawi said in 2011, "the country's economic performance is being called into question by the two groups because Ethiopia refuses to let outsiders dictate to them what economic policies should be put in place."[53]

"A License to Print Money"

Ethiopia's fierce independence has also created commercial opportunities for China, particularly in its telecommunications sector. Until Prime Minister Abiy Ahmed began privatization efforts in 2019, Ethiopia was among the last countries in the world to maintain a monopoly of its national telecommunications.[54]

Before Abiy took office, the government had been reluctant to relinquish this power. As Ethiopia's previous prime minister Hailemariam Desalegn said in 2013, "This sector is a cash cow, and that's why the private sector wants to get in there, and they're trying to tell us all kinds of stories . . . to get the license. . . . We want to use that money for infrastructure development."[55] His predecessor, Meles Zenawi, was even more forthcoming, calling telecommunications privatization "a license to print money."[56] Opponents of privatization have argued that the revenue is not only reinvested into the telecommunications sector but also subsidizes roads, railways, and other infrastructure.

Ethiopia's telecom monopoly was also terribly inefficent.[57] Despite large investments into the telecom sector, Ethiopia has one of the lowest telephone penetration rates in Africa, with two out of three citizens lacking cell-phone access in 2017.[58] The IMF and other international donors were willing to provide loans, but only if Ethiopia liberalized the sector.

Instead, Ethiopia turned to China for its telecommunications needs. In 2006, it struck a massive deal with China's ZTE that a World Bank study on corruption calls "highly unusual."[59] In return for $1.5 billion in financing from China Development Bank, Ethiopia granted ZTE an exclusive three-year contract to supply all of Ethiopia telecom's equipment.[60] The award even ignored Ethiopia's own rulebook for procurement. No competitive bidding process took place, and specifications and price were decided only after the award was announced. ZTE did not try to hide its delight. "This is the world's only project in which a national telecom network is built by a sole equipment supplier," Zhang Yanmeng, chief of ZTE's Ethiopia operations, said in 2009.[61]

The Ethiopian government, responding to criticism about its dependence on a single company, decided to work with two Chinese companies in 2012. China's Export-Import Bank provided the second loan, for $1.6 billion, for work by ZTE and Huawei. Over the course of these two loans, the Chinese firms built a 2G network that was later expanded and upgraded to 3G and 4G. They installed six thousand kilometers of fiber-optic cable, helping to increase Ethiopia's mobile penetration rate from 1 percent in 2006 to 41 percent in 2018.[62] The growth was impressive, but Ethiopia's network remained woefully inefficient, producing revenue that was two and a half times less per subscriber than networks in Kenya and Nigeria.[63]

Through these deals, Ethiopia's monopoly effectively became China's monopoly.[64] Chinese firms sell fiber-optic cables and other network equipment, they provide installation and maintenance services, and they market phones and other devices.[65] As a result, Ethiopia became dependent not only on Chinese hardware but also on the skills and expertise of Chinese technicians. Huawei trains roughly twelve thousand Africans each year, but two Ethiopian economists have found "extremely limited" evidence of Chinese firms providing meaningful skill or technology transfers.[66] An Ethiopian technician summarized the situation: "The system is not ours—it's Chinese. All the nitty-gritty: they know it, we don't. So we always need their support."[67]

The Ethiopian government was becoming reliant on China, but it had other reasons to feel secure. It not only retained a lucrative revenue source but also enhanced its ability to monitor Ethiopian citizens. Part of ZTE's package was a system called "ZSmart," which provided the Ethiopian government with access to customer account details as well as location information and content of text messages. ZTE also provided the ability to intercept emails and chat messages and to monitor web browsing. As Human Rights Watch detailed in 2014, the government faced little judicial or legislative oversight and used these capabilities to block opposition websites, to harass and threaten bloggers, and to cut telephone access during peaceful protests.[68]

Of course, the Ethiopian government could have looked to Western firms for its surveillance needs.[69] But China's telecommunications footprint has expanded, and overlapped with, its deepening security ties across Africa. As Michael Kovrig, an analyst at the International Crisis Group and former Canadian diplomat, wrote in October 2018, "Security sector cooperation risks transferring methods and technologies from Beijing's authoritarian playbook, in which the law and its enforcers are instruments of party and state power rather than constraints on it. That might help African states impose order and control, but at the cost of progress on accountable governance and human rights."[70] This was Kovrig's last publication for the International Crisis Group before Chinese security officers detained him in Beijing.

Kovrig did not mention that China's partners face another risk: the watchers being watched. In January 2018, the French paper *Le Monde* reported that the African Union headquarters, located in Addis Ababa, was bugged.[71] China provided $200 million to finance the building, which Chinese firms built, including its information technology (IT) system. Every night for five years, data from the building's servers were transferred to Chinese servers in Shanghai. After the breach was discovered, a sweep of the building reportedly discovered microphones hidden in desks and walls. For spooks, the building is a target-rich environment, hosting twelve thousand to fifteen thousand officials and representatives for meetings every year.[72]

Huawei was the African Union's IT services provider and proudly noted on its website, "The AU needed a robust solution to streamline their conference operations and protect their data from a variety of security threats. They chose Huawei's FusionCloud Desktop Solution, which offers computing, storage sharing, and resource allocation through cloud data centers."[73] Huawei also trained African Union technical experts and signed a partnership to deepen cooperation on information and communications technology infrastructure in 2015.[74]

Huawei's critics point to the incident as evidence that its systems cannot be trusted, along with other aspects of the firm's history. Its founder, Ren Zhengfei, was an engineer in China's PLA, and the company's relationships with the Chinese military were important for developing its early capabilities. It benefited from partnerships with military-affiliated research institutes, provided equipment for the PLA's first national communications network, and hosted military researchers.[75] Researchers have also questioned whether Huawei is truly owned by its employees and not the state, while others caution that even if Huawei is not currently cooperating with the Chinese government, it could be compelled to in the future.[76]

Chinese authorities denied the *Le Monde* report's allegations, but more tellingly, so did African officials. In one of the few official statements that hinted at regret, Paul Kagame, Rwanda's president and chairman of the African Union at the time, admitted, "I would only have wished that in Africa we had got our act together earlier on. We should have been able to build our own building."[77] African Union officials discovered the breach a year before it became public, according to *Le Monde*. Although they continued to insist that nothing was wrong, the African Union issued a call for new IT equipment. "The African Union's Data Center is a very critical asset," it emphasized. "The data stored and systems hosted in this data center need to be protected from any form of internal or external threats and unauthorized access."[78]

If African officials debated how to handle the breach in their home capitals, it is possible that China was listening. China has also helped finance, build, or renovate parliament buildings in Zimbabwe, Congo, Malawi, Guinea-Bissau, Lesotho, Gabon, and Sierra Leone—roughly one in every eight African countries.[79] In April 2018, less than three months after the *Le Monde* story, China announced it was providing the Commission of the Economic Community of West African States (ECOWAS), a regional economic union of fifteen West African countries, with $31 million for a new headquarters building in Nigeria.

Government buildings have always been attractive targets for espionage.[80] After spending $23 million to build an embassy in the Soviet Union during the 1970s and 1980s, the United States spent more than twice that trying to neutralize listening devices, including some that were so deeply planted that they could not be removed from the building's structure. A U.S. Senate committee in 1987 called it "the most massive and skillfully executed bugging operation in history."[81] Ultimately, the building was scrapped, and a new one was built that finally opened in 2000. Offering extensive financing tied to its firms, China may be taking this game to a new level.

"As Big Brother Monitors"

China's financing and flexibility have won its firms access to vastly different markets.[82] While Western firms wait for governments like Ethiopia's to liberalize their economy, Chinese firms work easily with state-owned monopolies. In countries that have liberalized their telecommunications sector, such as Kenya, Chinese firms undercut their competition on cost. Since 2007, Huawei has been building Kenya's national fiber-optic system, a deal that China helped secure by offering $60 million in financing.[83] With state subsidies and generous financing, Huawei routinely undercuts its Western competitors by offering discounts of 20–30 percent, according to an unpublished study by a European government.[84]

On top of these cost advantages, Chinese firms have excelled at connecting remote places. In Kenya and Ghana, Huawei has installed low-cost solar-powered units, called RuralStar, that bring mobile access to small communities with little existing infrastructure.[85] Customer service also helped build market share. "We brought a Chinese attitude to both work ethic and relationship building in Africa. The result was that clients soon realized they could rely on Huawei 24 hours a day, seven days a week," a former head of Huawei's operations in Africa recounts.[86] Ren Zhengfei claims to use military strategy to inform Huawei's business operations, especially Mao's focus on seizing the countryside before encircling and conquering cities.[87] One of Mao's ten principles of guerrilla warfare is, "Take small and medium cities and extensive rural areas first; take big cities later."[88]

"First the countryside, then the smart cities" might be Huawei's new mantra. In Nairobi, Huawei has installed eighteen hundred surveillance cameras that feed into central command centers for the local police. The system includes facial- and movement-recognition analysis and allows police officers to do real-time surveillance and browse recordings.[89] Huawei has installed similar systems in Mombasa, and it has highlighted these cases as examples of its "Safe City" technology, a suite of products advertised as reducing crime in urban environments. The smart-city market is projected to grow to nearly $3.5 trillion by 2026 as cities grow and acquire new technologies.[90] Smart cities, of course, are surveillance cities. It just depends on who is watching.

Huawei's promotional materials can seem oblivious to concerns about technology eroding civil liberties. One video opens like an espionage thriller, using satellite photos to zoom into Nairobi from above. Then footage shows cameras installed in public places. "For some time now, Kenyans have been thinking that these CCTV cameras installed both in Nairobi and Mombasa counties are inactive," a voice says. "However, this is far from the truth. Unbeknown to Kenyans, security agencies have already activated the new Safaricom security system." The video claims that crime has been dramatically reduced and that police officers do not need to travel as far. "As big brother monitors, they aren't going miles away," it says.[91]

Huawei's drive has occasionally put it at odds with its Chinese competitors, shattering the myth that Beijing carefully coordinates every move of China's largest companies. After the Kenyan government gave ZTE an award for a national surveillance and police communications system in 2012, it was Huawei that pushed for a review. The Kenyan government subsequently found that ZTE's prices were inflated to roughly twice the market cost. "It does not require rocket science in view of the evidence before the Board to establish that [ZTE's] financial proposal was highly exaggerated," the government explained.[92] ZTE's loss was Huawei's gain.

After the Westgate shopping mall attacks in 2013, the Kenyan government pushed through a similar contract for surveillance and communication equipment, justifying it as a national emergency. It required that the contractor be a national telecom operator, essentially giving the award to Safaricom, which then subcontracted the work to Huawei. Safaricom's deal with Huawei has also come under fire, with allegations raised that the companies followed improper procurement procedures and committed bribery.[93] Meanwhile, Huawei is building Kenya's national government cloud infrastructure, where government data, applications, and communications will be stored.[94]

"Where It Is Going to Nobody Knows"

In financial terms, Kenya's biggest and riskiest undertaking with China is its $3.3 billion standard-gauge railway, or SGR, its most expensive project since independence. Before the project was approved, international experts urged the Kenyan government to upgrade the existing meter-gauge railway, which had decayed after years of neglect and could be fixed at one-fifteenth the cost of laying a new railway. "There is no economic or financial case for standard gauge," a World Bank note concluded in 2013.[95]

But politics created the SGR. When President Uhuru Kenyatta took office in 2013, he promised that building the SGR would "greatly enhance [Kenya's] competitiveness."[96] China Export-Import Bank provided two loans totaling $3.2 billion in financing, over fifteen and twenty years, despite most railways taking longer to become profitable.[97] China Road and Bridge Corporation won the contract for building the railway despite a relatively thin track record outside China. The company is a subsidiary of CCCC, the same parent company that landed contracts for Malaysia's East Coast Rail Link and Sri Lanka's Hambantota Port after being blacklisted from the World Bank for fraud. Despite these red flags, no independent analysis of the railway's cost appears to have been undertaken.

Impressively, the project was completed ahead of time, unlike most megaprojects globally. Environmental groups, which objected to the line cutting through Tsavo National Park, failed to stop it. Some design changes were made, such as elevating tracks in some areas, in response to their concerns. The decision to build a new line rather than use the existing railway also created disputes over land ownership, which is poorly documented in some areas of Kenya. Plenty of court cases remained unsettled, but the railway was completed and opened to the public on June 1, 2017.

Kenyatta's reelection was just three weeks away, and the SGR's opening ceremony was tailor-made for his campaign. Kenyatta boarded the train in Mombasa and stopped in seven counties along the way to Nairobi, pausing to address Kenyans at each stop. "Change is here," he declared during the day-long event. "For over a century, Africans who gave birth to, and sustained a Pan-African dream of unity, have sought the free movement of African people and their goods."[98] The railway was opened to the public on Madaraka Day, a holiday celebrating Kenya's self-rule, and was even named the Madaraka Express.

It was not the time to worry about whether Kenya's debt could jeopardize its independence. Chinese officials were on board as well, but they understood that Kenyatta needed the spotlight. During the ceremony, Kenyan female drivers even appeared to take the train's controls, reaffirming the railway as a symbol of progress. But when the cameras left, Chinese workers were back at the helm. "We just sit at the back and watch. There is no actual transfer of skills that is happening here," an assistant locomotive driver said in July 2018.[99]

When I visited in April 2019, the atmosphere near the tracks felt like boarding a plane. Kenyan stewardesses, wearing red jackets, red hats, and black dresses, smiled and struck a pose next to the doors, cupping their hands with elbows outward. Male conductors, wearing dark-blue suits and hats, could have been mistaken for pilots. Dressed in simple white shirts, two Chinese supervisors milled about.

Chinese state media have publicized railway training efforts in Kenya, but the propaganda is also laced with paternalism. One article, for example, described a Chinese "station master" who "spends the bulk of his working hours monitoring the arrival and departure of the Mombasa-Nairobi train service while prodding Kenyan colleagues to be up to task."[100] Chinese staff will manage the railway until 2023.[101]

The SGR's dependency on an outside power recalls the British railway it replaced. The British railway was a characteristically imperial adventure, motivated by a mishmash of geopolitics, commercial interests, and missionary zeal. Britain wanted to protect its control of the Suez Canal by expanding its claims near the source of the Nile River, which flows northward from present-day South Sudan. "Whatever Power holds the Upper Nile Valley must, by mere force of its geographical situation, dominate Egypt," the British consul in Egypt warned in 1889.[102] Steam and steel would carry raw materials from the Great Lakes region to the coastline and "modernity" to East Africa by demonstrating the appeal of superior technology and eventually settling more British citizens.

When Britain began building the railway in 1896, it was woefully underprepared. The rush to claim and map land in political terms far outpaced the mapping of its physical features. Political maps can be works of social engineering, none more so than those drawn by outside powers in Africa, but they are shallow compared to what is required for technical engineering. When Britain decided to build a railway from Mombasa to the shore of Lake Victoria in Uganda, relatively little was known about the challenge that lay ahead. Citing these concerns, Henry Laboucher, a British parliamentarian and writer, panned the proposal and one of its advocates with a poem:

> What it will cost no words can express;
> What is its object no brain can suppose;
> Where it will start from no one can guess;
> Where it is going to nobody knows;
> What is the use of it none can conjecture;
> What it will carry there's none can define;
> And in spite of George Curzon's superior lecture,
> It clearly is naught but a lunatic line."[103]

At first glance, the new railway appears more futuristic than lunatic. Nairobi's new station is a gray metallic structure that looks like it was teleported from another country, if not another galaxy. It stands out amid the brown brush and red soil outside the city, like a giant computer component that could be plugged into a colossal motherboard. Large red letters above the station—"NAIROBI TERMINUS"—announce that it is an origin and destination. No train service leads into the city center, requiring passengers to trek to and from the station.

The Mombasa terminal is similarly inconvenient and outsized, including a massive control tower that looks like it was stolen from an airport. After arriving, passengers heading into the city must pay for a taxi or bus that moves from the station's new off-ramps onto crumbling roads choked with gridlock traffic and clouds of dirt.

Inside both stations, touch-screen machines dispense tickets, and turnstiles with ticket scanners provide access to the trains. On a Saturday morning in Nairobi, a large electronic board signaled that there were about thirty first-class tickets and four hundred second-class tickets still available half an hour before departure. Passengers can book their tickets in advance online and pay from their phones with M-Pesa, Kenya's mobile payment system that has become an inspirational example of how local innovation can catapult African economies ahead of developed economies. When M-Pesa was launched in 2007, nearly three out of four Kenyans lacked access to formal financial services. A decade later, the ratio was reversed, with three out of four having access.[104]

M-Pesa also reflects Kenya's shift toward China. A U.S. company, IBM, ran the system's original servers, which were based in Germany. As demand increased, Safaricom decided to move the servers to Kenya, expanded them, and made Huawei its technical partner. Huawei not only provided the servers but also helped to design the M-Pesa platform, an app that was installed on twenty-one million phones as of 2019.[105] In 2018, the equivalent of over 90 percent of Kenya's GDP went through M-Pesa and, by design, through Huawei's servers.[106]

The SGR's embrace of new tools should have resulted in productivity gains, but whether out of cautious planning or pressure to create jobs, the Nairobi station did not appear to have reaped those rewards. Attendants and police are stationed throughout the building, in numbers that suggest they are ready, like the cavernous building itself, for much-larger crowds. In 2018, Kenyan authorities discovered that China Road and Bridge Corporation employees were siphoning ticket revenue from the railway. Seven employees, including three senior Chinese employees, were arrested in connection with the scandal.

The SGR has big challenges to overcome, but that is not stopping both sides from using it as a symbol of closer ties. Kenyan and Chinese flags sit side by side above the doors in the first-class wagons. The side of the train, painted white with orange stripes, carries a lofty and unproven slogan: "connecting nations, prospering people." The SGR was intended to link Kenya with Rwanda and Uganda, a route that was projected to be responsible for over a third of the railway's traffic, but those connections have not materialized.[107]

The SGR's commercial future hinges on freight traffic, which is growing but not nearly fast enough. To increase freight activity, the Kenyan government mandated that container cargo arriving at the Port of Mombasa be transported to the Nairobi terminus, effectively requiring shippers to use the SGR.[108] The requirement dealt a heavy blow to the trucking industry that previously carried that cargo, and while the SGR's freight activities are increasing, it would need to move four to eleven times its 2018 levels to become profitable.[109] In the meantime, the clock is ticking on Kenya's payments for the railway, which begin in 2023.[110]

In December 2018, a leaked report from Kenya's auditor general warned that China could take control of the Port of Mombasa if Kenya defaulted on its loans.[111] The auditor general refused to confirm its authenticity, and President Kenyatta called it "pure propaganda."[112] Warnings about China's "debt-trap diplomacy" and Mombasa becoming the next Hambantota are politically potent but somewhat misleading. Because the "trap" for taking control of the port is being laid by a separate project, the railway, the comparison assumes that Beijing has an even greater degree of centralized control and strategic motivation than it did in Sri Lanka.

The stakes are even higher. Unlike Hambantota, Mombasa is an established regional hub, with an estimated 80 percent of East Africa's trade flowing through it.[113] It can more easily attract outside investment and does not need to rely on Chinese support alone. Indeed, just feet away from the new SGR railway connection into the Port of Mombasa is a terminal that Japan financed, a reminder that even competing visions for connectivity can overlap in complementary ways. The presence of other international investors in Mombasa also means the stakes are higher. Taking over Mombasa would be like taking over Sri Lanka's thriving Port of Colombo.

The Coming Collision

In the meantime, China is already building Kenya's next major port. Kenya's national development plan, Vision 2030, includes a $25 billion series of projects intended to connect South Sudan and Ethiopia with Kenya's coast, called the Lamu Port–South Sudan–Ethiopia Transport Corridor, or LAPSSET Corridor, for short. Among those projects is a new thirty-two-berth port that China Communications Construction Company (CCCC) is building. Under these plans, Lamu will have eight times Mombasa's capacity.[114]

Lamu brings China's engagement with Africa full circle. Zheng He, the Chinese Ming dynasty explorer, is believed to have landed there, as well as at Mombasa, with his fleet during the fifteenth century.[115] As Chinese officials are fond of reminding their Kenyan counterparts, their relations predated the Portuguese, and unlike the Portuguese, they claim to have arrived offering gifts rather than firing guns—an appealing message, even if embellished. But He's visit was temporary, and the bar for establishing an enduring presence has always been higher and much messier.

When I visited Manda Bay, in Lamu, a massive dredging machine, the Tian Jing Hao, was pumping sand onto the shore. Stretching over four hundred feet and built at a cost of $130 million, it can extract enough sand every hour to nearly fill two Olympic swimming pools.[116] It was Asia's largest dredging machine until 2018, and before it arrived in Lamu, China used it extensively to build artificial islands in the South China Sea. Dredging is one of the many concerns about Lamu Port raised by Kenyan activists, who claim that the activity is damaging the environment and livelihoods of local fishermen.[117]

As our boat weaved between newly installed piers, Kenyan workers in blue jackets, orange life vests, and yellow hard hats walked the partially finished dock closer to shore. "They have shifts going 24/7," a local fisherman explained. Underneath one section of the dock, and out of the hot sun, two security guards were taking a break on a small floating platform. On the way back to town, a speed boat raced by with piles of large brown sacks and three armed men. They were taking khat, grown in the Kenyan highlands, to sell in Somalia, just one hundred kilometers up the coast.

Lamu's proximity to Somalia is why it also hosts a U.S. military facility, which is located just miles from the new port. The facility, Camp Simba, is used for training East African security forces as well as supporting drone strikes and other counterterrorism missions into Somalia and Yemen. Since the base was established in 2004, it has expanded to become one of the largest U.S. facilities in Africa. The facility includes a long runway, expanded over the years, that can accommodate C-130s and other large aircraft.[118]

In January 2020, Somalia's al-Shabaab militant group attacked the facility, killing three Americans and destroying several aircraft and military vehicles before being repelled. After the attack, CCCC temporarily suspended construction at the port. Workers were asking for hazard pay, and CCCC was asking the Kenyan government for security guarantees.[119] This reality flips the *Wolf Warrior 2* script: rather than rescuing their African hosts from harm's way, the Chinese were looking to them for help and, indirectly, to the U.S. forces that support them.

Help may take longer to arrive in the future. When fully operational, the port may not be able to operate efficiently unless Camp Simba is relocated. Port cranes will compromise the flight path of the runway, according to a 2011 study prepared for the Kenyan government.[120] If Camp Simba remains, the study concluded, the port would need to be broken into two parts, one on either side of the military facility. That would be a losing proposition for everyone, compromising Camp Simba's security and making the port and inland transport inefficient.

These tensions at Lamu and Djibouti are likely to play out elsewhere around the world and especially in the Indian Ocean. U.S. security forces and Chinese state-owned enterprises are not simply operating in closer proximity but, increasingly, competing for strategic space. For their hosts, this contest is not zero-sum. But geography is finite, and there is only so much coastline and even fewer stretches of it that balance access to the ocean with proximity to other priorities. No country wants to choose between the world's leading military power and its rising economic power. But as their competition for access intensifies, so does the risk of collision.

CHAPTER TEN

Refining the Blueprint

XI LOOKED OUT FROM the podium and into the cavernous, red-carpeted hall. Below him, nearly forty heads of state sat in high-backed chairs in a long single line. Behind them stretched rows and rows of representatives hailing from 150 countries. They applauded as orchestra music came to a crescendo, cymbals ringing out. They clapped for him. The world clapped for him.

But as Xi prepared to address the second Belt and Road Forum in April 2019, he knew that not all was well. Australia, Canada, India, and the United States did not send high-level delegates. More conspicuously, missing among his friends in the front row was Recep Tayyip Erdogan, the Turkish president. At the first Belt and Road Forum, Erdogan had said, "This initiative, particularly in the face of the rising terrorism in the world, will be an initiative that will virtually eradicate terrorism. We, as Turkey, are ready to give all kinds of support for it."[1] Two years later, he may have been having all kinds of regret. Officially, Erdogan's absence at the second forum was unexplained, but China's detention of one to two million ethnic Uighurs, Kazakhs, and other minorities was becoming harder to ignore.[2]

If seats were Xi's scorecard, however, he was still winning. Even more of the world's most powerful people had assembled in Beijing.

Despite China's mass internment of Muslims, leaders from Egypt, Saudi Arabia, and the United Arab Emirates made the trek.³ Plenty of old friends remained faithful. Vladimir Putin was ready to take the podium next and would pitch his "Greater Eurasian Partnership," trying to stitch a frayed idea onto China's coattails. António Guterres, secretary general of the United Nations, spoke next. He failed to mention the two million missing people.

There were new faces, too. Italy's Prime Minister Giuseppe Conte and Switzerland's President Ueli Maurer wore wide grins in official photographs with Xi. A few weeks earlier, Italy and Switzerland became the first major European economies to sign BRI MOUs. Neither document was legally binding, but the approval of European governments carried symbolic value. Eager for British firms to finance projects and provide advisory services along the BRI, Phillip Hammond, head of the British Treasury, took the stage and gushed about a "Golden Era" of UK-China relations.⁴

Even leaders who shook their fists at the BRI while campaigning for office now took the stage to applaud it. "BRI marks a new and distinct phase in the onward march of nations of the world along the path of globalization," Pakistan's Prime Minister Imran Khan declared. "Pakistan is proud to have partnered and pioneered with China in this transformational endeavor."⁵ Malaysia's Prime Minister Mahathir Mohamad pledged, "I am fully in support of the Belt and Road initiative. I am sure my country, Malaysia, will benefit from the project."⁶

Their praise did not come free. Less than two weeks before the forum, China and Malaysia announced a new deal for the East Coast Rail Link. The cost was cut by a third, but the loan terms were not yet finalized.⁷ One month before the forum, Pakistan announced it received a $2.1 billion loan from China to help alleviate its balance-of-payments crisis.⁸ Along with endorsing Xi's vision, his former critics also came with ideas for improving it. To green the effort, Khan called for planting one hundred billion trees in two years. To supercharge east-west trade, Mahathir called again for building bigger trains.

Naturally, Xi agreed that the world needed more, not less, of the BRI. Cooperation, he emphasized, was the key. "Going ahead, we should focus on priorities and project execution, . . . just like an architect refining the blueprint, and jointly promote high-quality Belt and Road cooperation." He called for "multilateral cooperation." He called for "open, green, and clean cooperation." He called for "high standard cooperation." He called for everything that the BRI was not.[9]

Xi was doing his best to repair the Belt and Road brand, and these buzzwords were echoed in a mountain of announcements at the gathering. Among the "multilateral" accomplishments, Chinese officials noted the Network of Silk Road Arts Festivals, the Silk Road International League of Theatres, and the International Alliance of Museums of the Silk Road. To burnish their anticorruption and environmental credentials, they unveiled the Beijing Initiative for the Clean Silk Road and the Green Development International Alliance. Altogether, nearly three hundred deliverables were announced, as well as deals totaling some $64 billion.

It was savvy political theater, but each new effort further complicated a set of activities that was already unmanageable. Even an official BRI advisory group, composed mainly of former heads of state and other international officials, observed, "unlike many international platforms for economic cooperation, the [Belt and Road Forum] currently has neither a centralized coordinating mechanism . . . nor a clear set of underpinning work streams."[10] Beneath the diplomatic couching, the point was brutally honest. What happened between the forums, of course, was the BRI itself.

All Aboard

Even as Xi's vision gained support in foreign capitals, it was being skewed on the ground. "Thanks to the joint efforts of all of us involved in this initiative, a general connectivity framework consisting of six corridors, six connectivity routes and multiple countries and ports has been put in place," Xi said.[11] Corridors are economically valuable when transportation infrastructure connects cities and industrial hubs, helping facilitate the flow of people and goods.[12] In the BRI's case, there is also advertising value because the corridors lend credibility and a semblance of structure to an otherwise amorphous undertaking. The only problem is that they remain more myth than reality.

As China is learning, international corridors are as easy to imagine as they are difficult to implement. With the exception of the China-Pakistan Economic Corridor (CPEC), Xi's corridors remained mostly broad brushstrokes on an aspirational map. Unlike the corridors managed by the Asian Development Bank and other multilateral banks, the BRI's corridors were not defined below the national level to include specific cities and roadways. Around the BRI's five-year anniversary in 2018, as much Chinese-financed project activity was happening outside the corridors as inside them.[13] Either Chinese officials were not following these priorities, or they were struggling to bring them about.

Having never provided a detailed blueprint, Xi's initiative became a Rorschach blot. Everywhere, inside and outside China, interest groups have gazed upon it and seen different things. What they see often reveals more about themselves than anything else. Naturally, most interpret the BRI to suit their own interests.

China's massive state-owned enterprises grabbed the BRI banner but have not marched lockstep to Beijing's tune. Outside China, they often have more influence on the ground than Chinese officials. They have deeper local connections, more technical expertise, and more staff in recipient countries. They lobby local politicians and Chinese ministries to propose and approve projects. They bid on projects even when the Chinese embassy instructs them not to. Pushing back can be risky for Chinese officials who aspire to climb higher up the party ladder. The heads of China's biggest national champions are vice ministers, an administrative rank that few active Chinese ambassadors achieve.[14] With savvy and standing, they exploit fissures among Chinese ministries.

China's own government is far from united on the BRI's priorities, and its aid process is fragmented.[15] Among the main agencies, the Ministry of Commerce usually wields the most power and places a higher priority on profitability, resource extraction, and other economic considerations. The Chinese Ministry of Foreign Affairs is often the second most influential and more inclined to view projects as political tools to strengthen bilateral ties. The Ministry of Finance is charged with evaluating lending risks. China's largest lenders, China Development Bank and China Export-Import Bank, are dedicated to promoting exports and strengthening China's national champions. The PLA and other parts of the party-state bureaucracy have their own interests, as does every province. Rarely do projects check all these boxes. In the BRI's initial years, the universe of projects has been wide enough to give something to everyone. Competition among these perspectives will intensify if the pipeline shrinks.

Since the BRI left the station, it has become a gravy train without a conductor or adequate crew. The National Development and Reform Commission was initially tasked with coordinating the BRI. Its performance is self-evident. The Ministry of Commerce's Department of Foreign Aid, or DFA, has roughly seventy staff to oversee all aid.[16] To improve coordination, Chinese ministries and provinces have created working groups.[17] It is unclear whether these efforts are improving project outcomes or simply another reflection of political incentives for visibly supporting Xi's vision. None of these entities have adequate staff and expertise, particularly outside China, for managing the project of the century.

In 2018, China announced a new aid organization, the China International Development Cooperation Agency (CIDCA), that is unlikely to resolve these challenges.[18] It is intended to play a greater role in planning and oversight but sits uncomfortably in the shadow of more powerful agencies. The Ministry of Commerce's DFA makes up two-thirds of the new agency. The Ministries of Commerce and Foreign Affairs still control project implementation. When things go wrong, CIDCA could struggle to challenge either of them, since it is a more junior agency. More effective oversight would be costly, politically and financially. It would require shifting power away from those who currently hold it. It would also require raising a small army of management staff and technical advisers and deploying them across the world.

Recipient countries have their own priorities. Their participation should not be confused with consenting to Xi's version of the BRI. They face risks, of course, especially when China's offer is the only one on the table. Even those with forward-looking development plans can fall victim to politicians' universal impulses to build projects for personal gain. But China's checkbook is not the barrel of a gun, and every project is a negotiation. With greater technical capacity, planning, and oversight, recipient countries can incorporate responsible amounts of Chinese investment into their overall development plans while safeguarding their independence. More than anyone else, they hold the future of Xi's signature effort in their hands.

The Connectivity Conundrum

Of the BRI's six corridors, CPEC is the exception that proves the rule. Despite being called a corridor, its connectivity is weak, as Chapter 8 explained, and transportation is entirely cut off for several winter months each year. It is also the only corridor of the six that involves China and a single country. The others include as many as seven countries, making coordination even more difficult. Held up as the BRI's flagship corridor, CPEC showcases the limits of Chinese power.

The Chinese side of CPEC, which is rarely discussed, reveals what is perhaps the BRI's biggest contradiction. There is a fundamental tension between the connectivity that China says it seeks through the BRI and the control it is unwilling to give up. Even as China claims to be championing globalization and broadening ties, it is clamping down in areas that BRI routes are intended to pass through, potentially crippling its own projects.[19]

China's connectivity conundrum was painfully evident when I visited Kashgar, a historic city in southwestern China. Marco Polo once described it as "the biggest city, and the most splendid" in Turkestan.[20] It is now ground zero for Beijing's repression of ethnic minorities. Police stations, with lights flashing as if to convince the public of a constant state of emergency, were as common as Starbucks are in New York City. Cameras were everywhere. The Id Kah Mosque, the largest in China, seemed designed to catalogue those who are practicing Islam rather than to provide them a space to worship in peace. It can accommodate 20,000 people but was deserted.

Beijing has been ramping up security measures since July 2009, when ethnic riots in Urumqi, the capital of Xinjiang, resulted in at least two hundred deaths. The aftermath of the riots saw the internet cut off in the region for over a year. Thousands of police stations were built, and police recruitment has risen dramatically. By 2017, Xinjiang's police force was more than five times the size it had been a decade earlier, and the province's spending on surveillance technology skyrocketed to $3.5 billion.[21] That year, Xi called for building a "Great Wall of Iron" around the province.[22] While promoting a vision for connecting the world, Xi was raising a fortress at home.

Leaving Kashgar, I drove six hours to Tashkurgan, the last major town before China's border with Pakistan and a stop along ancient trading routes. It is perched at more than ten thousand feet in the Pamirs, a range where the Himalayas, Tian Shan, and other mountains meet. The places between these mountains are distinct worlds, connected only by a thread of pavement. The monotony of the dunes and desert was broken by switchbacks and long climbs. When the road levels, verdant pasture stretches to the horizon. Roaming freely, shaggy-haired yaks drank from a glacial blue river. Weighing over one thousand pounds, these beasts are so well adapted that Chinese security forces still use them to patrol the area's rugged terrain.

The beauty of the great open spaces outside Tashkurgan collides with a harsher reality inside it. The city felt like a remote outpost preparing for a siege that will never come. An armored vehicle cruised slowly along a main street. Walls, gates, and barbed wire surrounded hulking government buildings and a handful of hotels. Security guards sat inside buildings, halfheartedly patting down visitors after they passed through metal detectors. Shields, batons, and other riot gear were stashed near entrances.

Within this security bubble, commerce was sluggish and mostly local. There was no sign of activity at the Khunjerab Port, which aspires to become a logistics hub and is named after the three-mile-high mountain pass that links China and Pakistan. Economic activity ebbs and flows according to the seasons, holidays, and other factors, but Tashkurgan was undoubtedly sleepy.

One sector was thriving. Stern and oversized, local police and security buildings looked like foreign embassies. Spending on security-related construction in Xinjiang tripled in 2017, inflating the region's official growth rate.[23] The police themselves were busy at the local gas station, where a long line of cars and trucks were waiting for their approval to refuel. Words and handshakes allowed some vehicles to cut the line. The police seemed to be not only providing order but profiting from the demand to get in.

Dangerously, Xinjiang's GDP figures do not measure what matters. China's security-industrial complex artificially boosts growth while destroying value. It overbuilds, enlarging the scope of projects and delivering others that serve little purpose. But even worse are the projects that are used. After all, what is their purpose? Physical capital is erasing human capital. China does all of this in the name of security and growth. It may end up with less of both.

In addition to the monumental human cost of this security crackdown, domination of daily life by security forces stands in the way of greater economic activity. Intrusive security personnel and ubiquitous checkpoints make it difficult to send and receive packages. Local laws require citizens to participate in "antiterror" drills as often as three times a day, weekly flag-raising ceremonies, impromptu identification and appearance inspections (beards and hijabs are prohibited), and other intrusions that distract from running a business. The BRI is designed to enable trade, but Beijing's paranoia constrains commerce at every turn.

This is not a flaw limited to Xinjiang but one that runs to the very core of Xi's vision. He promises that the BRI will increase international financial flows, but its capital controls stand in the way. Hardest to reconcile may be Xi's promise to speed the flow of information and ideas. As he said at the first Belt and Road Forum, "The ancient silk routes were not for trade only, they boosted flow of knowledge as well."[24] But Chinese censorship and cybersecurity laws have become more intrusive. China is also offering to help other countries learn from its "Great Firewall"—in effect sharing knowledge to limit knowledge sharing.

Of course, greater connectivity of all kinds brings disruption as well as benefits. China's leaders, valuing their continued rule above all else, may have a high tolerance for forgoing economic gains from connectivity in the name of political stability. They would do well to recall, however, that the very "Silk Road" images they promote represent an improvement in connectivity: camels, caravans, and merchants. If the BRI's most powerful images are symbols of stasis—police checkpoints, long lines of trucks, and barbed wire— there will not be much to remember.

All empires have grappled with the challenge of balancing connectivity while maintaining control, and they have responded to it in different ways, from direct means such as colonies to indirect means such as proxies and treaty ports. Strikingly, China faces these challenges not merely in distant lands, and in its immediate neighborhood, but also at home.

Incremental Imperialism

China's BRI is clearest when measured against the imperial projects that came before it. It is a product of China's rise as well as a tool for exercising and increasing its power. Many of China's activities—seeking access to markets, cultivating influence in foreign capitals, and expanding its military footprint—are classic rising-power behaviors. There are historical parallels with the technology that China is using, the places it is going, and its advantages over weaker partners. Acknowledging that these activities are not entirely unique, however, does not mean writing them off as harmless. On the contrary, these imperial echoes should urge caution.

The longer China's rise continues, the more likely its overseas activities will take on a sharper military edge. Even more than providing a means for expanding Chinese military activities, the BRI provides a motive by placing Chinese workers and investments in dangerous environments. In the absence of adequate security, China could assume a greater role in protecting its workers and investments, if partner countries allow it. China's first official military base on foreign soil, in Djibouti, will not be its last. From ancient Rome to the Mongol Empire to the British Empire, trade has never traveled far, for long, without the flag.

"Imperialism" is so loaded, so heavy a term, that it can be distracting. It may be easier to think objectively about China's BRI purely in terms of power without the historical baggage. There have been different forms of imperialism, of course, and there is a rich debate about defining it.[25] The Oxford English Dictionary, which appropriately was created during imperial Britain's reign, offers one definition of "imperialism" that feels timeless: "the extension and maintenance of a country's power or influence through trade, diplomacy, military or cultural dominance, etc."[26] That "etc." demands more attention from scholars, particularly how new technologies provide avenues of influence, but China is, quite obviously, extending its power and influence through these means. The BRI's ambitions are imperial, even if they may not succeed.

Equally important is understanding how Chinese power and influence, extended through the BRI, are different. As Howard French observes when considering China's activities in Africa, "What one must grant is that every imperial project throughout history is distinctive."[27] Even more than its predecessors, China's imperialism is economic and incremental. This stems from China's capabilities as well as the constraints that it faces. The BRI is tailored to deploy China's comparative advantages, especially its massive state-owned firms. The world's needs for infrastructure and investment are insatiable, but China faces a much higher bar in its pursuit of influence beyond its borders.

Compared to the European powers that partitioned Africa, China's actions are more constrained by international norms. International law has developed, particularly after World War II, to protect the sovereignty of states and the rights of individuals. Taking territory by force, a preferred method of great powers past, is prohibited. These laws can be ignored, of course, as Russia seems to remind the world every few years, but doing so comes with a steeper cost. Instead, China relies on means short of force to advance its aims. It can co-opt, coerce, and gradually undermine the status quo, one artificial island at a time. But for the most part, foreign leaders must choose to participate in China's activities.

Unlike Truman's Point IV program, the BRI is often found wanting because it is measured against well-developed multilateral standards. When U.S. companies built massive dams in Pakistan during the 1960s that displaced large populations, environmental- and social-impact studies were comparatively underdeveloped. Corruption was treated more as a cost of doing business. Modern safeguards at the World Bank and other multilateral development banks may have become too cautious, overly expensive, and slow. But they also reflect an attempt to learn, perhaps overlearning, from decades of mistakes.[28] When China ignores international best practices, its errors look worse.

The world is watching even more closely. Imagine the British building a railway from Mombasa to Nairobi under the glare of cell-phone cameras and social media. Labor abuses, while still underreported, are easier to document with mobile communications. Satellite imagery, once accessible only to a handful of governments, is widely available to the public at low cost. Environmental groups can monitor changes in land from their desks. Journalists benefit from all these tools and larger document leaks. In the coming years, more efforts will throw light onto China's opaque practices.

Compared to Japan's infrastructure push in the 1980s, Chinese leaders are more insulated from internal and external pressure. Recent corruption scandals in Malaysia, unlike Japan's missteps in the Philippines during the 1980s, have generated comparatively little public outcry within China. Chinese state media are dedicated to amplifying BRI success stories and countering negative publicity. Publicly and privately, the United States pressed Japan to improve its foreign-aid practices, helping to strengthen reformers within the Japanese government.[29] China does not have a partner to provide that pressure, and its relations with the United States are only deteriorating.

Japan's experience suggests that Xi's assurances will not persuade Western skeptics. The fear that Japan inspired in the United States, a fellow democracy and ally, only subsided after Japan's economy tanked. At the peak of U.S. anxiety, some experts foresaw a coming war with Japan.[30] Their alarm blinded them to the pressures building within Japan's economy. In the early 1990s, a severe financial crisis halted Japan's three-decade-long "economic miracle" and began its "lost decade." In marveling at China's expanding global footprint, it is easy to overlook the challenges it faces. The BRI's risks run both ways, and recognizing it as an imperial project does not imply that it will succeed.

"When the Tide Goes Out"

China is likely to remain its own worst enemy. Its competitors are waking up but face coordination challenges. In 2018, the U.S. Congress passed the BUILD Act, which consolidates development-finance activities into a new agency, the U.S. International Development Finance Corporation (USDFC), with twice the resources and expanded authorities. The same year, the European Union announced its "EU-China Connectivity Platform."[31] Australia, India, and Japan have been active as well, and several bilateral and multilateral cooperation agreements have been signed. But even if these comparatively modest efforts are made into something greater than the sum of their parts, particularly for mobilizing private investment, the sheer demand for infrastructure globally guarantees that China will have ample opportunities.

Meanwhile, China is repeating the mistakes, and learning the lessons, of powers that came before it, especially the costs of going it alone. Xi's emphasis on multilateralism at the second forum could be strongly self-interested, just it was for Western powers to create multilateral development banks. Since the BRI has been mostly a cover for bilateral deal making, China bears the financial and reputational costs when things go wrong. Pulling in more partners would allow China to share the risks of hugely complex projects in risky business environments, but it is unclear how much China is willing to relinquish for those benefits.

China's interest in large projects beyond its borders will not end with Xi. Just as the "going out" policy preceded the BRI, someone could fashion yet another tagline to make Chinese power, projected through infrastructure and investment, appear more palatable. Like the great powers that have come before it, as long as China's rise continues, its companies will seek more market opportunities, and its leaders will crave the access and influence that large projects provide. These projects also take years to complete and decades to repay. If the BRI was magically paused and no more projects were announced, its current footprint would still take years to unfold.

Ultimately, China's economy will determine how long the BRI continues and in what form. China's foreign reserves have dropped substantially since the BRI was launched, and it faces rising costs and shrinking revenues at home. Even before the coronavirus pandemic, there were indications of a pullback on BRI-related projects, suggesting that project announcements could be slimmed down in the coming years. That is bad news for China's massive state-owned firms, but scarcity may also make oversight easier and encourage Beijing to increase the quality of its projects.

These headwinds may also lift China's "digital silk road." Compared to ports, railways, and other megaprojects, digital infrastructure is often less risky financially while offering distinct strategic benefits. Even in friendly Pakistan, it is much easier for China to lay a fiber-optic line than a pipeline across difficult terrain. Building and operating telecommunications networks offers commercial gains, intelligence, and the ability to disrupt enemy communications while protecting your own. Facing increased scrutiny in Western markets, China's tech champions may double down in developing and emerging markets.

Ironically, if the BRI is updated to genuinely reflect Xi's buzz-words and address his critics—adopting high standards in its projects, emphasizing multilateral deals, and so on—Western policy makers might eventually regret that Chinese officials took their advice.[32] A more focused, higher-quality BRI could turn China from a lender of last resort to a preferred partner. It could spread Chinese influence in more targeted areas, from setting technology standards to swaying foreign capitals. It could signal that China is succeeding where others have failed. Because of what that implies about China's ability to wield power, nothing would be more alarming than success.

In the coming years, it is even more likely that China's mistakes will shake the world. Its partners are counting on sustaining high growth to pay their debts, setting ambitious targets that leave little room for error or unexpected events. Early mistakes along the BRI occurred in a relatively forgiving global economy, and as Warren Buffet is fond of saying, "you only find out who is swimming naked when the tide goes out."[33] The risks are probably greater than Chinese officials appreciate. Most infrastructure booms have gone bust.

The coronavirus pandemic is laying bare the BRI's flaws, even as it creates new needs that China could exploit. Developing and emerging economies that borrowed heavily are being pushed beyond the brink. The same instinct for secrecy that hides the terms of China's deals along the BRI concealed the outbreak. Most troubling for Xi's vision, China shared the virus with the world through the very connections the BRI aims to strengthen. It lost control.

Without a doubt, putting forward a decades-long vision for global connectivity takes courage. On the world stage, nothing approaches the BRI's scale and ambition. But avoiding failure will require much greater skill, lower expectations, and a heavy dose of modesty. Otherwise, China's boldness will eventually look like hubris. The difference between the two will be determined not in grand halls but on the ground.

Notes

Chapter One. Project of the Century

1. Evan A. Feigenbaum, "Why China's Highly Strategic Brand of Revisionism Is More Challenging than Washington Thinks," *MacroPolo*, April 27, 2018, https://carnegieendowment.org/2018/04/27/reluctant-stakeholder-why-china-s-highly-strategic-brand-of-revisionism-is-more-challenging-than-washington-thinks-pub-76213.
2. "List of Countries That Have Signed a 'One Belt, One Road' Cooperation Document with China" (in Chinese), Belt and Road Portal, April 30, 2019, https://www.yidaiyilu.gov.cn/gbjg/gbgk/77073.htm.
3. Xinhua, "President Xi Eyes Bigger Role for California in China-U.S. Cooperation," *Xinhuanet*, June 6, 2017, http://www.xinhuanet.com//english/2017-06/06/c_136344690.htm.
4. Ana Swanson, "How China Used More Cement in 3 Years than the U.S. Did in the Entire 20th Century," *Washington Post*, March 24, 2015, https://www.washingtonpost.com/news/wonk/wp/2015/03/24/how-china-used-more-cement-in-3-years-than-the-u-s-did-in-the-entire-20th-century/?utm_term=.532ea924778f.
5. "ENR 2018 Top 250 Global Contractors 1–100," *Engineering News Record*, August 2018, https://www.enr.com/toplists/2018-Top-250-Global-Contractors-1.
6. Xinhua, "Belgrade Joins Belt and Road Marathon Series," *Xinhuanet*, April 21, 2018, http://www.xinhuanet.com/english/2018-04/21/c_137125888.htm.
7. The unreliability of Chinese data extends well beyond lending, as James Palmer argues in a sharp essay: "Nobody Knows Anything about China," *Foreign Policy*, March 21, 2018, https://foreignpolicy.com/2018/03/21/nobody-knows-anything-about-china/.

8. Xinhua, "Xinhua Commentary: Belt and Road for Joint Development Benefits," *Xinhuanet*, April 25, 2019, http://www.xinhuanet.com/english /2019-04/25/c_138009104.htm.

9. Jonathan Hillman, "Five Myths about China's Belt and Road Initiative," *Washington Post*, May 31, 2019, https://www.washingtonpost.com/outlook/ five-myths/five-myths-about-chinas-belt-and-road-initiative/2019/05/30/ d6870958-8223-11e9-bce7-40b4105f7cao_story.html?utm_term =.4d8d4f2cf86d.

10. Asian Development Bank, "Asia Infrastructure Needs Exceed $1.7 Trillion per Year, Double Previous Estimates," February 28, 2017, https:// www.adb.org/news/asia-infrastructure-needs-exceed-17-trillion-year-double-previous-estimates.

11. UNDP China, "UNDP Engagement with the Belt and Road Initiative," YouTube, May 12, 2017, https://www.youtube.com/watch?v=b6rWKnog7lg.

12. Herbert Smith Freehills, "Belt and Road, Paving the Way to Global Trade: Our Team," https://www.herbertsmithfreehills.com/latest-thinking/hubs/belt-and-road.

13. HSBC, "What do you think of when you hear the term Belt and Road," Twitter, May 16, 2019, 6:33 a.m., https://twitter.com/HSBC/status /1129017032488493056.

14. Patrick Shanahan, "Written Statement for the Record" (testimony presented to the U.S. Senate Armed Services Committee, Washington, DC, March 14, 2019), https://www.armed-services.senate.gov/imo/ media/doc/Shanahan_03-14-19.pdf.

15. Peter Wells and Don Weinland, "Fitch Warns on Expected Returns from One Belt, One Road," *Financial Times*, January 25, 2017, https://www.ft. com/content/c67b0c05-8f3f-3ba5-8219-e957a90646d1.

16. For insight into China's political and economic underpinnings, see Regina Abrami, William Kirby, and F. Warren McFarlan, *Can China Lead? Reaching the Limits of Power and Growth* (Boston: Harvard Business Review Press, 2014); Jude Blanchette, *China's New Red Guards: The Return of Radicalism and the Rebirth of Mao Zedong* (Oxford: Oxford University Press, 2019); Elizabeth Economy, *The Third Revolution: Xi Jinping and the New Chinese State* (Oxford: Oxford University Press, 2018); David M. Lampton, *Following the Leader: Ruling China, from Deng Xiaoping to Xi Jinping* (Berkeley: University of California Press, 2014); George Magnus, *Red Flags: Why Xi's China Is in Jeopardy* (New Haven, CT: Yale University Press, 2018); Dinny McMahon, *China's Great Wall of Debt: Shadow Banks, Ghost Cities, Massive Loans, and the End of the Chinese Miracle* (Boston: Houghton Mifflin Harcourt, 2018); Andrew Nathan, "China's Changing of the Guard: Authoritarian Resilience" and "A Factionalism Model for CCP Politics," in *Critical Readings on the Communist Party of China* (Leiden: Brill, 2017), 86–99, 849–886; David Shambaugh, *China's Future* (New York: Wiley, 2016).

17. For higher-level views, see Robert Kaplan, *The Return of Marco Polo's World* (New York: Random House, 2018); Nadège Rolland, *China's Eurasian Century? Political and Strategic Implications of the Belt and Road Initiative* (Seattle: National Bureau of Asian Research, 2017); Peter Frankopan, *The New Silk Roads: The Present and Future of the World* (New York: Knopf, 2019); Richard McGregor, *Asia's Reckoning: China, Japan, the Fate of U.S. Power in the Pacific Century* (New York: Penguin Books, 2018). Notable exceptions are Bruno Maçães, *The Dawn of Eurasia: On the Trail of the New World Order* (London: Penguin, 2018); Tom Miller, *China's Asian Dream: Empire Building along the New Silk Road* (London: Zed Books, 2017); Wade Shepard, *On the New Silk Road: Journeying through China's Artery of Power* (London: Zed Books, 2019). Several scholars have helpfully examined China's activities in more narrow geographies, and those are referenced in the chapters that follow. Journalists have provided some of the best on-the-ground coverage.

18. Derek Scissors, "China Global Investment Tracker," American Enterprise Institute and the Heritage Foundation, accessed February 2, 2020, https://www.aei.org/china-global-investment-tracker/.

19. Jonathan Hillman, "Influence and Infrastructure," Center for Strategic and International Studies, January 22, 2019, https://www.csis.org/analysis/influence-and-infrastructure-strategic-stakes-foreign-projects.

20. Bent Flyvbjerg, "Introduction: The Iron Law of Megaproject Management," in *The Oxford Handbook of Megaproject Management*, ed. Bent Flyvbjerg (Oxford: Oxford University Press, 2017), 1–18, https://papers.ssrn.com/sol3/papers.cfm?abstract_id=2742088; Atif Ansar, Bent Flyvbjerg, Alexander Budzier, and Daniel Lunn, "Does Infrastructure Investment Lead to Economic Growth or Economic Fragility? Evidence from China," *Oxford Review of Economic Policy* 32, no. 3 (2016): 360–390, https://arxiv.org/ftp/arxiv/papers/1609/1609.00415.pdf.

21. Ye Chen, Hongbin Li, and Li-An Zhou, "Relative Performance and the Turnover of Provincial Leaders in China," *Economic Letters* 88, no. 3 (September 2005): 421–425, https://core.ac.uk/download/pdf/6271011.pdf.

22. Veasna Kong, Steven G. Cochrane, Brendan Meighan, and Matthew Walsh, "The Belt and Road Initiative—Six Years On," Moody's Analytics (Sydney), June 2019, https://www.moodysanalytics.com/-/media/article/2019/Belt-and-Road-Initiative.pdf.

23. H. J. Mackinder, "The Geographical Pivot of History," *Geographical Journal* 23, no. 4 (April 1904): 434, https://www.jstor.org/stable/1775498?seq=1#page_scan_tab_contents.

24. Qiu Qianlin, "Trade Grows with Better Links," *China Daily*, April 28, 2019, http://www.chinadaily.com.cn/a/201904/28/WS5cc504f6a3104842260b8d58.html.

25. Zbigniew Brzezinski, *The Grand Chessboard*, vol. 1 (New York: Basic Books, 1997), xiv.

26. Deborah Brautigam, *The Dragon's Gift: The Real Story of China in Africa* (Oxford: Oxford University Press, 2009), 296.

27. Jonathan Hillman, "A Chinese World Order," *Washington Post*, July 23, 2018, https://www.washingtonpost.com/news/theworldpost/wp/2018/07/23/china-world-order/?utm_term=.d78ofdcbdafb.

28. European Commission, *Joint Communication to the European Parliament, the European Council and the Council: EU-China—A Strategic Outlook* (Strasbourg: European Commission, March 2019), 5, https://ec.europa.eu/commission/sites/beta-political/files/communication-eu-china-a-strategic-outlook.pdf.

29. Mackinder, "Geographical Pivot of History," 423.

30. For an excellent overview of Mahan's thinking and its relevance for today, see Michael J. Green, *By More than Providence: Grand Strategy and American Power in the Asia Pacific since 1783* (New York: Columbia University Press, 2017), 79–93. For commentary on Mackinder, Mahan, and the BRI, see Joseph S. Nye, "Xi Jinping's Marco Polo Strategy," Project Syndicate, June 12, 2017, https://www.project-syndicate.org/commentary/china-belt-and-road-grand-strategy-by-joseph-s--nye-2017-06?barrier=accesspaylog.

31. Alfred Thayer Mahan, *The Influence of Sea Power upon History, 1660–1783* (Boston: Little, Brown, 1890), 398.

32. China Power Project, "Is China the World's Top Trader?," Center for Strategic and International Studies, March 28, 2019, https://chinapower.csis.org/trade-partner/; Richard Scott, "China-Owned Fleet Becomes World's Second Largest," *Hellenic Shipping News*, September 13, 2018, https://www.hellenicshippingnews.com/china-owned-fleet-becomes-worlds-second-largest/.

33. Anna Coren, Ellana Lee, Jane Sit, and James Griffiths, "Malaysian PM Mahathir: 'Most of the Top Echelons in the Government Are Corrupt,' " CNN, July 26, 2018, https://www.cnn.com/2018/07/25/asia/malaysia-mahathir-mohamad-interview-intl/index.html.

34. Mike Pence, "Remarks by Vice President Pence on the Administration's Policy toward China" (Hudson Institute, Washington, DC), White House, October 4, 2018, https://www.whitehouse.gov/briefings-statements/remarks-vice-president-pence-administrations-policy-toward-china/.

35. Daniel Headrick, "A Double-Edged Sword: Communications and Imperial Control in British India," *Historical Social Research / Historische Sozialforschung* 35, no. 1 (2010): 52.

36. Andrew Small, "A Slimmer Belt and Road Is Even Scarier," *Bloomberg Opinion*, April 24, 2019, https://www.bloomberg.com/opinion/articles/2019-04-24/a-slimmed-down-belt-and-road-will-increase-china-s-influence.

Chapter Two. Imperial Echoes: Technology and the Struggle for Control

1. I am indebted to Daniel R. Headrick for his comments on this chapter and for his contributions, which inspired many of its historical connections, especially *The Tools of Empire: Technology and European Imperialism in the Nineteenth Century* (New York: Oxford University Press, 1981); *The Tentacles of Progress: Technology Transfer in the Age of Imperialism, 1850–1940* (Oxford: Oxford University Press, 1988); *The Invisible Weapon: Telecommunications and International Politics, 1851–1945* (Oxford: Oxford University Press, 1991).

2. Jonathan Hillman, "Influence and Infrastructure," Center for Strategic and International Studies, January 22, 2019, https://www.csis.org/analysis/influence-and-infrastructure-strategic-stakes-foreign-projects.

3. The project was later renamed the "Pakistan East Africa Connecting Europe" cable, keeping the acronym the same.

4. "Report: Kenya Risks Losing Port of Mombasa to China," *Maritime Executive*, December 20, 2018, https://www.maritime-executive.com/article/kenya-risks-losing-port-of-mombasa-to-china.

5. Jonathan Hillman, "The Hazards of China's Global Ambitions," *Washington Post*, February 5, 2018, https://www.washingtonpost.com/news/theworldpost/wp/2018/02/05/obor-china-asia/?utm_term=.0125830d87f3.

6. Headrick, *Tools of Empire*.

7. Irène Delage, "Inauguration Ceremony of the Suez Canal at Port-Said, 17 November, 1869," Fondation Napoléon, accessed November 15, 2018, https://www.napoleon.org/en/history-of-the-two-empires/paintings/inauguration-ceremony-of-the-suez-canal-at-port-said-17-november-1869/.

8. Fondation Napoléon, "Speech Given by Monsignor Bauer," November 16, 1869, https://www.napoleon.org/wp-content/themes/napoleon/annexes/hors-serie/suez/en/html-content/inauguration/ceremonie/discours.html.

9. Max E. Fletcher, "The Suez Canal and World Shipping, 1869–1914," *Journal of Economic History* 18, no. 4 (1958): 572.

10. Jean-Paul Calon, "The Suez Canal Re-visited: 19th Century Global Infrastructure," in *Macro-Engineering: MIT Brunel Lectures on Global Infrastructure*, ed. Frank P. Davidson, Ernst G. Frankel, and C. Lawrence Meador (Cambridge, UK: Woodhead, 1997), 11–24, https://www.sciencedirect.com/science/article/pii/B9781898563334500057.

11. "The Suez Ship Canal," *New York Times*, September 3, 1869, https://nyti.ms/2yJgXqG.

12. Zachary Karabell, *Parting the Desert: The Creation of the Suez Canal* (New York: Knopf, 2003).

13. Amal Soliman ElGhouty, "Public Debt and Economic Growth in Egypt," *Business and Economic Research* 8, no. 3 (2018): 183–200, http://www.macrothink.org/journal/index.php/ber/article/view/13443.

14. "Ismail Pasha," Encyclopedia.com, accessed February 4, 2020, https://www.encyclopedia.com/people/history/egyptian-history-biographies/khedive-egypt-ismail.

15. Caroline Piquet, "The Suez Company's Concession in Egypt, 1854–1956: Modern Infrastructure and Local Economic Development," *Enterprise and Society* 5, no. 1 (2004): 107–127, https://muse.jhu.edu/article/53850.

16. Isma'il would later agree to pay 130 million francs, roughly half of the company's capital, to revise these provisions. Olukoya Ogen, "The Economic Lifeline of British Global Empire: A Reconsideration of the Historical Dynamics of the Suez Canal, 1869–1956," *Journal of International Social Research* 1, no. 5 (Fall 2008): 527, http://www.sosyalarastirmalar.com/cilt1/sayi5/sayi5pdf/ogen_olukoya.pdf.

17. Piquet, "Suez Company's Concession in Egypt."

18. Fondation Napoléon, "Speech Given by Monsignor Bauer."

19. Eric Toussaint, "Debt as an Instrument of the Colonial Conquest of Egypt," Committee for the Abolition of Illegitimate Debt, June 6, 2016, http://www.cadtm.org/spip.php?page=imprimer&id_article=13562.

20. Fletcher, "Suez Canal and World Shipping," 564 (quoting the *Economist*).

21. In 1842, after a military defeat to the British, the Qing government had opened five treaty ports: Shanghai, Canton, Fuzhou, Xiamen, and Ningbo. These ports gave foreigners legal protection and tax advantages, allowing them to own land and conduct business in these zones.

22. Albert Feuerwerker, "The Foreign Presence in China," in *The Cambridge History of China*, vol. 12, *Republican China 1912–1949, Part 1*, ed. John K. Fairbank (Cambridge: Cambridge University Press, 1983), 128–207.

23. Shannon R. Brown, "The Transfer of Technology to China in the Nineteenth Century: The Role of Direct Foreign Investment," *Journal of Economic History* 39, no. 1 (1979): 181–197.

24. Liu Hsi-hung, quoted in Li Kuo-ch'i, *History of the Early Chinese Railway Development* (in Chinese) (Taipei, 1961); cited in Arthur L. Rosenbaum, "China's First Railway: The Imperial Railways of North China, 1880–1911" (PhD diss., Yale University, 1972), 17.

25. Jonathan Hillman, "Is China Making a Trillion-Dollar Mistake?," *Washington Post*, April 9, 2018, https://www.washingtonpost.com/news/theworldpost/wp/2018/04/09/one-belt-one-road/?utm_term=.fac88ad702df.

26. Chinese Railroad Workers in North America Project at Stanford University, "CPRR FAQs," accessed February 4, 2020, http://web.stanford.edu/group/chineserailroad/cgi-bin/wordpress/faqs/.

27. Edson T. Strobridge, "The Chinese at Promontory, Utah, April 30–May 10, 1869," Central Pacific Railroad Photographic History Museum, December 6, 2001, http://cprr.org/Museum/Chinese_at_Promontory_ETS.html.

28. Richard White, *Railroaded: The Transcontinentals and the Making of Modern America* (New York: Norton, 2012), 24.

29. Erle Hearth, "A Railroad Record That Defies Defeat: How Central Pacific Laid Ten Miles of Track in One Day Back in 1869," *Southern Pacific Bulletin* 16, no. 5 (May 1928): 3–5, http://cprr.org/Museum/Southern_Pacific_Bulletin/Ten_Mile_Day.html.

30. Edgar A. Haine, *Railroad Wrecks* (New York: Cornwall Books, 1993), 195.

31. White, *Railroaded*, 485.

32. T. Reed and A. Trubetskoy, "Assessing the Value of Market Access from Belt and Road Projects" (Policy Research Working Paper WPS 8815, World Bank, Washington, DC, 2019).

33. Michele Ruta, Matías Herrera Dappe, Chunlin Zhang, Erik Churchill, Cristina Constantinescu, Mathilde Lebrand, and Alen Mulabdic, *Belt and Road Economics: Opportunities and Risks of Transport Corridors* (Washington, DC: World Bank Group, 2019).

34. "A Journal of Civilization," *Harper's Weekly* 11 (November 16, 1867): 723.

35. "W. F. Mayers, memorandum of a conversation with Li Hung-chang," September 1, 1865, FO 223/78, Public Record Office, London.

36. Rosenbaum, "China's First Railway," 19 (quote), 270–308.

37. "Railways in China," *London and China Telegraph*, July 14, 1873, 465.

38. Bradford later faced charges of using his public office for private gain. "Statement of Richard Phoenix to G. Wiley Wells," October 15, 1877, Library of Congress, accessed February 4, 2020, https://memory.loc.gov/service/gdc/scd0001/2009/2009102100 1st/2009102100 1st.pdf.

39. Rosenbaum, "China's First Railway," 107.

40. David Pong, "Confucian Patriotism and the Destruction of the Woosung Railway, 1877," *Modern Asian Studies* 7, no. 3 (1973): 669–670, https://doi.org/10.1017/S0026749X00005333.

41. Hsien-Chun Wang, "Merchants, Mandarins, and the Railway: Institutional Failure and the Wusong Railway, 1974–1877," *International Journal of Asian Studies* 12, no. 1 (2015): 31–53, doi:10.1017/S1479591414000205.

42. Albert Feuerwerker, "Economic Trends in the Late Ch'ing Empire, 1870–1911," in *The Cambridge History of China*, vol. 11, *Late Chi'ing 1800–1911*, *Part 2*, ed. John K. Fairbank and Kwang-ching Liu (Cambridge: Cambridge University Press, 1980), 11–52.

43. In 1895, Zongli Yamen, the Qing government body in charge of foreign affairs assumed responsibility for railway matters. E-Tu Zen Sun, "The Pattern of Railway Development in China," *Far Eastern Quarterly* 14, no. 2 (1955): 179–199, www.jstor.org/stable/2941730.

44. Rosenbaum, "China's First Railway," 117.

45. Sun, "Pattern of Railway Development in China."

46. For foreign share of debt, see Sun. For default rates, see Chi-ming Hou, *The Evolution of International Business, 1800–1945*, vol. 8, *Foreign Investment and Economic Development in China, 1840–1937* (Cambridge, MA: Harvard University Press, 2000), 37.

47. Daniel R. Headrick, "A Double-Edged Sword: Communications and Imperial Control in British India," *Historical Social Research / Historische Sozialforschung* 35, no. 1 (131) (2010): 51–65, http://www.jstor.org/stable/20762428.

48. Headrick, *Invisible Weapon*.

49. Alan J. Richardson, "The Cost of a Telegram: The Evolution of the International Regulation of the Telegraph," *Accounting History* 20, no. 4 (2015): 405–429, https://core.ac.uk/download/pdf/72789463.pdf.

50. Bruce J. Hunt, "The Ohm Is Where the Art Is: British Telegraph Engineers and the Development of Electrical Standards," *Osiris* 9 (1994): 48–63.

51. Daniel R. Headrick, "Strategic and Military Aspects of Submarine Telegraph Cables," in *Communications under the Seas: The Evolving Cable Network and Its Implications*, ed. Bernard Finn and Daqing Yang (Cambridge, MA: MIT Press, 2009), 187.

52. Charles Bright and Edward Brailsford Bright, *The Life Story of Sir Charles Tilston Bright, Civil Engineer: With Which Is Incorporated the Story of the Atlantic Cable, and the First Telegraph to India and the Colonies* (London: A. Constable, 1908), 143.

53. Headrick, *Invisible Weapon* (quote on 22).

54. Siemens, "Building the Indo-European Telegraph Line 150 Years Ago," accessed February 4, 2020, https://www.siemens.com/global/en/home/company/about/history/news/indo-european-telegraph-line.html.

55. Headrick, *Invisible Weapon*, 24.

56. Paul M. Kennedy, "Imperial Cable Communications and Strategy, 1870–1914," *English Historical Review* 86, no. 341 (1971): 728–752.

57. Walter S. Rogers, "International Electrical Communications," *Foreign Affairs* 1, no. 2 (1922): 156, https://archive.org/stream/jstor-20028220/20028220#page/n13.

58. Hunt, "Ohm Is Where the Art Is."

59. Daniel R. Headrick and Pascal Griset, "Submarine Telegraph Cables: Business and Politics, 1838–1939," *Business History Review* 75, no. 3 (2001): 553.

60. Headrick, "Double-Edged Sword," 51–65.

61. Quoted in Erik Baark, *Lightning Wires: The Telegraph and China's Technological Modernization, 1860–1890* (Westport, CT: Greenwood, 1997), 74. Shen also became a major proponent for the introduction of railways and telegraph lines in later years.

62. Quoted in Baark, 81.

63. Jorma Ahvenainen, *The Far Eastern Telegraphs: The History of Telegraphic Communications between the Far East, Europe, and America before the First World War* (Helsinki: Suomalainen Tiedeakatemia, 1981), 59–60.

64. Ariane Knuesel, "British Diplomacy and the Telegraph in Nineteenth-Century China," *Diplomacy and Statecraft* 18, no. 3 (2007): 517–537, https://doi.org/10.1080/09592290701540249.

65. Baark, *Lightning Wires*, 80–81, 83–84.

66. Quoted in Baark, 108.

67. Baark, 177.

68. Baark, 194–195.

69. Xinhua, "Full Text of Xi Jinping's Report at 19th CPC National Congress," *China Daily*, updated on November 4, 2017, http://www.chinadaily.com.cn/china/19thcpcnationalcongress/2017-11/04/content_34115212.htm.

70. Zongyi Liu, "Khan's Visit Infuses Momentum in Ties," *Global Times*, November 4, 2018, http://www.globaltimes.cn/content/1125776.shtml.

71. Michael Adas, "Imperialism and Colonialism in Comparative Perspective," *International History Review* 20, no. 2 (1998): 371–388, http://www.jstor.org/stable/40108227.

72. Andrew Lawler, "How Europe Exported the Black Death," *Science Magazine*, April 26, 2016, https://www.sciencemag.org/news/2016/04/how-europe-exported-black-death.

Chapter Three. The Crossroads: Central Asia

1. City Extremes, "Center of World Population," accessed June 4, 2019, http://cityextremes.com/averagedistance.php.

2. Daniel Garcia-Castellanos and Umberto Lombardo, "Poles of Inaccessibility: A Calculation Algorithm for the Remotest Places on Earth," *Scottish Geographical Journal* 123, no. 3 (May 2007): 227–233, https://www.tandfonline.com/doi/abs/10.1080/14702540801897809.

3. Charles Stevens, "Along the New Silk Road—Khorgos: Where East Meets West," *Geographical*, October 25, 2018, https://geographical.co.uk/people/development/item/2979-along-the-new-silk-road-khorgos-where-east-meets-west.

4. Wade Shepard, "Khorgos: Why Kazakhstan Is Building a 'New Dubai' on the Chinese Border," *Forbes*, February 28, 2016, https://www.forbes.com/sites/wadeshepard/2016/02/28/will-a-place-called-khorgos-become-the-next-dubai/#22ab2a27f4b7.

5. Andrew Higgins, "China's Ambitious New 'Port': Landlocked Kazakhstan," *New York Times*, January 1, 2018, https://www.nytimes.com/2018/01/01/world/asia/china-kazakhstan-silk-road.html.

6. "Why Railway Gauge in Russia Is Wider than in Europe" (in Russian), FactorЭ, accessed February 4, 2020, http://factor-e.ru/samopoznanie/istoriya/pochemu-zheleznodorozhnaya-koleya-v-rossii-shire-chem-v-evrope.html.

7. Vladimir Kosoy, "A Future of EU-EAEU-China Cooperation in Trade and Railway Transport" (presentation at the Working Party on Transport Trends and Economics 5, thirtieth session, United Nations Economic Commission for Europe, Geneva, 2017), https://www.unece.org/fileadmin/DAM/trans/doc/2017/wp5/WP5_30th_session_Mr_Kosoy.pdf.

8. Shigeru Otsuka, "Central Asia's Rail Network and the Eurasian Land Bridge," *Japan Railway & Transport Review* 28 (September 2001), http://www.ejrcf.or.jp/jrtr/jrtr28/pdf/f42_ots.pdf.

9. Vladimir Kontorovich, "The Railroads," in *The Disintegration of the Soviet Economic System*, ed. Michael Ellman and Vladimir Kontorovich (London: Routledge, 1992), 174–189.

10. For an account of this economic collapse, see Johannes F. Linn, "Economic (Dis)Integration Matters: The Soviet Collapse Revisited" (paper presented at the "Transition in the CIS: Achievements and Challenges" conference, Academy for National Economy, Moscow, September 13–14, 2004), https://www.brookings.edu/wp-content/uploads/2016/06/200410linn.pdf; see also Ellman and Kontorovich, *Destruction of the Soviet Economic System.*

11. Richard Pomfret, *The Economies of Central Asia* (Princeton, NJ: Princeton University Press, 1995), 39.

12. Julien Thorez, "The Post-Soviet Space between North and South: Discontinuities, Disparities and Migrations," in *Development in Central Asia and the Caucasus—Migration, Democratisation and Inequality in the Post-Soviet Era*, ed. Sophie Hohman, Claire Mouradian, Silvia Serrano, and Julien Thorez (New York: I. B. Tauris, 2014), 215–241, https://hal.archives-ouvertes.fr/hal-01482275/document.

13. "Uzbekistan Resumes Flights to Dushanbe after 25 Years," Radio Free Europe / Radio Liberty, April 11, 2017, https://www.rferl.org/a/uzbekistan-resumes-flights-to-dushanbe-after-25-years/28422811.html.

14. Richard Pomfret, "Trade and Transport in Central Asia" (paper presented at Eurasia Emerging Markets Forum, Thun, Switzerland, January 23–25, 2010), http://citeseerx.ist.psu.edu/viewdoc/download?doi=10.1.1.831.1845&rep=rep1&type=pdf.

15. United Nations Economic and Social Council, *Fifty Years of the Asian Highway* (Bangkok: United Nations, 2018), https://digitallibrary.un.org/record/651570/files/E_ESCAP_CTR_5-EN.pdf?version=1.

16. These include the European Bank for Reconstruction and Development (EBRD), the International Monetary Fund (IMF), the Islamic Development Bank (IsDB), the United Nations Development Programme (UNDP), and the World Bank.

17. U.S. Congress, Senate, *Silk Road Strategy Act of 1999*, S. Rept. 106-4, 1st sess., introduced by Sen. Sam Brownback (R-KS) in Senate, March 10, 1999, https://www.congress.gov/bill/106th-congress/senate-bill/579/text.

18. David Michael Gould, *Critical Connections: Promoting Economic Growth and Resilience in Europe and Central Asia* (Washington, DC: World Bank, 2018), 203, https://openknowledge.worldbank.org/bitstream/handle/10986/30245/9781464811579.pdf?sequence=6&isAllowed=y.

19. KTZ-Freight Transportation Joint Stock Company, "The Volume of Rail Traffic between Kazakhstan and China Grew by 33%" (in Russian), May 16, 2018, https://www.ktzh-gp.kz/ru/media/news/news_main_section_ru/11560/.

20. Vitaly Lobyrev, Andrey Tikhomirov, Taras Tsukarev, and Evgeny Vinoku-rov, *Belt and Road Transport Corridors: Barriers and Investments* (Saint Petersburg, Russia: Eurasian Development Bank, 2018), 22, https://eabr.org/upload/iblock/245/EDB-Centre_2018_Report-50_Transport-Corridors_Barriers-and-Investments_ENG.pdf.

21. "COSCO Shipping Invests in the Development of the Khorgos–Eastern Gate FEZ" (in Russian), Kazakh TV, May 22, 2017, https://kazakh-tv.kz/ru/view/business/page_185044_cosco-shipping-investiruet-v-razvitie-sez-.

22. Jonathan E. Hillman, "Trains from China Laden with Hype and Subsidies," *Financial Times*, July 26, 2017, https://www.ft.com/content/dd6196f8-715e-11e7-aca6-c6bd07df1a3c; Hillman, "The Rise of China-Europe Railways," Center for Strategic and International Studies, March 6, 2018, https://www.csis.org/analysis/rise-china-europe-railways.

23. UN Economic Commission for Europe, "Information from Participants on Recent Developments in Transport Infrastructure Priority Projects on EATL Routes," May 28, 2015, https://www.unece.org/fileadmin/DAM/trans/doc/2015/wp5-eatl/id15-05e.pdf.

24. Xinhua, "Xinhua Headlines: China, Europe on Path of Expanding Belt and Road Cooperation," *Xinhuanet*, March 17, 2019, http://www.xinhuanet.com/english/2019-03/17/c_137902322.htm.

25. Xu Zhang and Hans-Joachim Schramm, "Eurasian Rail Freight in the One Belt One Road Era" (paper presented at the Nordic Logistics Research Network Conference, Kolding, Denmark, June 2018), https://www.researchgate.net/publication/328880505_Eurasian_Rail_Freight_in_the_One_Belt_One_Road_Era.

26. Roland Berger, "Eurasian Rail Corridors: What Opportunities for Freight Stakeholders?," International Union of Railways, October 2017, https://uic.org/IMG/pdf/corridors_exe_sum2017_web.pdf.

27. Babak Besharati, Gansakh Gansakh, Feifei Liu, Xiaomin Zhang, and Ming Xu, "The Ways to Maintain Sustainable China-Europe Block Train Operation," *Business and Management Studies* 3, no. 3 (September 2017): https://doi.org/10.11114/bms.v3i3.2490.

28. Xinhua, "New China-Europe Freight Train Links China's Jiangxi, Uzbekistan," *Xinhuanet*, July 9, 2017, http://www.xinhuanet.com/english/2017-07/09/c_136429735.htm.

29. Patrick Sawer, "East Wind Train Blows In from China to Re-open Silk Road Trail," *Telegraph*, January 18, 2017, http://www.telegraph.co.uk/news/2017/01/18/east-wind-train-blows-china-re-open-silk-road-trail/; Tracy McVeigh, "Silk Road Route Back in Business as China Train Rolls into London," *Guardian*, January 14, 2017, https://www.theguardian.com/world/2017/jan/14/china-silk-road-trade-train-rolls-london.

30. Hans-Joachim Schramm and Sabrina Zhang, "Eurasian Rail Freight in the One Belt One Road Era" (paper presented at the thirtieth annual NOFOMA Conference: Relevant Logistics and Supply Chain Management,

Kolding, Denmark, July 13–15, 2018), https://www.researchgate.net/publication/328880505_Eurasian_Rail_Freight_in_the_One_Belt_One_Road_Era.

31. This is not a new problem, nor is it one that is limited to rail or even trade between China and Europe. At any time, some 45 percent of dry-bulk cargo ships, which typically carry commodities, are traveling without cargo. The shipping giant Maersk estimates that it spends $1 billion repositioning empty containers each year.

32. Edward Schatz, "When Capital Cities Move: The Political Geography of Nation and State Building," Helen Kellogg Institute for International Studies, February 2003, https://kellogg.nd.edu/sites/default/files/old_files/documents/303.pdf.

33. Xi Jinping, "Speech by H. E. Xi Jinping, President of the People's Republic of China, at Nazarbayev University," Ministry of Foreign Affairs of the People's Republic of China, September 7, 2013, http://www.fmprc.gov.cn/mfa_eng/wjdt_665385/zyjh_665391/t1078088.shtml.

34. "Each Region of Kazakhstan Will Benefit from the EXPO 2017 in Astana—Nazarbayev" (in Russian), Zakon.kz, November 28, 2012, http://www.zakon.kz/4527418-vygodu-ot-provedenija-expo-2017-v.html.

35. Trading Economics, "Kazakhstan Average Monthly Wages," accessed February 4, 2020, https://tradingeconomics.com/kazakhstan/wages.

36. Zhazira Dyussembekova, "In Astana, Hilton's VP for Operations Talks New Hotel and Industry Trends," *Astana Times*, December 4, 2017, https://astanatimes.com/2017/12/in-astana-hiltons-vp-for-operations-talks-new-hotel-and-industry-trends/.

37. Expo 2017 Astana, "Infographics," accessed February 4, 2020, https://www.expo2017astana.com/en/page_id=65.

38. Xinhua, "Xi Visits Chinese Pavilion at Astana Expo, Eyes Better Cross-Border Transportation," *Xinhuanet*, September 6, 2017, http://www.xinhuanet.com/english/2017-06/09/c_136350902.htm.

39. Expo 2017 Astana, "USA Pavilion Welcomes Presidential Delegation from United States to Expo 2017," August 28, 2017, http://www.usapavilion2017.org/usa-pavilion-welcomes-presidential-delegation-from-the-united-states-to-expo-2017/.

40. Ed Zuckerman, "In Kazakhstan, a World Expo Is All about Energy (and Dancing)," *New York Times*, August 23, 2017, https://www.nytimes.com/2017/08/23/travel/kazakhstan-world-expo-astana.html/.

41. Eric McGlinchey, "New Policy Memo: Central Asia's Autocrats: Geopolitically Stuck, Politically Free," PONARS Eurasia: New Approaches to Research and Security in Eurasia, August 17, 2015, http://www.ponarseurasia.org/article/new-policy-memo-central-asias-autocrats-geopolitically-stuck-politically-free.

42. Raffaello Pantucci and Sarah Lain, *China's Eurasian Pivot: The Silk Road Economic Belt* (New York: Routledge, 2017); Nadège Rolland, "Securing

the Belt and Road: Prospects for Chinese Military Engagement along the
Silk Roads" (NBR Special Report 80, National Bureau of Asian Research,
Seattle, WA, September 3, 2019), https://www.nbr.org/publication/
securing-the-belt-and-road-prospects-for-chinese-military-engagement-
along-the-silk-roads/.

43. Craig Nelson and Thomas Grove, "Russia and China Vie for Influence in
Central Asia as U.S. Plans Afghan Exit," *Wall Street Journal*, June 18,
2019, https://www.wsj.com/articles/russia-china-vie-for-influence-in-
central-asia-as-u-s-plans-afghan-exit-11560850203.

44. Sebastian Peyrouse, "The Evolution of Russia's Views on the Belt and
Road Initiative," *Asia Policy* 24, no. 1 (2017): 96–102; Safovudin Jaborov,
"Chinese Loans in Central Asia: Development Assistance or 'Predatory
Lending'?," in *China's Belt and Road Initiative and Its Impact in Central
Asia*, ed. Marlène Laruelle (Washington, DC: George Washington Uni-
versity, Central Asia Program, 2018), 34–40.

45. Harinder S. Koli, Johannes Lynn, and Leo Zucker, *China's Belt and Road
Initiative: Potential Transformation of Central Asia and the South Caucus*
(Thousand Oaks, CA: Sage, 2019).

46. Until Kyrgyzstan joined the Eurasian Economic Union, it played the role
of a trade entrepôt for China, leveraging its World Trade Organization
status to then reexport goods into the Commonwealth of Independent
States. Almazbek Atambayev, quoted in "Kyrgyzstan in the Project 'One
Belt, One Road': Perspectives and Opportunities" (in Russian), CA-por-
tal, May 19, 2017, http://www.ca-portal.ru/article:35040.

47. "Interview of President of Tajikistan Emomali Rahmon to the Newspaper *Renmin Ribao* [The People's Daily]" (in Russian), Press Service of
President of Republic of Tajikistan, September 4, 2017, http://www.presi
dent.tj/ru/node/16094; "Meetings and Negotiations of the Highest Level
between Tajikistan and China" (in Russian), Press Service of President of
Republic of Tajikistan, August 31, 2017, http://www.prezident.tj/ru/
node/16060.

48. "Shavkat Mirziyoyev: Our Peoples Must in Reality Feel the Effects of
Our Joint Efforts," official website of the president of Uzbekistan, April
27, 2019, https://president.uz/en/lists/view/2533.

49. Government of Turkmenistan, "'Turkmenistan Is the Heart of the Great
Silk Road': The New Book of President of Turkmenistan," accessed June
25, 2019, http://pubdocs.worldbank.org/en/911041512488377918/TURK
MENISTAN-IS-THE-HEART-OF-THE-GREAT-SILK-ROAD.pdf.

50. Center for Insights in Survey Research, "Public Opinion Survey Residents
of Kyrgyzstan," February 5, 2018 (data was collected from November 19
to December 2, 2017), http://www.iri.org/sites/default/files/2018-2-5
_iri_poll_presentation_kyrgyzstan.pdf.

51. Steve LeVine, *The Oil and the Glory: The Pursuit of Empire and Fortune on
the Caspian Sea* (New York: Random House, 2007).

52. "Kazakhstan Inaugurates Automobile Ferry Terminal on Caspian Sea," Agencia EFE, December 7, 2017, https://www.efe.com/efe/english/business/kazakhstan-inaugurates-automobile-ferry-terminal-on-caspian-sea/50000265-3460021.

53. For more detailed accounts of these dynamics around the Caspian region, see work by Natalie Koch, especially "Urban Boosterism in Closed Contexts: Spectacular Urbanization and Second-Tier Mega-Events in Three Caspian Capitals," *Eurasian Geography and Economics* 56, no. 5 (2015): 575–598.

54. Transparency International, "Global Corruption Report 2005: Corruption in Construction and Post-Conflict Reconstruction," March 16, 2005, https://www.transparency.org/whatwedo/publication/global_corruption_report_2005_corruption_in_construction_and_post_conflict.

55. "Tajik President's Son-in-Law Denies Ties to Company," Radio Free Europe / Radio Liberty, July 12, 2010, https://www.rferl.org/a/Tajik_Presidents_SonIn Law_Denies_Ties_To_Company/2097815.html.

56. Konrad Mathesius, "Tajik Toll Road Raises Public Ire, Stokes Corruption Concerns," *Eurasianet*, September 17, 2010, https://eurasianet.org/tajik-toll-road-raises-public-ire-stokes-corruption-concerns.

57. "Tajik President Sacks Official Who Criticized Toll Road," Radio Free Europe / Radio Liberty, January 24, 2011, https://www.rferl.org/a/tajik_ashur_sacking_toll_road/2285206.html; "Tajik Court Frees Journalist, Reduces Sentence to Fine and Community Service," Radio Free Europe / Radio Liberty, August 22, 2018, https://www.rferl.org/a/tajik-court-frees-journalist-mirsaidov-reduces-sentence-fine-community-service/29447571.html.

58. Hélène Thibault, *Transforming Tajikistan: State-Building and Islam in Post-Soviet Central Asia* (New York: Bloomsbury, 2018).

59. Elnura Alkanova, "Abuse of Power? On the Trail of China's Mystery Millions in Kyrgyzstan," Open Democracy, October 24, 2018, https://www.opendemocracy.net/od-russia/elnura-alkanova/what-happened-at-bishkek-power-plant.

60. Alexander Cooley, "The Emerging Political Economy of OBOR: The Challenges of Promoting Connectivity in Central Asia and Beyond" (report of the SCIS Simon Chair in Political Economy, Center for Strategic and International Studies, Washington, DC, October 2016), https://csis-prod.s3.amazonaws.com/s3fs-public/publication/161021_Cooley_OBOR_Web.pdf; Alexander Cooley and John Heathershaw, *Dictators without Borders: Power and Money in Central Asia* (New Haven, CT: Yale University Press, 2017).

61. Special Inspector General for Afghanistan Reconstruction (SIGAR), *Quarterly Report to the United States Congress* (Washington, DC: SIGAR, 2018), https://www.sigar.mil/pdf/quarterlyreports/2018-07-30qr.pdf.

62. Transparency International, "Transparency in Corporate Reporting: Assessing Emerging Market Multinationals," July 11, 2016, https://issuu.

com/transparencyinternational/docs/2016_transparencyincorporaterepor ti?e=2496456/37122985.

63. Kevin P. Gallagher, Rohini Kamal, Junda Jin, Yanning Chen, and Xinyue Ma, "Energizing Development Finance? The Benefits and Risks of China's Development Finance in the Global Energy Sector," *Energy Policy* 122 (November 2018), 313–321, https://www.sciencedirect.com/science/ article/pii/S0301421518303975; Geoff Dyer and Jamil Anderlini, "China's Lending Hits New Heights," *Financial Times*, January 17, 2011, https://www.ft.com/content/488c60f4-2281-11e0-b6a2-00144feab49a.

64. Christopher Balding, "Why Democracies Are Turning against Belt and Road: Corruption, Debt, and Backlash," *Foreign Affairs*, October 24, 2018, https://www.foreignaffairs.com/articles/china/2018-10-24/why-de mocracies-are-turning-against-belt-and-road.

Chapter Four. The Gatekeeper: Russia

1. James Forsyth, *A History of the Peoples of Siberia: Russia's North Asian Colony, 1581–1990* (Cambridge: Cambridge University Press, 1994), 222.

2. U.S. State Department, "Comments of Soviet Embassy Officer on China and Vietnam," memorandum of conversation, June 13, 1969, National Archives, SN 67-69, Pol Chicom-US, http://nsarchive.gwu.edu/NSAEBB /NSAEBB49/sino.sov.5.pdf.

3. "Work Starts on First China-Russia Highway Bridge," Radio Free Europe / Radio Liberty, December 25, 2016, https://www.rferl.org/a/russia-china-amur-river-highway-bridge-border-trade/28195627.html.

4. Tim Marshall, "Russia and the Curse of Geography," *Atlantic*, October 31, 2015, https://www.theatlantic.com/international/archive/2015/10/ russia-geography-ukraine-syria/413248/.

5. National Security Archive, George Washington University, "The Charge in the Soviet Union (Kennan) to the Secretary of State," February 22, 1946, https://nsarchive2.gwu.edu/coldwar/documents/episode-1/ kennan.htm.

6. Quoted in Benn Steil, *The Marshall Plan: Dawn of the Cold War* (New York: Oxford University Press, 2018), 251.

7. George F. Kennan, "A Fateful Error," *New York Times*, February 5, 1997, https://www.nytimes.com/1997/02/05/opinion/a-fateful-error.html/.

8. Yevgeny Primakov, *Russian Crossroads: Toward the New Millennium* (New Haven, CT: Yale University Press, 2008), 135.

9. Sergey Lavrov and Yang Jiechi, "Transcript of Remarks and Response to Media Questions by Russian Minister of Foreign Affairs Sergey Lavrov at Press Conference Following Talks with PRC Minister of Foreign Affairs Yang Jiechi," Ministry of Foreign Affairs of the Russian Federation, July 21, 2008, http://www.mid.ru/en/vistupleniya_ministra/-/asset_publisher/ MCZ7HQuMdqBY/content/id/330178.

10. Christopher Miller, "The New Cold War's Warm Friends," *Foreign Policy*, March 1, 2019, https://foreignpolicy.com/2019/03/01/the-new-cold-wars-warm-friends/.

11. Kremlin: President of Russia, "Presenting the Order of St Andrew the Apostle to President of China Xi Jinping," July 4, 2017, http://en.kremlin.ru/events/president/transcripts/54973.

12. Cheang Ming, "'Best Time in History' for China-Russia Relationship: Xi and Putin Boost Ties," CNBC, July 5, 2017, http://www.cnbc.com/2017/07/04/china-russia-ties-reaffirmed-after-xi-jinping-and-vladimir-putin-meet.html.

13. Cao Desheng, "Xi Presents Friendship Medal to Putin," *China Daily*, June 8, 2018, http://www.chinadaily.com.cn/a/201806/09/WS5b1af610a31001b82571foc6.html.

14. Ministry of Defense of the Russian Federation, "The Defense Ministers of Russia and China Noted the Special Significance of Russian-Chinese Relations for International Security" (in Russian), April 3, 2018, https://function.mil.ru/news_page/country/more.htm?id=12169612@egNews.

15. Brad Lendon and Steve George, "China's Navy Expands Reach: Ships in Baltic for Drills with Russia," CNN, July 21, 2017, http://www.cnn.com/2017/07/20/asia/china-navy-expansion-baltic-russia-drills/index.html; "Russia Launches Biggest War Games since Cold War," BBC, September 11, 2018, https://www.bbc.com/news/world-europe-45470460.

16. Jon Ostrower, "China and Russia Are Coming for Boeing and Airbus," CNN, May 23, 2107, http://money.cnn.com/2017/05/23/news/companies/china-russia-airplane-partnership/index.html.

17. "The Central Bank of Russia Shifts Its Reserves Away from the Dollar," *Economist*, January 17, 2019, https://www.economist.com/finance-and-economics/2019/01/17/the-central-bank-of-russia-shifts-its-reserves-away-from-the-dollar.

18. Alexander Gabuev, "Crouching Bear, Hidden Dragon: 'One Belt One Road' and Chinese-Russian Jostling for Power in Central Asia," *Journal of Contemporary East Asia Studies* 5, no. 2 (2016): 61–78.

19. For an inside account of how these sanctions came into place, see Michael McFaul, *From Cold War to Hot Peace: An American Ambassador in Putin's Russia* (Boston: Houghton Mifflin Harcourt, 2018).

20. Alexander Gabuev, "Donald Trump's Plan to Play Russia against China Is a Fool's Errand," Carnegie Moscow Center, May 24, 2017, https://carnegie.ru/2017/05/24/donald-trump-s-plan-to-play-russia-against-china-is-fool-s-errand-pub-70067; Gabuev, "A 'Soft Alliance'? Russia-China Relations after the Ukraine Crisis" (policy brief, European Council on Foreign Relations, Berlin, 2015), https://www.ecfr.eu/page/-/ECFR126_-_A_Soft_Alliance_Russia-China_Relations_After_the_Ukraine_Crisis.pdf.

21. Sebastien Peyrouse, "The Evolution of Russia's Views on the Belt and Road Initiative," *Asia Policy* 24, no. 1 (2017): 96–102.

22. Gerry Shih, "In Central Asia's Forbidding Highlands, a Quiet Newcomer: Chinese Troops," *Washington Post*, February 18, 2019, https://www.washingtonpost.com/world/asia_pacific/in-central-asias-forbidding-highlands-a-quiet-newcomer-chinese-troops/2019/02/18/78d4a8d0-1e62-11e9-a759-2b8541bbbe20_story.html.

23. Defense Intelligence Agency, *Russia Military Power: Building a Military to Support Great Power Aspirations* (Washington, DC: Defense Intelligence Agency, 2017), 16, https://www.hsdl.org/?abstract&did=801968.

24. White House, *National Security Strategy of the United States of America* (Washington, DC: White House, December 2017), https://www.whitehouse.gov/wp-content/uploads/2017/12/NSS-Final-12-18-2017-0905.pdf.

25. For insight into Putin's economic policies, including the EAEU, see Christopher Miller, *Putinomics: Power and Money in Resurgent Russia* (Chapel Hill: University of North Carolina Press), 2018.

26. "A New Integration Project for Eurasia: The Future in the Making," *Izvestia*, October 4, 2011, European Parliament, accessed February 4, 2020, http://www.europarl.europa.eu/meetdocs/2009_2014/documents/d-ru/dv/dru_2013_0320_06_/dru_2013_0320_06_en.pdf.

27. Sean P. Roberts and Arkady Moshes, "The Eurasian Economic Union: A Case of Reproductive Integration?," *Post-Soviet Affairs* 32, no. 6 (2016), https://researchportal.port.ac.uk/portal/files/3430174/The_Eurasian_Economic_Union_A_case_of_reproductive_integration.pdf.

28. Bruno S. Sergi, "Putin's and Russian-Led Eurasian Economic Union: A Hybrid Half-Economics and Half-Political 'Janus Bifrons,' " *Journal of Eurasian Studies* 9 (2018): 52–60, https://journals.sagepub.com/doi/pdf/10.1016/j.euras.2017.12.005.

29. Despite the name, the New Eurasian Land Bridge is operational largely because it relies heavily on infrastructure that predates the BRI. The Trans-Siberian Railway, opened over a century ago, constitutes the corridor's longest section. There have been proposals for upgrading that component to high-speed rail, but the astronomical price tag, estimated at $230 billion, is prohibitive.

30. Xi Jinping, "Full Text of President Xi's Speech at Opening of Belt and Road Forum," *Xinhuanet*, May 14, 2017, http://news.xinhuanet.com/english/2017-05/14/c_136282982.htm.

31. Kremlin: President of Russia, "Belt and Road International Forum," May 14, 2017, http://en.kremlin.ru/events/president/news/54491.

32. Marlene Laruelle, "The China-Russia Relationship in Central Asia and Afghanistan" (testimony prepared for the U.S.-China Economic and Security Review Commission, Washington, DC, March 21, 2019), https://www.uscc.gov/sites/default/files/Laruelle_Testimony.pdf.

33. Xi Jinping, "President Xi's Speech to Davos in Full," World Economic Forum, January 17, 2017, https://www.weforum.org/agenda/2017/01/full-text-of-xi-jinping-keynote-at-the-world-economic-forum.

34. Kremlin: President of Russia, "Belt and Road International Forum."
35. See memos by Hilary Appel and Elizabeth Wishnick, prepared for PONARS Policy Conference 2019, Washington, DC, http://www.ponarseurasia.org.
36. "Matchmakers See Chinese-Russian Intermarriages as More Links on Belt and Road," Sputnik, March 4, 2018, https://sputniknews.com/society/201803041062200297-china-russian-marriage-booming-business/.
37. Evgeny Vinokurov, "Eurasian Economic Union: Current State and Preliminary Results," *Russian Journal of Economics* 3, no. 1 (March 2017): 54–70, http://www.sciencedirect.com/science/article/pii/S2405473917300041#bib0085.
38. Ministry of Transport of the Russian Federation, "Railway Checkpoints," https://www.rosgranstroy.ru/checkpoints/list.php?bitrix_include_areas=Y&SECTION_ID=188.
39. Gordon Graham, "Cross-Border Intermodal," Canadian National Railway Company, http://www.theccib.com/files/4_CN_CrossBorder_GordonGraham.pdf.
40. Henry Sanderson, "Jay Hambro: Bridge to a Future in Russia," *Financial Times*, January 26, 2016, https://www.ft.com/content/033a2f7a-b955-11e5-bf7e-8a339b6f2164.
41. Wei He, "Program of Cooperation between the Regions of the Far East Siberia of the Russian Federation and the Northeast of the Chinese People's Republic (2009–2018)" (in Russian), Xin Da Li, May 3, 2010, http://www.chinaruslaw.com/RU/CnRuTreaty/004/201035210624_735729.htm.
42. A tally of cross-border projects announced between 2009 and 2018 found that only eight out of thirty-two had been completed, slightly better but not very encouraging.
43. Vita Spivak and Henry Foy, "Russia Struggles to Attract Chinese Capital to Its Far East," *Financial Times*, May 5, 2019, https://www.ft.com/content/d4cf3486-681b-11e9-a79d-04f350474d62.
44. The Kremlin: President of Russia, "Opening Remarks at the Meeting 'On the Development Prospects of the Far East and Transbaikalia'" (in Russian), Blagoveshchensk, July 21, 2000, http://kremlin.ru/events/president/transcripts/21494.
45. "Russia Gives Free Land, Incentives to Invest in Asian Far East," Russia Briefing, June 8, 2017, http://www.russia-briefing.com/news/russia-gives-free-land-incentives-invest-asian-far-east.html/.
46. Alexander Gabuev and Maria Repnikova, "Why Forecasts of a Chinese Takeover of the Russian Far East Are Just Dramatic Myth," Carnegie Moscow Center, July 14, 2017, https://carnegie.ru/2017/07/14/why-forecasts-of-chinese-takeover-of-russian-far-east-are-just-dramatic-myth-pub-71550.

47. "Sberbank Says Average Russian Salary Lower than Chinese," *Moscow Times*, May 19, 2016, https://www.themoscowtimes.com/2016/05/19/sberbank-says-average-russian-salary-lower-than-chinese-a52939.

48. Erica Downs, "China-Russia Energy Relations" (testimony prepared for the U.S.-China Economic and Security Review Commission hearing "An Emerging China-Russia Axis," Washington, DC, March 21, 2019), https://www.uscc.gov/sites/default/files/Downs_Testimony...pdf.

49. Henry Foy, "Russia's $55bn Pipeline Gamble on China's Demand for Gas," *Financial Times*, April 3, 2018, https://ig.ft.com/gazprom-pipeline-power-of-siberia/.

50. Lucy Hornby, Jamil Anderlini, and Guy Chazan, "China and Russia Sign $400bn Gas Deal," *Financial Times*, May 21, 2014, https://www.ft.com/content/d9a8b800-e09a-11e3-9534-00144feabdco.

51. Foy, "Russia's $55bn Pipeline Gamble."

52. On China in the Arctic, see Anne-Marie Brady, *China as a Polar Great Power* (Cambridge: Cambridge University Press, 2017); Heather Conley, "China's Arctic Dream," Center for Strategic and International Studies, February 26, 2018, https://www.csis.org/analysis/chinas-arctic-dream.

53. Stephanie Pezard, "The New Geopolitics of the Arctic: Russia's and China's Evolving Role in the Region" (testimony presented before the Standing Committee on Foreign Affairs and International Development of the Canadian House of Commons, Toronto, November 26, 2018), 6, https://www.rand.org/content/dam/rand/pubs/testimonies/CT500/CT500/RAND_CT500.pdf.

54. Gabuev, "Crouching Bear, Hidden Dragon," 76.

55. China Ministry of Commerce, "China and Eurasian Economic Union Officially Sign Trade and Economic Cooperation Agreement," May 18, 2019, http://english.mofcom.gov.cn/article/newsrelease/significantnews/201805/20180502746079.shtml.

56. Viktor Shakhmatov, "The EAEU: A Core Element of the Greater Eurasian Partnership," Valdai, March 14, 2019, http://valdaiclub.com/a/highlights/eaeu-a-core-element-of-the-greater-eurasian/.

57. Shanghai Cooperation Organization, "Development Strategy of the Shanghai Cooperation Organization until 2025," 2015, http://eng.sectsco.org/load/200162/.

58. Nargis Kassenova, "China's Belt and Road at Five" (panel presentation at the Center for Strategic and International Studies, Washington, DC, October 1, 2018), https://www.csis.org/events/chinas-belt-and-road-five-0.

Chapter Five. The Bridgehead: Central and Eastern Europe

1. James Kynge, Arthur Beesley, and Andrew Byrne, "EU Sets Collision Course with China over 'Silk Road' Rail Project," *Financial Times*, February 19, 2017, https://www.ft.com/content/003bad14-f52f-11e6-95ee-f14e55513608.

Total cost estimates for the two sections have ranged between $2.8 billion and $3.8 billion.

2. Ryan Hearth and Andrew Gray, "Beware Chinese Trojan Horses in the Balkans, EU Warns," *Politico*, July 27, 2018, https://www.politico.eu/article/johannes-hahn-beware-chinese-trojan-horses-in-the-balkans-eu-warns-enlargement-politico-podcast/.

3. Sigmar Gabriel, "Speech by Foreign Minister Sigmar Gabriel at the Munich Security Conference" (speech given at the Munich Security Conference, Munich, February 17, 2018), Federal Foreign Office of Germany, https://www.auswaertiges-amt.de/en/newsroom/news/rede-muenchner-sicherheitskonferenz/1602662.

4. See Phillipe Le Corre, "On China's Expanding Influence in Europe and Eurasia" (testimony to the U.S. Congress, Washington, DC, May 9, 2019), Carnegie Endowment, https://carnegieendowment.org/2019/05/09/on-china-s-expanding-influence-in-europe-and-eurasia-pub-79094; Le Corre, "China's Rise as a Geoeconomic Influencer: Four European Case Studies," Carnegie Endowment, October 15, 2018, https://carnegieendowment.org/2018/10/15/china-s-rise-as-geoeconomic-influencer-four-european-case-studies-pub-77462.

5. Michel Rose, "China's New 'Silk Road' Cannot Be One-Way, France's Macron Says," Reuters, January 8, 2018, https://www.reuters.com/article/us-china-france-idUSKBN1EX0FU.

6. George Parker, James Kynge, and Lucy Hornby, "May Resists Pressure to Endorse China's 'New Silk Road' Project," *Financial Times*, January 31, 2018, https://www.ft.com/content/3e79ae14-0681-11e8-9650-9c0ad2d7c5b5.

7. Dana Heide, Till Hoppe, Stephan Scheuer, and Klaus Stratmann, "EU Ambassadors Band Together against Silk Road," *Handelsblatt Today*, April 17, 2018, https://www.handelsblatt.com/today/politics/china-first-eu-ambassadors-band-together-against-silk-road/23581860.html?ticket=ST-2635619-iQxmRQU2eGxAwjKCAbTo-ap2.

8. David Barboza, Marc Santora, and Alexandra Stevenson, "China Seeks Influence in Europe, One Business Deal at a Time," *New York Times*, August 12, 2018, https://www.nytimes.com/2018/08/12/business/china-influence-europe-czech-republic.html.

9. Jason Horowitz and Liz Alderman, "Chastised by E.U., a Resentful Greece Embraces China's Cash and Interests," *New York Times*, August 26, 2017, https://www.nytimes.com/2017/08/26/world/europe/greece-china-piraeus-alexis-tsipras.html.

10. MTI, "Orbán: If EU Doesn't Pay, Hungary Will Turn to China," *Budapest Business Journal*, January 11, 2018, https://bbj.hu/economy/orban-if-eu-doesnt-pay-hungary-will-turn-to-china_143836.

11. Le Corre, "China's Rise as a Geoeconomic Influencer"; Thilo Hanemann, Mikko Huotari, and Agatha Kratz, *China FDI in Europe: 2018 Trends and Impact of New Screening Policies* (Berlin: Mercator Institute for

China Studies and Rhodium Group, 2019), https://www.merics.org/en/papers-on-china/chinese-fdi-in-europe-2018.

12. "Hungarian PM Viktor Orban's Friend Seals €2.3bn Railway Contract with Chinese Firms," BNE Intellinews, April 29, 2019, https://www.intel linews.com/hungarian-pm-viktor-orban-s-friend-seals-2-3bn-railway-contract-with-chinese-firms-160334/.

13. Michael Peel, James Kynge, and Lucy Hornby, "China's Balkan Investment Pledges Stoke EU Concern," *Financial Times*, July 1, 2018, https://www.ft.com/content/6c646a3e-7d29-11e8-bc55-50daf 1 1b720d.

14. Barbara Surk, "As China Moves In, Serbia Reaps Benefits, with Strings Attached," *New York Times*, September 9, 2017, https://www.nytimes.com/2017/09/09/world/europe/china-serbia-european-union.html.

15. Momir Samardžić, *Roads to Europe: Serbian Politics and the Railway Issue (1878–1881)* (Pisa: Pisa University Press, 2010), 59, https://www.academia.edu/2759935/Roads_to_Europe._Serbian_Politics_and_the_Railway_Issue_1878-1881.

16. Samardžić, 104.

17. Samardžić, 102.

18. Dragana Gnjatoviæ, "Foreign Long Term Government Loans of Serbia 1862–1914" (SEEMHN Papers 11, National Bank of Serbia, Belgrade, 2009).

19. Author interview, March 4, 2019.

20. Inke Piegsa-Quischotte, "Memories of the Orient Express," Travel Thru History, accessed April 1, 2019, http://www.travelthruhistory.com/html/exotic47.html.

21. Simon Calder, "Murder of the Orient Express," *Independent*, August 22, 2009, https://www.independent.co.uk/travel/news-and-advice/murder-of-the-orient-express-1775809.html.

22. Radomir Ralev, "Hungary Hopes Belgrade-Budapest Rail Project to Be Completed in 2023," *See News*, June 11, 2018, https://seenews.com/news/hungary-hopes-belgrade-budapest-rail-project-to-be-complet ed-in-2023-615874; Aleksandar Vasovic, "Belgrade-Budapest Railway Part of Chinese 'Express Lane' to Europe," Reuters, December 17, 2014, https://www.reuters.com/article/europe-china-east-idUSL6N0U11ZN20141217.

23. One estimate puts the average speed of Serbia's modern passenger trains at forty-four kilometers an hour, barely changed since the 1880s, when the first trains traveled just under forty kilometers an hour. See Federico Sicurella, "40 km an Hour: The Slow Modernization of the Serbian Railways," OBC Transeuropa, October 28, 2013, https://www.balcanicaucaso.org/eng/Areas/Serbia/40-km-an-hour.-The-slow-modernization-of-the-Serbian-railways-142933.

24. Bent Flyvbjerg, "What You Should Know about Megaprojects, and Why: An Overview," *Project Management Journal* 45, no. 2 (April–May 2014): 6–19, https://arxiv.org/ftp/arxiv/papers/1409/1409.0003.pdf.

25. Jamil Anderlini, "High-Speed China Changes Rail Landscape," *Financial Times*, March 16, 2010, https://www.ft.com/content/a04d14cc-310b-11df-b057-00144feabdco.

26. James McGregor, *China's Drive for "Indigenous Innovation": A Web of Industrial Policies* (Washington, DC: U.S. Chamber of Commerce, 2010), https://www.uschamber.com/sites/default/files/documents/files/100728chinareport_0_0.pdf.

27. DW staff, "China Masters German Train Technology, Will Cut Costs," *Deutsche Welle*, April 28, 2006, https://www.dw.com/en/china-masters-german-train-technology-will-cut-costs/a-1982476.

28. McGregor, *China's Drive for "Indigenous Innovation."*

29. Wendy Wu, "China Says Its Bullet Train Technology Was Stolen, Days after US Trade Probe Move," *South China Morning Post*, August 17, 2017, https://www.scmp.com/news/china/economy/article/2107096/china-says-its-bullet-train-technology-was-stolen-days-after-us.

30. Jean-Paul Rodrigue, "The Economics and Politics of High-Speed Rail: Lessons from Experiences," *AAG Review of Books* 4, no. 1 (2016): 17–18, DOI: 10.1080/2325548X.2016.1117342.

31. Ignacio Barrón, Javier Campos, Philippe Gagnepain, Chris Nash, Andreu Ulied, and Roger Vickerman, *Economic Analysis of High Speed Rail in Europe*, ed. Ginés de Rus (Bilbao: Fundación BBVA, 2009), https://www.fbbva.es/wp-content/uploads/2017/05/dat/inf_web_economic_analysis.pdf.

32. Baruch Feigenbaum, "High-Speed Rail in Europe and Asia: Lessons for the United States" (Policy Study 418, Reason Foundation, Los Angeles, CA, May 2013), https://reason.org/wp-content/uploads/files/high_speed_rail_lessons.pdf.

33. Nick Miller, "'Why Are They Giving Us the Money?' Behind China's Plans to 'Rescue' a Decrepit Rail Link," *Sydney Morning Herald*, June 20, 2018, https://www.smh.com.au/world/europe/why-are-they-giving-us-the-money-behind-china-s-plans-to-rescue-a-decrepit-rail-link-20180606-p4zjwk.html.

34. Mu Xuequan, "China-Europe Land-Sea Fast Transport Route Opens," *Xinhuanet*, February 7, 2017, http://www.xinhuanet.com/english/2017-02/08/c_136039012.htm.

35. Jens Bastian, *The Potential for Growth through Chinese Infrastructure Investments in Central and South-Eastern Europe along the "Balkan Silk Road"* (Athens and London: European Bank for Reconstruction and Development, July 2017), https://www.ebrd.com/documents/policy/the-balkan-silk-road.pdf.

36. Piraeus Port Authority, "Official Visit of China's Minister of Transport at the Port of Piraeus," October 16, 2018, http://www.olp.gr/en/press-releases/item/4159-official-visit-of-china-s-minister-of-transport-at-the-port-of-piraeus; Bian Jing, "China Transportation Infrastructure Three-Year Plan Released: Overall Investment around RMB 4.7 Trillion"

(Chinese), Reuters, May 11, 2016, https://cn.reuters.com/article/cn-in frastructure-plan-idCNKCS0Y302B; Helena Smith, "Xi Jinping Comes to Greeks Bearings Gifts," *Guardian*, November 11, 2019, https://www .theguardian.com/world/2019/nov/12/xi-jinping-comes-to-greeks-bear ings-gifts.

37. World Port Source, "Port of Piraeus," accessed April 1, 2019, http://www. worldportsource.com/ports/review/GRC_Port_of_Piraeus_1041.php.

38. Nektaria Stamouli, "What's Derailing Greece's Plan to Sell State Assets? Its Own Government," *Wall Street Journal*, October 3, 2016, https://www. wsj.com/articles/the-greek-government-is-both-for-and-against-its-own-privatization-plan-1475428917.

39. David Blair, "Greek PM Faces Revolt from His Own Left-Wing over Bail-Out Crisis," *Telegraph*, June 5, 2015, https://www.telegraph.co.uk/ news/worldnews/europe/greece/11652502/Greek-PM-faces-revolt-from-his-own-Left-wing-over-bail-out-crisis.html; Kerin Hope, "Greece Sells Controlling Stake in Piraeus Port," *Financial Times*, April 8, 2016, https://www.ft.com/content/895aac42-fd98-11e5-b5f5-070dca6d0a0d.

40. George Georgiopoulos, "China's COSCO Acquires 51 Pct Stake in Greece's Piraeus Port," Reuters, August 10, 2016, https://www.reuters. com/article/greece-privatisation-port/chinas-cosco-acquires-51-pct-stake-in-greeces-piraeus-port-idUSL8N1AR252.

41. Ports Europe, "Piraeus Port Reported Back to Normal after Strike Action," June 4, 2018, https://www.portseurope.com/piraeus-port-reported-back-to-normal-after-strike-action/.

42. Piraeus Port Authority S.A., "Annual Financial Report for the Year Ended December 31, 2017," February 13, 2018, https://www.worl dreginfo.com/wdoc.aspx?file=Piraeus_Port/1/13F11B98-07E2-4580-871C-F03720179186/394262_rfa_2017_en_grs470003013.pdf.

43. Simon Marks, "Greece Faces €200M Fine for Failing to Stop Chinese Fraud Network," *Politico*, January 14, 2019, https://www.politico.eu/article/ greece-faces-e200m-fine-for-failing-to-stop-chinese-fraud-network/.

44. Ilias Belos, "Cosco's Piraeus Plan Approved, in Part," *Ekathimerini*, October 13, 2019, http://www.ekathimerini.com/245471/article/ekathimerini/ business/coscos-piraeus-plan-approved-in-part.

45. Angelos Bentis, Caroline Carulas, Christ Mihalaris, and George Papoutsas, *China's Image in Greece: 2008–2018*, ed. Plamen Tonchev (Athens: Institute of International Economic Relations, October 2018), http://idos. gr/wp-content/uploads/2018/10/China-Image-in-Greece_9-10-2018.pdf.

46. GTP Editing Team, "Piraeus Port Development Plan Runs into New Hurdle," GTP Headlines, March 5, 2019, https://news.gtp.gr/2019/03/05/ piraeus-port-development-plan-runs-new-hurdle/.

47. Jonathan Hillman, "A Chinese World Order," *Washington Post*, July 23, 2018, https://www.washingtonpost.com/news/theworldpost/wp/2018/07/23/ china-world-order/?utm_term=.d780fdcbdafb.

48. Ministry of Foreign Affairs of the People's Republic of China, "The Sofia Guidelines for Cooperation between China and Central and Eastern European Countries," July 9, 2018, http://www.fmprc.gov.cn/mfa_eng/zxxx_662805/t1577455.shtml.

49. "Chinese Premier Praises EU, Says Free Trade Must Be Upheld," Associated Press, July 7, 2018, https://apnews.com/d641da055d7248e39d34ae49615c822b.

50. Thornsten Benner, Jan Gaspers, Mareike Ohlberg, Lucrezia Poggetti, and Kristin Shi-Kupfer, "Authoritarian Advance: Responding to China's Growing Political Influence in Europe," Global Public Policy Institute, February 5, 2018, https://www.gppi.net/2018/02/05/authoritarian-advance-responding-to-chinas-growing-political-influence-in-europe.

51. Asian Infrastructure Investment Bank, "Quick Facts," accessed February 2, 2020, https://www.aiib.org/en/index.html.

52. Nikki Sun, "China Development Bank Commits $250bn to Belt and Road," *Nikkei Asian Review*, January 15, 2018, https://asia.nikkei.com/Politics-Economy/Economy/China-Development-Bank-commits-250bn-to-Belt-and-Road.

53. Peel, Kynge, and Hornby, "China's Balkan Investment Pledges Stoke EU Concern."

54. Beta, "Salaries in Serbia among Lowest in Europe," N1, May 21, 2018, http://rs.n1info.com/English/NEWS/a389833/Serbian-salaries-among-lowest-in-Europe.html.

55. Holger Hansen and Michael Nienaber, "With Eye on China, Germany Tightens Foreign Investment Rules," Reuters, December 19, 2018, https://www.reuters.com/article/us-germany-security-m-a/with-eye-on-china-germany-tightens-foreign-investment-rules-idUSKBN1OI0UP.

56. Rochelle Toplensky, "EU Blocks Planned Siemens-Alstom Rail Deal in Landmark Decision," *Financial Times*, February 6, 2019, https://www.ft.com/content/6e344f6a-29fd-11e9-88a4-c32129756dd8.

57. Silvia Amaro, "EU Blocks Alston-Siemens Rail Merger Due to 'Serious Competition Concerns,'" CNBC, February 9, 2019, https://www.cnbc.com/2019/02/06/eu-blocks-plan-for-alstom-siemens-rail-merger.html.

58. Tara Patel and Aoife White, "Siemens-Alstom's Expected EU Veto Unleashes Political Storm," *Bloomberg*, February 4, 2019, https://www.bloomberg.com/news/articles/2019-02-04/european-champions-may-yet-rise-from-the-siemens-alstom-rubble.

59. BDI, "Partner and Systemic Competitor: How Do We Deal with China's State-Controlled Economy" (policy paper, BDI, Berlin, January 2019), https://english.bdi.eu/media/publications/#/publication/news/china-partner-and-systemic-competitor.

60. This estimate includes only BRI-specific documents. Chinese state media cite higher estimates, which often count MOUs on related topics, such as infrastructure, transport, and customs cooperation. Policy Department

for Structural and Cohesion Policies, *Research for TRAN Committee: The New Silk Route—Opportunities and Challenges for EU Transport* (Brussels: European Parliament, 2018), http://www.europarl.europa.eu/RegData/etudes/STUD/2018/585907/IPOL_STU(2018)585907_EN.pdf.

61. Shi Jiangtao, "China, France Sign US$45 Billion of Deals including Airbus Order," *South China Morning Post*, March 26, 2019, https://www.scmp.com/news/china/diplomacy/article/3003384/china-france-sign-us45-billion-deals-including-airbus-order; Giselda Vagnoni and Francesca Landini, "Italy Signs Deals Worth 2.5 Billion Euros with China," Reuters, March 23, 2019, https://www.reuters.com/article/us-italy-china-deals-factbox/italy-signs-deals-worth-2-5-billion-euros-with-china-idUSKCN1R40KN.

62. Andrew Small, "Why Europe Is Getting Tough on China: And What It Means for Washington," *Foreign Affairs*, April 3, 2019, https://www.foreignaffairs.com/articles/china/2019-04-03/why-europe-getting-tough-china.

63. European Commission, *Joint Communication to the European Parliament and the Council* (Brussels: European Commission, 2016), http://eeas.europa.eu/archives/docs/china/docs/joint_communication_to_the_european_parliament_and_the_council_-_elements_for_a_new_eu_strategy_on_china.pdf.

64. European Commission, *EU-China—A Strategic Outlook* (Brussels: European Commission, 2019), https://ec.europa.eu/commission/sites/beta-political/files/communication-eu-china-a-strategic-outlook.pdf.

65. Valerie Hopkins, "Brussels Says EU Has 'Underestimated' China's Reach in Balkans," *Financial Times*, March 5, 2019, https://www.ft.com/content/4ba18efa-377b-11e9-b72b-2c7f526ca5do.

66. Jacob Poushter and Christine Huang, "Climate Change Still Seen as the Top Global Threat, but Cyberattacks a Rising Concern," Pew Research Center, February 10, 2019, https://www.pewresearch.org/global/2019/02/10/climate-change-still-seen-as-the-top-global-threat-but-cyberattacks-a-rising-concern/.

67. Noah Barkin, "The U.S. Is Losing Europe in Its Battle with China," *Atlantic*, June 4, 2019, https://www.theatlantic.com/international/archive/2019/06/united-states-needs-europe-against-china/590887/.

68. Halford John Mackinder, "The Geographical Pivot of History," *Geographical Journal* 23, no. 4 (April 1904), https://www.iwp.edu/docLib/20131016_MackinderTheGeographicalJournal.pdf.

Chapter Six. The Weak Are Powerful: Southeast Asia

1. Anna Coren, Ellana Lee, Jane Sit, and James Griffiths, "Malaysian PM Mahathir: 'Most of the Top Echelons in the Government Are Corrupt,'" CNN, July 26, 2018, https://www.cnn.com/2018/07/25/asia/malaysia-mahathir-mohamad-interview-intl/index.html.

2. Russell Fifield, "Southeast Asia as a Regional Concept," *Asian Journal of Social Science* 11, no. 1 (1983): 1–14.
3. International Monetary Fund, "World Economic Outlook Database," October 2018, https://www.imf.org/external/pubs/ft/weo/2018/02/weodata/index.aspx.
4. International Monetary Fund; US-ASEAN Business Council, "Growth Projections," accessed January 7, 2019, https://www.usasean.org/why-asean/growth.
5. Krishnadev Calamur, "High Traffic, High Risk in the Strait of Malacca," *Atlantic*, August 21, 2017, https://www.theatlantic.com/international/archive/2017/08/strait-of-malacca-uss-john-mccain/537471/.
6. Owen Lattimore, "Yunnan, Pivot of Southeast Asia," *Foreign Affairs* 21, no. 3 (1943): 476–493.
7. John Pomfret, "U.S. Takes a Tougher Tone with China," *Washington Post*, July 30, 2010, http://www.washingtonpost.com/wp-dyn/content/article/2010/07/29/AR2010072906416.html.
8. Eleanor Ross, "How and Why China Is Building Islands in the South China Sea," *Newsweek*, March 29, 2017, https://www.newsweek.com/china-south-china-sea-islands-build-military-territory-expand-575161.
9. Mission of Japan to the Association of Southeast Asian Nations, "Japan's Cooperation on ASEAN 2025 (Connectivity)," May 2016, https://www.asean.emb-japan.go.jp/asean2025/jpasean-eco3.html.
10. Yukio Tajima, "Abe Softens Tone on Indo-Pacific to Coax China's ASEAN Friends," *Nikkei Asian Review*, November 13, 2018, https://asia.nikkei.com/Politics/International-Relations/Abe-softens-tone-on-Indo-Pacific-to-coax-China-s-ASEAN-friends.
11. Matthew Goodman and Jonathan Hillman, "Is China Winning the Scramble for Eurasia?," *National Interest*, August 21, 2017, https://nationalinterest.org/feature/the-new-cold-war-was-never-inevitable-21994.
12. "Mahathir: A Winner in the War of Words?," CNN, October 31, 2003, http://www.cnn.com/2003/WORLD/asiapcf/southeast/10/29/mahathir.west/index.html.
13. Mahathir bin Mohamad, *A Doctor in the House: The Memoirs of Tun Dr. Mahathir Mohamad* (Petaling Jaya, Malaysia: MPH, 2011), 336–337.
14. Karminder Dhillon Singh, *Malaysian Foreign Policy in the Mahathir Era, 1981–2003* (Singapore: National University of Singapore Press, 2009), 59–60.
15. Mahathir, *Doctor in the House*, 160–161.
16. Japan Ministry of Foreign Affairs, *Japan's Official Development Assistance White Paper 2014* (Tokyo: Ministry of Foreign Affairs, 2014), 3, https://www.mofa.go.jp/files/000119315.pdf.
17. Robert M. Orr Jr., "The Rising Sun: Japan's Foreign Aid to ASEAN, the Pacific Basin and the Republic of Korea," *Journal of International Affairs* 41, no. 1 (Summer–Fall 1987): 39–62.

18. Robert M. Orr Jr., *The Emergence of Japan's Foreign Aid Power* (New York: Columbia University Press, 1990).

19. Richard Ellings and Sheldon Simon, *Southeast Asian Security in the New Millennium* (London: Routledge, 2016), 131.

20. Tadao Chino, quoted in Edward Lincoln, *Japan's New Global Role* (Washington, DC: Brookings Institution, 1993), 124.

21. Edith Terry, "How Asia Got Rich: World Bank vs. Japanese Industrial Policy" (JPRI Working Paper 10, Japan Policy Research Institute, Oakland, CA, June 1995), http://www.jpri.org/publications/workingpapers/wp10.html.

22. Walter Hatch and Kozo Yamamura, *Asia in Japan's Embrace: Building a Regional Production Alliance*, vol. 3 (Cambridge: Cambridge University Press, 1996), 110.

23. Hatch and Yamamura.

24. Hatch and Yamamura, 126.

25. David Arase, *Buying Power: The Political Economy of Japan's Foreign Aid* (Boulder, CO: Lynne Rienner, 1995), 109–110.

26. James Brown and Jeff Kingston, eds., *Japan's Foreign Relations in Asia* (New York: Routledge, 2018).

27. Mark Taylor, "Dominance through Technology: Is Japan Creating a Yen Bloc in Southeast Asia?," *Foreign Affairs* 74, no. 6 (1995): 14–20, https://www.jstor.org/stable/20047376?seq=1#metadata_info_tab_contents.

28. Mahathir Mohamad, "The First Malaysia-Japan Colloquium," Speech Collection Archives of Chief Executives, Prime Minister's Office of Malaysia, August 27, 1984, http://www.pmo.gov.my/ucapan/?m=p&p=mahathir&id=1128.

29. Mahathir.

30. U.S. Congress, House, *A Concurrent Resolution Relating to Predatory Tied Aid Credit*, H. Con. Res. 316, introduced by Rep. Stephen L. Neal (D-NC-5), April 10, 1986, https://www.govinfo.gov/content/pkg/STATUTE-100/pdf/STATUTE-100-Pg4347.pdf.

31. Bernard Wysocki Jr., "Guiding Hand: In Asia, the Japanese Hope to 'Coordinate' What Nations Produce," *Wall Street Journal*, Eastern Edition, August 20, 1990, A1.

32. As cited in Terry, "How Asia Got Rich."

33. Shafiqul Islam, "Foreign Aid and Burdensharing: Is Japan Free Riding to a Coprosperity Sphere in Pacific Asia?," National Bureau of Economic Research, January 1993, https://www.nber.org/chapters/c7842.pdf.

34. Wysocki, "Guiding Hand."

35. Hatch and Yamamura, *Asia in Japan's Embrace*, 203.

36. Orr, *Emergence of Japan's Foreign Aid Power*, 138.

37. Robert M. Orr Jr., "Collaboration or Conflict? Foreign Aid and U.S.-Japan Relations," *Pacific Affairs* 62, no. 4 (1989): 481, https://www.jstor.org/stable/2759671.

38. Hatch and Yamamura, *Asia in Japan's Embrace*, 125.

39. William Grimes, "The Belt & Road Initiative as Power Resource: Lessons from Japan," Asan Forum, April 15, 2016, http://www.theasanforum. org/the-belt-road-initiative-as-power-resource-lessons-from-japan/.
40. Orr, *Emergence of Japan's Foreign Aid Power*, 132.
41. Zhigang Wu, "Research on Japan's ODA to China and Its Contribution to China's Development" (presentation paper, Kyoto Sangyo University, Kyoto, March 21, 2008), https://www.cc.kyoto-su.ac.jp/project/orc/econ public/china/documents/WUDP28.pdf.
42. Howard French, "China's Premier, on Japan Visit, Wears a Friendly Face," *New York Times*, October 16, 2000, https://www.nytimes.com/2000/10/16/ world/china-s-premier-on-japan-visit-wears-a-friendly-face.html.
43. Bernard Gwertzman, "Malaysia, Seeing a Threat, Urges U.S. to Stop Building Up Power of China," *New York Times*, July 10, 1984, https:// www.nytimes.com/1984/07/10/world/malaysia-seeing-a-threat-urges-us- to-stop-building-up-power-of-china.html.
44. Zuraidah Ibrahim, "Nothing to Fear from China, Says Malaysia's Mahathir Mohamad, but Lopsided Deals Must End," *South China Morning Post*, June 19, 2018, https://www.scmp.com/week-asia/geopolitics/article/2151451/ nothing-fear-china-says-malaysias-mahathir-mohamad-lopsided.
45. Deborah Brautigam, *The Dragon's Gift: The Real Story of China in Africa* (Oxford: Oxford University Press, 2011), 47, 50–51.
46. Terry, "How Asia Got Rich."
47. Eugene Moosa, "Hosokawa to Visit China Next Month," Reuters, February 24, 1994, accessed February 2, 2020, through Factiva, document ID: lba0000020011119dq2002u3u.
48. Export-Import Bank of the United States, *Report to the U.S. Congress on the Export Credit Competition and the Export-Import Bank of the United States* (Washington, DC: Export-Import Bank of the United States, 2007), https://www.exim.gov/sites/default/files/newsreleases/2006Compe titivenessReport-1.pdf. China has become a major provider of technical assistance as well, training nearly fifty thousand people from developing countries from 2012 to 2014, by its own count. One of its leadership academies offers ten-day programs for ASEAN officials. See Xinhua, "China's Foreign Aid," Reliefweb, July 10, 2014, https://reliefweb.int/re port/china/chinas-foreign-aid; He Huifeng, "In a Remote Corner of China, Beijing Is Trying to Export Its Model by Training Foreign Officials the Chinese Way," *South China Morning Post*, July 14, 2018, https:// www.scmp.com/news/china/economy/article/2155203/remote-corner- china-beijing-trying-export-its-model-training.
49. "SE-Asia Railway Idea Revived," BBC, November 4, 2001, http://news. bbc.co.uk/2/hi/asia-pacific/1637032.stm.
50. Working Group on the Trans-Asian Railway Network, *Building the Missing Links in the Trans-Asian Railway Network* (Busan, South Korea: United Nations, Economic and Social Commission for Asia and the Pacific,

2017), https://www.unescap.org/sites/default/files/e-E_ESCAP_TARN_WG(5)4_E.pdf.

51. United Nations Economic and Social Commission for Asia and the Pacific, *Trans-Asian Railway Route Requirements: Development of the Trans-Asian Railway in the Indo-China and ASEAN Subregion* (New York: United Nations, 1996), https://www.unescap.org/asean/publications/Trans-Asian_V3.pdf.

52. Francis Chan and Wahyudi Soeriaatmadja, "Indonesia's National Rail Network Aims for More Growth, Less Inequality," *Straits Times*, September 4, 2017, https://www.straitstimes.com/asia/se-asia/aim-more-growth-less-inequality.

53. Clark has produced a second version of the Southeast Asia railway map that distinguishes between existing and proposed lines.

54. Working Group on the Trans-Asian Railway Network, *Building the Missing Links*.

55. Shawn Crispin, "Misaligned Rails Keep SEAsia Delinked from China," *Asia Times*, May 4, 2018, https://cms.ati.ms/2018/05/misaligned-rails-keep-seasia-delinked-from-china/.

56. Mahathir Mohamad, "The Occasion of the Official Visit to the Republic of Kazakhstan," Speech Collection Archives of Chief Executives, Prime Minister's Office of Malaysia, July 18, 1996, http://www.pmo.gov.my/ucapan/index.php?qt=railway&m=p&p=all&id=1304.

57. Mahathir.

58. "Study: China Section of Pan-Asian Railway Feasible," China.org.cn, June 6, 2006, http://www.china.org.cn/english/2006/Jun/170560.htm.

59. Ministry of Foreign Affairs of the People's Republic of China, "Work Together to Open a New Chapter in China-ASEAN Relations," January 14, 2007, https://www.fmprc.gov.cn/mfa_eng/wjdt_665385/zyjh_665391/t290185.shtml; "Wen: China to Speed Up Pan-Asian Rail Link," *China Daily*, January 15, 2007, http://www.chinadaily.com.cn/bizchina/2007-01/15/content_783295.htm.

60. Ministry of Foreign Affairs, "Remarks by Ambassador Xu Bu at Seminar on the 25th Anniversary of China-ASEAN," June 5, 2016, https://www.fmprc.gov.cn/mfa_eng/wjb_663304/zwjg_665342/zwbd_665378/t1369567.shtml.

61. James Reilly, "A Norm-Taker or a Norm-Maker? Chinese Aid in Southeast Asia," *Journal of Contemporary China* 21, no. 73 (2012): 89.

62. Joshua Lipes, "High-Speed Railway Delay," Radio Free Asia, April 26, 2011, https://www.rfa.org/english/news/laos/railway-04262011171130.html.

63. "China's Fast Track to Influence: Building a Railway in Laos," Radio Free Asia Laos Service, March 15, 2018, https://www.rfa.org/english/news/special/laoschinarailway/.

64. Patpon Sabpaitoon, "The Great Rail Dilemma," *Bangkok Post*, July 22, 2018, https://www.bangkokpost.com/news/special-reports/1507722/the-great-rail-dilemma.

65. New China TV, "Life-Changing! China-Laos Railway Brings New Hope to Lao Single Mum," YouTube, August 30, 2018, https://www.youtube.com/watch?v=AOvX7ozsgE8.

66. Will Doig, *High-Speed Empire: Chinese Expansion and the Future of Southeast Asia* (New York: Columbia University Press, 2018), 37.

67. Agatha Kratz, "Exporting 'Harmony' and 'Rejuvenation': Explaining the Uneven Track Record of China's Global High-Speed Rail Expansion" (PhD diss., King's College London, 2019), 236.

68. Murray Hiebert, *Under Beijing's Shadow: Southeast Asia's China Challenge*, (Lanham, MD: Rowman and Littlefield, 2020).

69. World Bank, *Indonesia Economic Quarterly: Closing the Gap* (Jakarta: World Bank, October 2017), http://pubdocs.worldbank.org/en/677741506935868706/IEQ-Oct-2017-ENG.pdf.

70. Kratz, "Exporting 'Harmony' and 'Rejuvenation,' " 171; Leo Jegho, "China to Invest US$50 Billion in Indonesia's Infrastructure Projects," Global Indonesian Voices, April 27, 2015, http://web.archive.org/web/20160422234034/http://www.globalindonesianvoices.com/20456/china-to-invest-us50-billion-in-indonesias-infrastructure-projects/.

71. Kratz, "Exporting 'Harmony' and 'Rejuvenation.' "

72. Hong Zhao, "Chinese and Japanese Infrastructure Investment in Southeast Asia: From Rivalry to Cooperation?" (IDE Discussion Paper, Institute of Developing Economies, Japan External Trade Organization [IDE-JETRO], Chiba City, Japan, 2018), http://hdl.handle.net/2344/00050160; Kratz, "Exporting 'Harmony' and 'Rejuvenation,' " 155.

73. Shotaro Tani, "Widodo Slammed for Infrastructure Policy in Second TV Debate," *Nikkei Asian Review*, February 18, 2019, https://asia.nikkei.com/Politics/Widodo-slammed-for-infrastructure-policy-in-second-TV-debate.

74. Nur Asyiqin Mohamad Salleh, "Jakarta-Bandung High-Speed Rail Project Back on Track, Says Indonesia's Investment Chief," *Straits Times*, May 8, 2019, https://www.straitstimes.com/asia/se-asia/jakarta-bandung-high-speed-rail-project-back-on-track-says-indonesias-investment-chief.

75. Kratz, "Exporting 'Harmony' and 'Rejuvenation,' " 235–236.

76. Shotaro Tani, "Indonesia Minister: Japan, China Rivalry Good for Asian Infrastructure," *Nikkei Asian Review*, May 5, 2017, https://asia.nikkei.com/Economy/Indonesia-minister-Japan-China-rivalry-good-for-Asian-infrastructure.

77. Doig, *High-Speed Empire*.

78. Chester Tay, "Mustapa: Malaysia-China RM144 Bil Deal Involves Three Components," *Edge Markets*, November 10, 2016, http://www.theedgemarkets.com/article/mustapa-malaysia-china-rm144-bil-deal-involves-three-components.

79. Najib Razak, "Fruits Harvested from Seeds of Trust," *China Daily*, November 2, 2016, http://www.chinadaily.com.cn/opinion/2016-11/02/content_27245852.htm.

80. Tom Wright and Bradley Hope, *Billion Dollar Whale: The Man Who Fooled Wall Street, Hollywood, and the World* (New York: Hachette Books, 2018).

81. Tom Wright and Simon Clark, "Investigators Believe Money Flowed to Malaysian Leader Najib's Accounts amid 1MDB Probe," *Wall Street Journal*, July 2, 2015, https://www.wsj.com/articles/SB10130211123459277486 9404581083700187014570. For a timeline and additional coverage, see "Malaysia's 1MDB Decoded," *Wall Street Journal*, http://graphics.wsj.com/1mdb-decoded/.

82. Sarawak Report, "How Najib Nearly Sold Out Malaysia to China," October 26, 2018, http://www.sarawakreport.org/2018/10/how-najib-nearly-sold-out-malaysia-to-china/; Rozanna Latiff and Joseph Sipalan, "Malaysia Had Plan to Use Chinese Money to Bail Out 1MDB Court Hears," Reuters, September 4, 2019, https://www.reuters.com/article/us-malaysia-politics-najib/malaysia-had-plan-to-use-chinese-money-to-bail-out-1mdb-court-hears-idUSKCN1VP1DS.

83. Bandar Malaysia, "Key Features," accessed January 7, 2019, https://web.archive.org/web/20160725121420/http://www.bandarmalaysia.my:80/key-features.

84. "Bandar Malaysia in Turmoil as Government Cancels Development Deal," *Global Construction Review*, May 10, 2017, http://www.globalconstructionreview.com/news/bandar-malaysia-turm7oil-gover7nment-canc7els/.

85. Tony Pua, "Tony Pua: Who Authorised Termination of Bandar Malaysia Deal?," *Edge Markets*, May 11, 2017, http://www.theedgemarkets.com/article/tony-pua-who-authorised-termination-bandar-malaysia-deal.

86. Najib Razak, "Why Malaysia Supports China's Belt and Road," *South China Morning Post*, May 12, 2017, updated July 7, 2017, https://www.scmp.com/comment/insight-opinion/article/2094094/why-malaysia-supports-chinas-belt-and-road.

87. Mahathir bin Mohamad, "FDI," *Chedet* (blog), January 6, 2017, http://chedet.cc/?p=2394.

88. Stefania Palma, "Malaysia Suspends $22bn China-Backed Projects," *Financial Times*, July 4, 2018, https://www.ft.com/content/409942a4-7f80-11e8-bc55-50daf11b720d.

89. Mahathir, *Doctor in the House*, 756–757.

90. Yiswaree Palansamy, "Dr M: We Support China's Belt and Road Initiative, but . . . ," *Malay Mail*, May 10, 2018, https://www.malaymail.com/news/malaysia/2018/05/10/dr-m-we-support-chinas-belt-and-road-initiative-but/1629327.

91. Prime Minister's Office of Malaysia, "Press Statement by YAB Prime Minister Tun Dr. Mahathir Bin Mohamad on East Coast Rail Link (ECRL) Project," April 15, 2019, https://www.pmo.gov.my/2019/04/press-statement-by-yab-prime-minister-tun-dr-mahathir-bin-mohamad-on-east-coast-rail-link-ecrl-project/.

92. Joseph Sipalan, "Malaysia to Revive Multi-Billion Dollar Project Linked to China," Reuters, April 19, 2019, https://www.reuters.com/article/us-malaysia-china-project/malaysia-to-revive-multi-billion-dollar-project-linked-to-china-idUSKCN1RV0K0.

93. Prime Minister's Office of Malaysia, "Belt and Road Initiative Not China's Plan to Dominate—PM," April 28, 2019, https://www.pmo.gov.my/2019/04/belt-and-road-initiative-not-chinas-plan-to-dominate-pm/.

94. Bent Flyvbjerg, "What You Should Know about Megaprojects, and Why: An Overview," *Project Management Journal* 45, no. 2 (April–May 2014): 6–19, https://arxiv.org/ftp/arxiv/papers/1409/1409.0003.pdf.

95. Prime Minister's Office of Malaysia, "Speech at the High-Level Meeting of Belt and Road Forum for International Cooperation," April 26, 2019, https://www.pmo.gov.my/2019/04/speech-at-the-high-level-meeting-of-belt-and-road-forum-for-international-cooperation/.

Chapter Seven. The Black Hole: Pakistan

1. For an authoritative account of China-Pakistan relations in the years leading up to the BRI's formal announcement, see Andrew Small, *The China-Pakistan Axis: Asia's New Geopolitics* (Oxford: Oxford University Press, 2015).

2. Jeremy Page and Saeed Shah, "China Readies $46 Billion for Pakistan Trade Route," *Wall Street Journal*, April 16, 2015, https://www.wsj.com/articles/china-to-unveil-billions-of-dollars-in-pakistan-investment-1429214705.

3. USAID, "Foreign Aid Explorer: Data (Country Summary)," accessed June 26, 2019, https://explorer.usaid.gov/data.

4. Prime Minister's Office, Islamic Republic of Pakistan, "Visit of President Xi to Start a New Chapter in Pak-China Friendship: PM," press release, April 20, 2015, http://www.pmo.gov.pk/press_release_detailes.php?pr_id=917.

5. China-Pakistan Economic Corridor, "Official Message," accessed April 19, 2019, http://cpec.gov.pk/messages/1.

6. Prime Minister's Office, Islamic Republic of Pakistan, "Prime Minister Imran Khan Has Said That the Government Accords Top Priority to the China-Pakistan Economic Corridor (CPEC) Project," press release, April 11, 2019, http://pmo.gov.pk/press_release_detailes.php?pr_id=2791.

7. Christine Lagarde, "Pakistan and Emerging Market in the World Economy" (speech, Islamabad, Pakistan, October 24, 2016), International Monetary Fund, October 24, 2016, https://www.imf.org/en/News/Articles/2016/10/24/SP102416-Pakistan-Emerging-Markets-in-the-World-Economy.

8. World Bank, "CPEC Offers Enormous Potential to Boost Pakistan Economy, Report Says," press release, March 22, 2018, https://www.worldbank.org/en/news/press-release/2018/03/22/cpec-offers-enormous-potential-boost-pakistan-economy.

9. Daniel Markey, "Why the China-Pakistan Economic Corridor Will Worsen Tensions in South Asia," War on the Rocks, September 28, 2017, https://warontherocks.com/2017/09/why-the-china-pakistan-economic-corridor-will-worsen-tensions-in-south-asia/.

10. Khurram Husain, "Exclusive: CPEC Master Plan Revealed," *Dawn*, June 21, 2017, https://www.dawn.com/news/1333101.

11. Robert D. Kaplan, *The Return of Marco Polo's World: War, Strategy, and American Interests in the Twenty-First Century* (New York: Random House, 2019), 28.

12. Pew Research Center, "Opinion of China," Global Indicators Database, accessed February 2, 2020, https://www.pewresearch.org/global/database/indicator/24/country/pk. See also R. J. Reinhard and Zacc Ritter, "China's Leadership Gains Global Admirers," Gallup, March 4, 2019, https://news.gallup.com/poll/247196/china-leadership-gains-global-admirers.aspx.

13. Gustav F. Papanek, *Pakistan's Development: Social Goals and Private Incentives* (Cambridge, MA: Harvard University Press, 1967), 1.

14. Harry S. Truman, "Inaugural Address," January 20, 1949, Avalon Project, accessed February 4, 2020, https://avalon.law.yale.edu/20th_century/truman.asp.

15. Mussarat Jabeen and Muhammad Saleem Mazhar, "Security Game: SEATO and CENTO as Instrument of Economic and Military Assistance to Encircle Pakistan," *Pakistan Economic and Social Review* 49, no. 1 (Summer 2011): 109–132, https://www.jstor.org/stable/41762426.

16. "East-West Teamwork Goes on Trial in Pakistan," *Businessweek*, June 30, 1956, 99.

17. John O. Bell, "Chief of U.S. Operations Mission, ICA 29 Karachi (1955–1957)," in *Pakistan: Country Reader* (Arlington, VA: Association for Diplomatic Studies, 2018), 29, https://adst.org/wp-content/uploads/2018/02/Pakistan.pdf.

18. Paul Beckett to David Bell, November 23–25, 1960, Ford Foundation Archives, Rockefeller Archive Center, Sleepy Hollow, NY.

19. Adam Curle, *Planning for Education in Pakistan* (Cambridge, MA: Harvard University Press, 1966), 1.

20. David Bell, "Interview with David E. Bell for the Ford Foundation Oral History Project," interview by Charles T. Morrissey and Ronald J. Grele, New York, November 16, 1972, Ford Foundation Archives, Rockefeller Archive Center, Sleepy Hollow, NY.

21. Albert Waterson, *Planning in Pakistan* (Baltimore: Johns Hopkins University Press, 1963), 114, http://documents.worldbank.org/curated/en/766851468758721256/pdf/multiopage.pdf.

22. David E. Bell, "Allocating Development Resources: Some Observations Based on Pakistan Experience," *Public Policy* 9 (1959): 93–94.

23. Gustav Papanek, interview by author, January 26, 2019.

24. Papanek.

25. George Rosen, *Western Economists and Eastern Societies: Agents of Change in South Asia* (Baltimore: Johns Hopkins University Press, 1985), 63.

26. Rosen, 136.

27. Forrest F. Hill, Office files, Box 1, Folder 2, International division, Ford Foundation Archives.

28. Director of Central Intelligence, "Probable Developments in Pakistan," National Intelligence Estimate, no. 52-56, November 13, 1956, https://www.cia.gov/library/readingroom/docs/CIA-RDP79R01012A007900030001-3.pdf.

29. Hill, Office files.

30. J. Bell, "Chief of U.S. Operations Mission," 30–31.

31. "Letter from the Ambassador in Pakistan (Langley) to the Assistant Secretary of State for Near Eastern, South Asian, and African Affairs (Rountree)," December 27, 1957, Office of the Historian, Department of State, accessed April 19, 2019, https://history.state.gov/historicaldocuments/frus1955-57v08/d224.

32. Dennis Kux, "Economic Office Karachi (1957–1960); Political Office Islamabad (1969–1971)," in *Pakistan: Country Reader*, 55.

33. "Excerpts from Ayub's Address to Congress Warning against Foreign-Aid Cut," *New York Times*, July 13, 1961, https://www.nytimes.com/1961/07/13/archives/excerpts-from-ayubs-address-to-congress-warning-against-foreignaid.html.

34. Azeem Ibrahim, *U.S. Aid to Pakistan—U.S. Taxpayers Have Funded Pakistani Corruption* (Cambridge, MA: Belfer Center for Science and International Affairs, 2009), https://www.belfercenter.org/sites/default/files/legacy/files/Final_DP_2009_06_08092009.pdf.

35. World Bank, "Pakistan, GDP (Current US $)," World Bank Open Data, accessed April 19, 2019, https://data.worldbank.org/indicator/NY.GDP.MKTP.CD?locations=PK.

36. Papanek, *Pakistan's Development*, 87.

37. J. Bell, "Chief of U.S. Operations Mission," 30–31.

38. Office of the Historian, Department of State, "The India-Pakistan War of 1965," Office of the Historian, Department of State, accessed April 19, 2019, https://history.state.gov/milestones/1961-1968/india-pakistan-war.

39. Ghlulam Ali, *China-Pakistan Relations: A Historical Analysis* (Oxford: Oxford University Press, 2016), 55.

40. Mohammad Ayub Khan, *Friends Not Masters: A Political Autobiography* (Karachi: Oxford University Press, 1967), 158–159.

41. John F. Copper, *China's Foreign Aid and Investment Diplomacy*, vol. 2 (New York: Palgrave Macmillan, 2015), 202.

42. Muhammad Mumtaz Khalid, *History of the Karakoram Highway*, 2 vols. (Rawalpindi, Pakistan: Hamza Pervez, 2006–2009), 2:2.

43. Khalid, 2:5.

44. Khalid, 2:22.

45. Barry Naughton, "The Third Front: Defence Industrialisation in the Chinese Interior," *China Quarterly* 115 (September 1988): 351–386, http://journals.cambridge.org/action/displayAbstract?fromPage=online&aid=3546864.

46. Khalid, *History of the Karakoram Highway*, 2:14.

47. Khalid, 1:320.

48. Khalid, 2:16, 23.

49. Khalid, 2:12.

50. Khalid, 2:42.

51. Khalid, 2:22.

52. Khalid, 2:172.

53. "Keng Piao Visits Pakistan and Sri Lanka," *Peking Review*, July 7, 1978, 3, http://massline.org/PekingReview/PR1978/PR1978-27.pdf.

54. "Documents March–August 1978," *Pakistan Horizon* 31, nos. 2–3 (1978): 232–274, https://www.jstor.org/stable/41393590.

55. Tim Craig, "Pakistan's Route to China Sees Ferrymen's Livelihoods Dry Up," *Guardian*, October 12, 2015, https://www.theguardian.com/world/2015/oct/12/landslide-closed-road-ferry-pakistan-china.

56. "Nawaz Inaugurates Rs144bn Havelian-Thakot Motorway in Mansehra," *Dawn*, April 28, 2016, https://www.dawn.com/news/1255003.

57. Office of the Historian, U.S. Department of State, "Memorandum of Conversation, Washington, September 18, 1973, 11 a.m.–12:45 p.m.," September 18, 1973, https://history.state.gov/historicaldocuments/frus1969-76ve08/d147.

58. U.S. Department of State, telegram from US Embassy Islamabad to Secretary of State, January 11, 1974, Richard Nixon Presidential Archives, Yorba Linda, CA.

59. Office of the Historian, U.S. Department of State, "Memorandum of Conversation, Washington, September 19, 1973, 10–11:05 a.m.," September 19, 1973, https://history.state.gov/historicaldocuments/frus1969-76ve08/d148.

60. Henry Kissinger, memorandum for the president, "Your Second Meeting with Prime Minister Bhutto, Wednesday, September 19, 10:00 a.m., 1973," September 19, 1973, Nixon Presidential Archives.

61. Kissinger.

62. See, for example, Daniel S. Markey, *No Exit from Pakistan: America's Tortured Relationship with Islamabad* (Cambridge: Cambridge University Press, 2013); Dennis Kux, *The United States and Pakistan, 1947–2000: Disenchanted Allies* (Baltimore: Johns Hopkins University Press, 2001); and Husain Haqqani, *Magnificent Delusions: Pakistan, the United States, and an Epic History of Misunderstanding* (New York: PublicAffairs, 2013).

63. Haqqani, *Magnificent Delusions*, 6.

64. National Commission on Terrorist Attacks upon the United States, *The 9/11 Commission Report* (Washington, DC: Government Printing Office, 2004), https://www.9-11commission.gov/report/911Report.pdf.

65. U.S. Agency for International Development, Department of State, and Department of Defense, "Quarterly Progress and Oversight Report on the Civilian Assistance Program in Pakistan," Reliefweb, December 31, 2010, https://reliefweb.int/sites/reliefweb.int/files/resources/CB0B64 A77D433E0485257833006BA5C2-Full_Report.pdf.

66. U.S. House of Representatives, "Pakistan Assistance Strategy Report," December 14, 2009, https://propublica.s3.amazonaws.com/assets/pakistan_contracts/121409_Pakistan_assistance_strategy%20reportFINAL. pdf?_ga=2.157913530.1071857353.1546874721-1561684278.1546874721/.

67. U.S. House of Representatives, 2.

68. Starr even shaped the "Silk Road Strategy Act," congressional legislation sponsored by Senator Sam Brownback of Kansas in 1999 and 2006 that aimed to target assistance to support the economic and political independence of Central Asia and South Caucasus countries. U.S. Congress, "Silk Road Strategy Act of 2006," 109th Congress, 2005–2006, https://www.congress.gov/bill/109th-congress/senate-bill/2749/all-info; see also S. Frederick Starr and Andrew C. Kuchins, *The Key to Success in Afghanistan: A Modern Silk Road Strategy* (Washington, DC: Central Asia–Caucasus Institute and Silk Road Studies Program, 2010), https://www.silkroadstudies.org/resources/pdf/SilkRoadPapers/2010_05_SRP_StarrKuchins_Success-Afghanistan.pdf.

69. Hillary Rodham Clinton, "Remarks on India and the United States: A Vision for the 21st Century" (speech, Chennai, India, July 20, 2011), U.S. Department of State, July 20, 2011, https://2009-2017.state.gov/secretary/20092013clinton/rm/2011/07/168840.htm.

70. "The Great Endgame," *Economist*, July 22, 2010, https://www.economist.com/asia/2010/07/22/the-great-endgame.

71. U.S. Department of State, "U.S. Support for the New Silk Road," accessed February 4, 2020, https://2009-2017.state.gov/p/sca/ci/af/newsilkroad/index.htm.

72. Hillary Rodham Clinton, "Remarks at the New Silk Road Ministerial" (speech, New York City, NY, September 11, 2011), U.S. Department of State, September 11, 2011, https://2009-2017.state.gov/secretary/20092013clinton/rm/2011/09/173807.htm.

73. USAID, "U.S. Foreign Aid by Country: Pakistan," accessed February 2, 2020, https://explorer.usaid.gov/cd/PAK?measure=Obligations&fiscal_year=2017&implementing_agency_id=1.

74. Barack Obama, "Remarks by President Obama in Address to the People of India," New Delhi, India, January 27, 2015, https://obamawhitehouse.archives.gov/the-press-office/2015/01/27/remarks-president-obama-address-people-india.

75. Nancy Birdsall, Wren Elhai, and Molly Kinder, *Beyond Bullets and Bombs: Fixing the U.S. Approach to Development in Pakistan* (Washington, DC: Center for Global Development, June 2011), https://www.cgdev.org/sites/default/files/1425136_file_CGD_Pakistan_FINAL_web.pdf.

76. Anum Pasha, "Unmasking USAID Pakistan's Elite Stakeholder Discourses: Towards an Evaluation of the Agency's Development Interventions" (Media@LSE MSc Dissertation Series, London School of Economics, 2017), http://www.lse.ac.uk/media-and-communications/assets/documents/research/msc-dissertations/2016/Dissertation-Anum-Pasha.pdf.

77. Office of Inspector General, USAID, "Competing Priorities Have Complicated USAID/Pakistan's Efforts to Achieve Long-Term Development under EPPA," September 8, 2016, https://oig.usaid.gov/sites/default/files/2018-06/g-391-16-003-p_0.pdf.

78. Office of Inspector General.

79. Office of Inspector General.

80. In a separate study, researchers at the University of Oxford, after considering the likelihood of delays and cost overruns, concluded that the project is "a non-starter." "This is without even discussing potential effects of inflation and interest rates, potential social and environmental costs, and opportunity cost Pakistan could earn by committing such vast amount of capital to more prudent investments," they cautioned. Atif Ansar, Bent Flyvbjerg, Alexander Budzier, and Daniel Lunn, "Should We Build More Large Dams? The Actual Costs of Hydropower Megaproject Development," *Energy Policy*, March 2014, 13, https://papers.ssrn.com/sol3/papers.cfm?abstract_id=2406852.

81. AidData, William and Mary College, "China's Global Development Footprint," accessed February 4, 2020, https://www.aiddata.org/china-official-finance.

82. Irfan Haider and Mateen Haider, "Economic Corridor in Focus as Pakistan, China Sign 51 MOUs," *Dawn*, April 20, 2015, https://www.dawn.com/news/1177109.

83. Nadia Naviwala, "Pakistan's $100B Deal with China: What Does It Amount To?," Devex, August 24, 2017, https://www.devex.com/news/pakistan-s-100b-deal-with-china-what-does-it-amount-to-90872.

84. Associated Press, "China-Driven Silk Road Project Hits Political, Financial Hurdles," *Dawn*, January 12, 2018, https://www.dawn.com/news/1382334.

85. Abid Hussain, "The Mega-Dam Being Crowdfunded by Pakistan's Top Judge," BBC Urdu, October 30, 2018, https://www.bbc.com/news/world-asia-45968574; "Akon Voices Support for Diamer-Bhasha Dam Fund," *Daily Times Monitor*, January 16, 2019, https://dailytimes.com.pk/344693/akon-voices-support-for-diamer-bhasha-dam-fund/.

86. Ministry of Water Resources, "Diamer Basha Dam Project," accessed February 4, 2020, htts://mowr.gov.pk/index.php/diamer-basha-dam-project/; Supreme Court of Pakistan, "Fund Raising Status for the Supreme Court of Pakistan and the Prime Minister of Pakistan Diamer-Bhasha and Mohmand Dams Fund," April 19, 2019, http://www.supremecourt.gov.pk/web/page.asp?id=2757.

87. Saeed Shah, "Pakistan Requests IMF Bailout Talks," *Wall Street Journal*, October 8, 2018, https://www.wsj.com/articles/pakistan-to-hold-bailout-talks-with-imf-1539018792; International Monetary Fund, "Pakistan: History of Lending Arrangements," April 30, 2018, https://www.imf.org/external/np/fin/tad/extarr2.aspx?memberKey1=760&date1key=2018-04-30; International Monetary Fund, "SDR Valuation," April 16, 2019, https://www.imf.org/external/np/fin/data/rms_sdrv.aspx.

88. Embassy of the People's Republic of China in the Islamic Republic of Pakistan, "Statement from Chinese Embassy," December 29, 2018, https://pk.chineseembassy.org/eng/zbgx/CPEC/t1625941.htm; Embassy of the People's Republic of China in the Islamic Republic of Pakistan, "Financing Run Down of 22 CPEC Projects," December 29, 2018, https://pk.chineseembassy.org/eng/zbgx/CPEC/t1625940.htm.

89. Arif Rafiq, "The China-Pakistan Economic Corridor: The Lure of Easy Financing and the Perils of Poor Planning," *Asian Affairs* 50, no. 2 (2019): 236–248.

90. Husain, "Exclusive: CPEC Master Plan Revealed."

91. Saeed Shah, "Pakistan Turns to China in Energy Binge," *Wall Street Journal*, December 18, 2016, https://www.wsj.com/articles/pakistan-turns-to-china-in-energy-binge-1482062404; Jeremy Page and Saeed Shah, "China's Global Building Spree Runs into Trouble in Pakistan," *Wall Street Journal*, July 22, 2018, https://www.wsj.com/articles/chinas-global-building-spree-runs-into-trouble-in-pakistan-1532280460.

92. Ali, *China-Pakistan Relations*, 189.

93. "Gwadar Port: 'History-Making Milestones,'" *Dawn*, April 14, 2008, https://www.dawn.com/news/297994/gwadar-port; CPECWire, "Timeline: The History of CPEC," accessed February 4, 2020, https://cpecwire.com/cpec-history-timeline/.

94. "'Today Marks Dawn of a New Era': CPEC Dreams Come True as Gwadar Port Goes Operational," *Dawn*, November 13, 2016, https://www.dawn.com/news/1296098/today-marks-dawn-of-new-era-cpec-dreams-come-true-as-gwadar-port-goes-operational.

95. "Pakistan's Gwadar Port Sees First Container Vessel, a Milestone for Belt and Road Initiative," *Hellenic Shipping News*, October 3, 2018, https://www.hellenicshippingnews.com/pakistans-gwadar-port-sees-first-container-vessel-a-milestone-for-belt-and-road-initiative/.

96. International Crisis Group, *China-Pakistan Economic Corridor: Opportunities and Risks*, Asia Report 297 (Brussels: International Crisis Group, June 29, 2018), https://www.crisisgroup.org/asia/south-asia/pakistan/297-china-pakistan-economic-corridor-opportunities-and-risks.

97. Adnan Aamir, "China's Belt and Road Plans Dismay Pakistan's Poorest Province," *Financial Times*, June 14, 2018, https://www.ft.com/content/c4b78fe0-5399-11e8-84f4-43d65af59d43.

98. Meher Ahmad and Salman Masood, "Chinese Presence in Pakistan Is Targeted in Strike on Consulate in Karachi," *New York Times*, November 23, 2018, https://www.nytimes.com/2018/11/23/world/asia/pakistan-karachi-attack-chinese-consulate.html.

99. Small, *China-Pakistan Axis*, 115.

100. Helena Legarda and Meia Nouwens, "Guardians of the Belt and Road: The Internationalization of China's Private Security Companies," Mercator Institute for China Studies, August 16, 2018, https://www.merics.org/en/china-monitor/guardians-of-belt-and-road.

101. Others expect China to build a separate facility in nearby Jiwani. See, for example, "China Plans New Naval Base in Pakistan," *Maritime Executive*, January 8, 2018, https://www.maritime-executive.com/article/china-plans-new-naval-base-in-pakistan.

102. Farhan Bokhari and Kathrin Hille, "Pakistan Turns to China for Naval Base," *Financial Times*, May 22, 2011, https://www.ft.com/content/3914bd36-8467-11e0-afcb-00144feabdc0.

103. See, for example, "China Denies Plans to Set Up Military Base in Pakistan," *Economic Times*, January 9, 2018, https://economictimes.indiatimes.com/news/defence/china-denies-plans-to-set-up-military-base-in-pakistan/articleshow/62427995.cms; "China Did Not Ask for Military Access to Gwadar, Says Pakistani Admiral," *Economic Times*, October 26, 2018, https://economictimes.indiatimes.com/news/defence/china-not-asked-for-military-access-to-gwadar-pakistan-admiral-says/articleshow/66375908.cms?from=mdr.

104. Office of the Historian, U.S. Department of State, "Telegram 2213 from the Embassy in Pakistan to the Department of State, March 10, 1972, 0725Z1," March 10, 1972, https://history.state.gov/historicaldocuments/frus1969-76ve07/d235.

105. Sushant Sareen, *Corridor Calculus: China Pakistan Economic Corridor and China's Comprador Investment Model in Pakistan* (New Delhi: Vivekanada International Foundation, 2016), https://www.vifindia.org/sites/default/files/corridor-calculus-china-pakistan-economic-corridor-and-china-s-comprador-investment-model-in-pakistan.pdf.

106. Zafar Bhutta, "From Gwadar-Kashgar: Crude Oil Pipeline Requires $10 Billion Investment," *Express Tribune*, May 18, 2018, https://tribune.com.pk/story/1712888/2-gwadar-kashgar-crude-oil-pipeline-requires-10-billion-investment/.

107. Gateway House, "Gwadar: Trade Hub or Military Asset?—Analysis," *Eurasia Review*, February 8, 2019, https://www.eurasiareview.com/08022019-gwadar-trade-hub-or-military-asset-analysis/.

108. Andrew S. Erickson and Gabriel B. Collins, "China's Oil Security Pipe Dream: The Reality, and Strategic Consequences, of Seaborne Imports," *Naval War College Review* 63, no. 2 (Spring 2010): 88–111; Guy

C. K. Leung, "China's Energy Security: Perception and Reality," *Energy Policy* 39, no. 3 (2011): 1330–1337.

109. "PR and CRCC to Cooperate on (ML) II (Kotri-Attock Line) and ML III (Rohri Chaman Line) Projects," Times International News Service, May 10, 2018, https://tns.world/pr-and-crcc-to-cooperate-on-ml-ii-kotri-attock-line-and-ml-iii-rohri-chaman-line-projects/.

110. Sayed Munaway Shah, "1st Meeting of Railway Working Group," CAREC, November 24, 2015, https://web.archive.org/web/20160803101654/https://www.carecprogram.org/uploads/events/2015/035-Railway-WG-Meeting/Presentation-Materials/Day-1/2015-RWG-Meeting-P07_PPresentation%20by%20PAK_EN.pdf.

111. Amin Yusufzai, "Rail Connectivity of Gwadar with Other Parts of Pakistan Not a Priority: Officials," ProPakistani, April 6, 2019, https://propakistani.pk/2019/04/06/rail-connectivity-of-gwadar-with-other-parts-of-pakistan-not-a-priority-officials/.

112. Zafar Bhutta, "Optic Fibre Cable Connecting Pakistan, China to Be Inaugurated Today," *Express Tribune*, July 13, 2018, https://tribune.com.pk/story/1756458/2-optic-fibre-cable-connecting-pakistan-china-inaugurated-today/.

113. "$44m Pakistan-China Optic Fibre Project," *Dawn*, August 3, 2013, https://www.dawn.com/news/1033788.

114. Jamil Anderlini, Henny Sender, and Farhan Bokhari, "Pakistan Rethinks Its Role in Xi's Belt and Road Plan," *Financial Times*, September 9, 2018, https://www.ft.com/content/d4a3e7f8-b282-11e8-99ca-68cf89602132.

115. "CPEC Project: Chinese Companies Frustrated by Delayed Payments by Pakistan Government," *Eurasian Times*, December 19, 2018, https://eurasiantimes.com/cpec-project-chinese-companies-frustrated-by-delayed-payments-by-pakistan-government-for/; Omer Farooq Khan, "Chinese Companies Warn Pakistan against Delay in CPEC Project," *Times of India*, January 21, 2019, https://timesofindia.indiatimes.com/world/pakistan/chinese-companies-warn-pakistan-against-delay-in-cpec-project/articleshow/67627895.cms.

116. Press Trust of India, "China Stops Funds for China-Pakistan Economic Corridor over Corruption," NDTV, December 5, 2017, https://www.ndtv.com/world-news/china-stops-funds-for-china-pak-economic-corridor-over-corruption-report-1783849.

117. Fan Zhang, *In the Dark: How Much Do Power Sector Distortions Cost South Asia?* (Washington, DC: World Bank, 2019), 23, https://openknowledge.worldbank.org/bitstream/handle/10986/30923/9781464811548.pdf.

118. C. Christine Fair, "Pakistan's Sham Election: How the Army Chose Imran Khan," *Foreign Affairs*, July 27, 2018, https://www.foreignaffairs.com/articles/pakistan/2018-07-27/pakistans-sham-election.

119. Embassy of the Islamic Republic of Pakistan Beijing, "Pakistan to Become Energy Sufficient Country Soon: Omar Ayub Khan," October 18, 2018, http://www.pakbj.org/index.php?m=content&c=index&a=show&c atid=12&id=259.

120. Page and Shah, "China's Global Building Spree."

121. AFP, "Pakistan, China Vow to Promote Regional Peace, Cooperation," *Dawn*, July 5, 2013, https://www.dawn.com/news/1022999.

Chapter Eight. Game of Loans: Sri Lanka

1. "Sri Lanka-China Industrial Zone Office in Hambantota Port Kicks Off Industrialisation of Ruhuna," *Daily FT*, November 6, 2017, http://www. ft.lk/business/Sri-Lanka-China-Industrial-Zone-Office-in-Hambantota-Port-kicks-off-industrialisation-of-Ruhuna/34-642838.

2. Mike Pence, "Remarks by Vice President Pence on the Administration's Policy toward China" (Hudson Institute, Washington, DC), White House, October 4, 2018, https://www.whitehouse.gov/briefings-statements/remarks-vice-president-pence-administrations-policy-toward-china/.

3. Mahinda Rajapaksa, "A Brighter Future, Presidential Election—2010: Mahinda Chintana, Vision for the Future," PreventionWeb, accessed June 26, 2019, https://www.preventionweb.net/files/mahinda_chintana_vision_for_the_future_eng%5B1%5D.pdf.

4. Saliya Wickramasuriya, interviewed by Meg Rithmire and Yihao Li, "Chinese Infrastructure Investments in Sri Lanka: A Pearl or a Teardrop on the Belt and Road?" (Harvard Business School Case 719-046, January 2019, revised July 2019).

5. Government of Sri Lanka, "Regaining Sri Lanka: Vision and Strategy for Accelerated Development," December 2002, http://siteresources.worldbank. org/INTPRS1/Resources/Country-Papers-and-JSAs/Sri_Lanka_PRSP.pdf.

6. "Hambantota Port Feasibility Study Rejected," *Island*, November 21, 2003, http://www.island.lk/2003/11/21/news03.html.

7. "25 Colombo (Sri Lanka)," *Lloyd's List*, August 2, 2017, https://lloydslist. maritimeintelligence.informa.com/articles/2017/one-hundred-ports/25-colombo-sri-lanka.

8. "Sri Lanka Colombo Plans for 35mn TEU Capacity with North Port," *Economy Next*, September 22, 2016, http://www.economynext.com/Sri_Lanka_Colombo_plans_for_35mn_TEU_capacity_with_north_port-3-6175.html.

9. "Hardliner Wins Sri Lanka Election," BBC News, November 18, 2005, http://news.bbc.co.uk/2/hi/south_asia/4447794.stm.

10. "I've Honoured My First Two Promises Made 5 Yrs Ago—MR First Vessel Ceremonially Berthed at Hambantota Port," *Island*, November 18, 2010, http://www.island.lk/index.php?page_cat=article-details&page=article-details&code_title=11569.

11. Guinness World Records, "Most Cabinet Ministers Appointed by a Government," accessed February 19, 2019, http://www.guinnessworldrecords.com/world-records/most-cabinet-ministers-appointed-by-a-government/.

12. Maria Abi-Habib, "How China Got Sri Lanka to Cough Up a Port," *New York Times*, June 25, 2018, https://www.nytimes.com/2018/06/25/world/asia/china-sri-lanka-port.html.

13. Colum Lynch, "U.N.: Sri Lanka's Crushing of Tamil Tigers May Have Killed 40,000 Civilians," *Washington Post*, April 21, 2011, https://www.washingtonpost.com/world/un-sri-lankas-crushing-of-tamil-tigers-may-have-killed-40000-civilians/2011/04/21/AFU14hJE_story.html?utm_term=.07d228a67783.

14. Central Intelligence Agency, "The World Factbook—Sri Lanka," last updated February 8, 2019, https://www.cia.gov/library/publications/the-world-factbook/geos/ce.html.

15. Sonali Samarasinghe, "Helping Hambantota Investigation," *Lanka Standard*, July 3, 2005, http://www.lankastandard.com/vault/helping-hambantota-investigation/.

16. "Bribery Complaint Filed against Former Sri Lankan President over Misappropriating Tsunami Funds," *Colombo Page*, April 24, 2015, http://www.colombopage.com/archive_15A/Apr24_1429883356CH.php.

17. Nieman Foundation, "Louis M. Lyons Award for Conscience and Integrity in Journalism," November 17, 2009, https://nieman.harvard.edu/events/louis-m-lyons-award-for-conscience-and-integrity-in-journalism/.

18. Amal S. Kumarage, "Feasibility Study for the Road Network for Hambantota Development Plan," Department of Transport & Logistics Management, University of Moratuwa, December 2010, https://kumarage.files.wordpress.com/2015/03/2010-ucr-2-te-feasibility-of-road-network-for-hambantota-develoment-rda-186pp.pdf.

19. Central Bank of Sri Lanka, *Economic and Social Statistics of Sri Lanka 2010* (Colombo: Central Bank of Sri Lanka Statistics Department, 2010), https://web.archive.org/web/20190605142032/https:/www.cbsl.gov.lk/sites/default/files/cbslweb_documents/statistics/otherpub/econ_%26_ss_2010_e-min.pdf; World Shipping Council, "Top 50 World Container Ports," accessed February 19, 2019, http://www.worldshipping.org/about-the-industry/global-trade/top-50-world-container-ports.

20. James Kynge, Chris Campbell, Amy Kazmin, and Farhan Bokhari, "How China Rules the Waves," *Financial Times*, January 12, 2017, https://ig.ft.com/sites/china-ports/.

21. Karthik Sivaram, *"Locked-In" to China: The Colombo Port City Project* (Stanford, CA: Leadership Academy for Development, 2016), https://fsi-live.s3.us-west-1.amazonaws.com/s3fs-public/colombo_port_city.pdf; China Harbour Engineering Company, "President of China and President of Sri Lanka Attended the Commencement Ceremony of Colombo Port City Project," September 18, 2014, http://www.chec.bj.cn/pub/chec_pc/en/Media/PressReleases/2014/201903/t20190306_7046.html.

22. Matthew Funaiole and Jonathan Hillman, "China's Maritime Silk Road Initiative: Economic Drivers and Challenges," Center for Strategic and International Studies, April 2, 2018, https://www.csis.org/analysis/chinas-maritime-silk-road-initiative-economic-drivers-and-challenges.

23. Diresh Jayasuriya, "Lotus Tower to Open Soon," *Daily News*, March 2, 2018, http://www.dailynews.lk/2018/03/02/business/144350/lotus-tower-open-soon.

24. Telecommunications Regulatory Commission of Sri Lanka, *Cumulative Number of Licenses Granted under Section 17 of the Sri Lanka Telecommunications Act No 25 of 1991 as Amended* (Colombo: Telecommunications Regulatory Commission of Sri Lanka, December 2018), http://www.trc.gov.lk/images/pdf/statis_q42018.pdf; Ministry of Mass Media and Information, *Media Licence Issued for Television Transmission* (Colombo: Ministry of Mass Media and Information, November 2018), https://media.gov.lk/images/pdf_word/2019/english-tv.pdf; Ministry of Mass Media and Information, *Media Licence Issued for Radio Broadcasting* (Colombo: Ministry of Mass Media and Information, November 2018), https://www.media.gov.lk/images/pdf_word/2019/english-radio.pdf.

25. External Resources Department, Government of Sri Lanka, *Global Partnership in Development* (Colombo: External Resources Department, 2011), http://www.erd.gov.lk/images/pdf/global_partnership_in_development_2011.pdf.

26. "Mattala Rajapaksa International Airport Opens Tomorrow with Pomp and Pageantry," *Sunday Times*, March 17, 2013, http://www.sundaytimes.lk/130317/news/mattala-rajapaksa-international-airport-opens-tomorrow-with-pomp-and-pageantry-37247.html.

27. Allison Hope, "This $200 Million Airport Sees an Average of 7 Passengers a Day," *Forbes*, October 10, 2017, https://www.cntraveler.com/story/this-200-million-dollar-airport-sees-an-average-of-7-passengers-a-day.

28. Eric Ellis, "The Brothers' Grip," *Global Mail*, accessed February 19, 2019, http://tgm-archive.github.io/sri-lanka/brothers-grip.html.

29. Ellis, "Brothers' Grip."

30. "Buddha's 'Blood Relative' Tolerates His Tattoo but His Officials Can't Tolerate Buddha Tattoo," *Colombo Telegraph*, March 19, 2013, https://www.colombotelegraph.com/index.php/buddhas-blood-relative-tolerates-his-tattoo-but-his-officials-cant-tolerate-buddha-tattoo/.

31. "I've Honoured My First Two Promises Made 5 Yrs Ago."

32. China Harbour Engineering Company, "Opening Ceremony of Hambantota Port in Sri Lanka Was Held," November 22, 2010, https://www.ccdz056.com/zg/tabid/81/InfoID/2666/Default.aspx&hl=en&gl=us&strip=1&vwsrc=0.

33. Abi-Habib, "How China Got Sri Lanka to Cough Up a Port."

34. Maithripala Sirisena, "A Compassionate Maithri Governance: A Stable Country," New Democratic Front, December 2014, https://www.onlanka.

com/wp-content/uploads/2014/12/maithripala-election-manifesto-english.pdf.

35. Ranga Sirilal, "Chinese Firm Pays $584 Million in Sri Lanka Debt-to-Equity Deal," Reuters, June 28, 2018, https://www.reuters.com/article/us-sri-lanka-china-ports/chinese-firm-pays-584-million-in-sri-lanka-port-debt-to-equity-deal-idUSKBN1JG2Z6.

36. Shihar Aneez, "China's 'Silk Road' Push Stirs Resentment and Protest in Sri Lanka," Reuters, February 1, 2017, https://www.reuters.com/article/us-sri-lanka-china-insight/chinas-silk-road-push-stirs-resentment-and-protest-in-sri-lanka-idUSKBN15G5UT.

37. "458 Employees Shut Out of Hambantota Port: Labour Minister Slams Port Company," *Sunday Times*, December 3, 2017, http://www.sunday-times.lk/171203/news/458-employees-shut-out-of-hambantota-port-labour-minister-slams-port-company-271604.html.

38. China Xinhua News, "Another milestone along path of #BeltandRoad. Sri Lanka officially hands over southern port of Hambantota to China on 99-year lease," Twitter, December 9, 2017, 11:09 p.m., https://twitter.com/XHNews/status/939753813115789312/.

39. Jonathan Hillman, "The Hazards of China's Global Ambitions," *Washington Post*, February 5, 2018, https://www.washingtonpost.com/news/theworldpost/wp/2018/02/05/obor-china-asia/?utm_term=.fdf8206fbd98.

40. Abi-Habib, "How China Got Sri Lanka to Cough Up a Port."

41. Brahma Chellaney, "China's Debt-Trap Diplomacy," Project Syndicate, January 23, 2017, https://www.project-syndicate.org/commentary/china-one-belt-one-road-loans-debt-by-brahma-chellaney-2017-01.

42. Sri Lanka faced "significant" risk from Chinese lending, according to a study by the Center for Global Development, but was not among the eight countries at greatest risk. See John Hurley, Scott Morris, and Gailyn Portelance, *Examining the Debt Implications of the Belt and Road Initiative from a Policy Perspective* (Washington, DC: Center for Global Development, March 2018), https://www.cgdev.org/sites/default/files/examining-debt-implications-belt-and-road-initiative-policy-perspective.pdf.

43. Christine Lagarde, "Belt and Road Initiative: Strategies to Deliver in the Next Phase," International Monetary Fund, April 12, 2018, https://www.imf.org/en/News/Articles/2018/04/11/sp041218-belt-and-road-initiative-strategies-to-deliver-in-the-next-phase.

44. Marwaan Macan Markar, "Sri Lanka Sinks Deeper into China's Grasp as Debt Woes Spiral," *Nikkei Asian Review*, August 29, 2018, https://asia.nikkei.com/Spotlight/Belt-and-Road/Sri-Lanka-sinks-deeper-into-China-s-grasp-as-debt-woes-spiral.

45. Kiran Stacey, "China Signs 99-Year Lease on Sri Lanka's Hambantota Port," *Financial Times*, December 11, 2017, https://www.ft.com/content/e150efoc-de37-11e7-a8a4-0a1e63a52f9c.

46. Deng Xiaoci, "China's Blue Helmets Help Maintain Peace," *Global Times*, May 29, 2018, http://www.globaltimes.cn/content/1104710.shtml.

47. Press Trust of India, "Hambantota Port Not a Military Base for Foreign Countries: Lanka PM Assures," *Hindustan Times*, September 1, 2017, https://www.hindustantimes.com/world-news/hambantota-port-not-a-military-base-for-foreign-countries-lanka-pm-assures/story-rXxlFtYiz REefdRRotDacO.html.

48. Press Trust of India, "Hambantota Port Won't Be Used as Military Base: Lankan Official," *India Today*, February 27, 2018, https://www.indiatoday.in/pti-feed/story/hambantota-port-wont-be-used-as-military-base-lankan-official-1178931-2018-02-27.

49. Ryan D. McLearnon, "Spruance Arrives in Sri Lanka for the 25th Anniversary of CARAT 2019 Series," United States Navy, April 22, 2019, https://www.public.navy.mil/surfor/ddg111/Pages/Spruance-arrives-in-Sri-Lanka-for-the-25th-anniversary-of-CARAT-2019-series.aspx; "Japanese Naval Ship 'Ikazuchi' Arrives at Hambantota Port," *Daily FT*, January 16, 2019, http://www.ft.lk/news/Japanese-Naval-Ship--Ikazuchi--arrives-at-Hambantota-Port/56-670932.

50. Abi-Habib, "How China Got Sri Lanka to Cough Up a Port."

51. Yogita Limaye, "Sri Lanka: A Country Trapped in Debt," BBC, May 26, 2017, https://www.bbc.com/news/business-40044113.

52. Department of External Resources, Government of Sri Lanka, "Debt Indicators Summary," last modified September 6, 2018, http://www.erd.gov.lk/index.php?option=com_content&view=article&id=86&Itemid=307&lang=en#debt-stock.

53. Yusuf Ariff, "Sri Lanka Facing a Massive Debt Crisis—Auditor General," *Ada Derana*, February 7, 2018, http://www.adaderana.lk/news/45829/sri-lanka-facing-a-massive-debt-crisis-auditor-general.

54. "India Firm's Interest in Sri Lankan Port Upgrade Advances," *Journal of Commerce*, September 17, 2018, https://www.joc.com/port-news/india-firm%E2%80%99s-interest-sri-lanka-port-upgrade-advances_20180917.html.

55. Zulfath Saheed, "Eastern Gateway Prepare for Takeoff or Landing?," *LMD*, accessed February 4, 2020, https://lmd.lk/eastern-gateway/.

56. Sanjeev Miglani and Mohamed Junayd, "After Building Spree, Just How Much Does the Maldives Owe China?," Reuters, November 23, 2018, https://www.reuters.com/article/us-maldives-politics-china/after-building-spree-just-how-much-does-the-maldives-owe-china-idUSKCN1NS1J2.

57. Quoted in "Inspiring Speeches at Gaining Independence," *Sunday Observer*, February 14, 2016, http://archives.sundayobserver.lk/2016/02/14/fea02.asp.

58. Shihar Aneez and Ranga Sirilal, "Sri Lanka Signs Port Deals with China amid Political Upheaval," Reuters, November 29, 2018, https://www.reuters.

com/article/us-sri-lanka-china/sri-lanka-signs-port-deals-with-china-amid-political-upheaval-idUSKCN1NY19S.

59. Shihar Aneez and Ranga Sirilal, "Sri Lanka PM Rajapaksa Resigns amid Government Shut Down Fears," Reuters, December 15, 2018, https://www.reuters.com/article/us-sri-lanka-politics-rajapaksa-idUSK-BN1OE068.

60. "MR Blasts Govt. for Diluting Intelligence Services," *Daily Mirror,* April 23, 2019, http://www.dailymirror.lk/breaking_news/MR-blasts-govt-for-diluting-intelligence-services/108-165806.

61. "Minister Instructs to Resume Operations at Mattala Airport Soon," *Colombo Page,* January 12, 2020, http://www.colombopage.com/archive_20A/Jan12_1578848662CH.php.

Chapter Nine. War and PEACE: East Africa

1. Charles W. Koburger, *Naval Strategy East of Suez: The Role of Djibouti* (New York: Greenwood, 1992), xvii.

2. International Development Association, "Project Appraisal Document on a Proposed Credit to the Republic of Djibouti," World Bank, April 4, 2018, 9, http://documents.worldbank.org/curated/en/826531523301322820/pdf/Djibouti-Public-Admin-PAD-PAD2604-04062018.pdf.

3. Julian Ryall, "Japan to Expand Djibouti Base Despite Decline in Piracy," *Deutsche Welle,* November 19, 2018, https://www.dw.com/en/japan-to-expand-djibouti-base-despite-decline-in-piracy/a-46356825?maca=en-rss-en-all-1573-rdf.

4. Adam Satariano, "How the Internet Travels across Oceans," *New York Times,* March 10, 2019, https://www.nytimes.com/interactive/2019/03/10/technology/internet-cables-oceans.html.

5. International Telecommunications Union, "ICT Data for the World, by Geographic Regions and by Level of Development," accessed December 20, 2019, https://www.itu.int/en/ITU-D/Statistics/Pages/stat/default.aspx.

6. Jiangsu Stock, "600487 Hengtong Optoelectronics—PEACE-Information Silk Road—Information Is Power" (in Chinese), Sina, April 10, 2017, http://guba.sina.com.cn/?s=thread&tid=370073&bid=357.

7. China's military has been a powerful force behind its technological rise. For an excellent history, see Evan A. Feigenbaum, *China's Techno-Warriors: National Security and Strategic Competition from the Nuclear to the Information Age* (Stanford, CA: Stanford University Press, 2003).

8. Mission Information Office, "The Prosperous Civil-Military Integration of Leading Enterprises into the 'People's Participation Army' in Suzhou: The Accumulation of Products, an Industry to Serve the Country" (in Chinese), Suzhou Chamber of Commerce, September 11, 2018, http://www.szcc.org.cn/news-micro/su-zhou-min-can-jun-ling-jun-qi-ye-de-4706.html [link broken].

9. Cheng, "Hengtong Group Won 2015 China Innovation Model Award" (in Chinese), *China Economic Weekly*, December 28, 2015, https://web.archive.org/web/20190812090014/http://tech.hexun.com/2015-12-28/181467366.html; Hengtong Group, "OFweek Optical Communication Network: Joint Laboratory of Underwater Optical Network Established Hengtong Layout Underwater Optical Network" (in Chinese), November 1, 2016, http://www.hengtonggroup.com/news/497604.htm.

10. "PEACE Cable," interview with Xiaohua Sun, *Capacity*, December–January 2019, 60, https://edition.pagesuite-professional.co.uk/html5/reader/production/default.aspx?pubname=&edid=bbc7ec88-c0e4-4ce6-b30b-95513cc7091c.

11. "Report: Kenya Risks Losing Port of Mombasa to China," *Maritime Executive*, December 20, 2018, https://www.maritime-executive.com/article/kenya-risks-losing-port-of-mombasa-to-china.

12. Charles Miller, *The Lunatic Express: The Magnificent Saga of the Railway's Journey into Africa* (London: Head of Zeus, 2017).

13. Su Zhou, "Number of Chinese Immigrants in Africa Rapidly Increasing," *China Daily*, January 14, 2017, http://www.chinadaily.com.cn/world/2017-01/14/content_27952426.htm; Brendon J. Cannon, "Is China Undermining Its Own Success in Africa?," *Diplomat*, February 8, 2019, https://thediplomat.com/2019/02/is-china-undermining-its-own-success-in-africa/.

14. Geoff Hill, "Chinese Military Taking 'Irresponsible Actions' toward U.S. Forces in Djibouti, Intel Chief Says," *Washington Times*, June 16, 2019, https://www.washingtontimes.com/news/2019/jun/16/china-us-military-clash-over-djibouti-airspace/; Paul Sonne, "U.S. Accuses China of Directing Blinding Lasers at American Military Aircraft in Djibouti," *Washington Post*, May 4, 2018, https://www.washingtonpost.com/news/checkpoint/wp/2018/05/03/u-s-accuses-china-of-directing-blinding-lasers-at-american-military-aircraft-in-djibouti/?utm_term=.750dcff99870.

15. Michael R. Gordon, "Russian Lasers Reported Aimed at U.S. Planes," *New York Times*, October 3, 1987, https://www.nytimes.com/1987/10/03/world/russian-lasers-reported-aimed-at-us-planes.html.

16. Neil Melvin, "The Foreign Military Presence in the Horn of Africa Region," SIPRI, April 2019, 4, https://sipri.org/sites/default/files/2019-04/sipribp1904.pdf.

17. Mahamoud Ali Youssouf, quoted in Max Bearak, "In Strategic Djibouti, a Microcosm of China's Growing Foothold in Africa," *Washington Post*, December 30, 2019, https://www.washingtonpost.com/world/africa/in-strategic-djibouti-a-microcosm-of-chinas-growing-foothold-in-africa/2019/12/29/a6e664ea-beab-11e9-a8b0-7ed8aod5dc5d_story.html.

18. United Nations Conference on Trade and Development, *The Djibouti City–Addis Ababa Transit and Transport Corridor: Turning Diagnostics into Action* (Geneva: United Nations, 2018), 20, https://unctad.org/en/PublicationsLibrary/aldc2018d6_en.pdf.

19. China Merchants Holdings, "Acquisition of 23.5% Interests in Joint Venture in Djibouti," December 30, 2012, http://www3.hkexnews.hk/listedco/listconews/sehk/2012/1230/ltn20121230025.pdf.

20. FactWire, "The First 'One Belt, One Road' Project Was on the Hong Kong Court: The China Merchants Port Was Accused of Ignoring the Franchise" (in Chinese), *FactWire*, February 10, 2019, https://www.factwire.org/single-post/2019/02/10/Legal-battle-for-control-of-Djibouti-ports-comes-to-Hong-Kong.

21. Author interview, April 29, 2019.

22. John R. Bolton, "Remarks on the Trump Administration's New Africa Strategy," White House, December 13, 2018, https://www.whitehouse.gov/briefings-statements/remarks-national-security-advisor-ambassador-john-r-bolton-trump-administrations-new-africa-strategy/.

23. "Djibouti Inaugurates Africa's Largest Free Trade Zone," *Maritime Executive*, July 5, 2018, https://maritime-executive.com/article/djibouti-inaugurates-africa-s-largest-free-trade-zone.

24. DP World, "What We Do: Berbera-Somaliland," accessed February 4, 2020, https://www.dpworld.com/what-we-do/our-locations/Middle-East-Africa/Berbera/somaliland.

25. TeleGeography, "Submarine Cable Map," Primetrica Inc., accessed February 4, 2020, https://www.submarinecablemap.com/#/landing-point/djibouti-city-djibouti.

26. Bolton, "Remarks on the Trump Administration's New Africa Strategy." These principles were put forth by Zhou Enlai during his 1963–1964 visit to Africa.

27. Virginia Thompson and Richard Adloff, *Djibouti and the Horn of Africa* (Stanford, CA: Stanford University Press, 1968), 206.

28. Alberto Sbacchi, *Legacy of Bitterness: Ethiopia and Fascist Italy, 1935–1941* (Trenton, NJ: Red Sea, 1997); Suez Canal Authority, Government of Egypt, "Canal History: Historical Outline," accessed February 4, 2020, https://www.suezcanal.gov.eg/English/About/SuezCanal/Pages/CanalHistory.aspx.

29. John Irish, "Macron Warns of Chinese Risk to African Sovereignty," Reuters, March 11, 2019, https://www.reuters.com/article/us-djibouti-france/macron-warns-of-chinese-risk-to-african-sovereignty-idUSKBN1QS2QP.

30. Office of African and Latin American Analysis, U.S. Central Intelligence Agency, *Djibouti: Gouled under Pressure* (Washington, DC: Directorate of Intelligence, 1986), 2, https://www.cia.gov/library/readingroom/docs/CIA-RDP88T00768R000200240001-8.pdf.

31. United Nations Conference on Trade and Development, "UNCTAD FDI/TNC Database: Djibouti," accessed February 4, 2020, https://unctad.org/Sections/dite_fdistat/docs/webdiaeia2014d3_DJI.pdf.

32. "China to Sign $3.3 Bln Loan for Addis-Djibouti Railway Project," *Ethiopia First*, April 29, 2013, https://web.archive.org/web/20130503190450/

http://www.ethiopiafirst.info/etnews/index.php/component/k2/item/222-china-to-sign-$-33-bln-loan-for-addis-djibouti-railway-project.html; Istvan Tarrosy and Zoltán Vörös, "China and Ethiopia, Part 2: The Addis Ababa–Djibouti Railway," *Diplomat*, February 22, 2018, https://thediplomat.com/2018/02/china-and-ethiopia-part-2-the-addis-ababa-djibouti-railway/.

33. "Camel Trains Are Holding Up Ethiopia's New Railway Line," *Economist*, February 10, 2018, https://www.economist.com/middle-east-and-africa/2018/02/10/camel-trains-are-holding-up-ethiopias-new-railway-line.

34. Thompson and Adloff, *Djibouti and the Horn of Africa*, 205–206.

35. Tewodros W. Workneh, "The Politics of Telecommunications and Development in Ethiopia" (PhD diss., University of Oregon, 2014), 148–151.

36. Raymond Jonas, *The Battle of Adwa: African Victory in the Age of Empire* (Cambridge, MA: Harvard University Press, 2015).

37. United Nations Conference on Trade and Development, *Djibouti City–Addis Ababa Transit and Transport Corridor*.

38. Robert Peet Skinner, *Abyssinia of To-Day: An Account of the First Mission Sent by the American Government to the Court of the King of Kings, 1903–1904* (New York: Longmans, Green, 1906), 86–90, https://archive.org/stream/abyssiniaoftodayooskinrich/abyssiniaoftodayooskinrich_djvu.txt.

39. Amanda Kay McVety, "Pursuing Progress: Point Four in Ethiopia," *Diplomatic History* 32, no. 3 (June 2008), 371–403, https://www.jstor.org/stable/24915879.

40. Lemmu Baissa, "United States Military Assistance to Ethiopia, 1953–1974: A Reappraisal of a Difficult Patron-Client Relationship," *Northeast African Studies* 11, no. 3 (1989): 51–70, https://www.jstor.org/stable/43660384.

41. "Revolution and Military Government," in *Ethiopia: A Country Study*, rev. ed., ed. Harold D. Nelson and Irving Kaplan (Washington, DC: Library of Congress, 1993), accessed February 4, 2020, http://memory.loc.gov/frd/etsave/et_01_07.html.

42. Office of African and Latin American Analysis, U.S. Central Intelligence Agency, *Ethiopia: The Impact of Soviet Military Assistance* (Washington, DC: Directorate of National Intelligence, January 1983), https://www.cia.gov/library/readingroom/docs/DOC_0000496797.pdf.

43. Minor agreements preceded Zemin's visit, including technical, economic, and trade agreements, but their impact was limited. China also provided a $15 million loan in 1988, for a national stadium and ring road.

44. Zeng Aiping and Shu Zhan, "Origin, Achievements, and Prospects of the Forum on China-Africa Cooperation," *China International Studies*, no. 72 (September–October 2018): 88–108, https://www.focac.org/eng/lhyj_1/yjcg/P020181026382446204313.pdf.

45. Yun Sun, "China's 2018 Financial Commitments to Africa: Adjustment and Recalibration," *Africa in Focus* (blog), Brookings Institution, September 5, 2018, https://www.brookings.edu/blog/africa-in-focus/2018/09/

05/chinas-2018-financial-commitments-to-africa-adjustment-and-recali
bration/.

46. Nana Addo Dankwa Akufo-Addo, "Ghana Aiming to Replicate China's
Success Story," Presidency: Republic of Ghana, September 4, 2018,
http://presidency.gov.gh/index.php/briefing-room/news-style-2/809-
ghana-aiming-to-replicate-china-s-success-story-president-akufo-addo.

47. Deborah Brautigam, *The Dragon's Gift: The Real Story of China in Africa*
(New York: Oxford University Press, 2009), 114.

48. Irene Yuan Sun, *The Next Factory of the World: How Chinese Investment Is
Reshaping Africa* (Boston: Harvard Business Press, 2017).

49. Howard W. French, *China's Second Continent: How a Million Migrants Are
Building a New Empire in Africa* (New York: Knopf, 2014), 42.

50. Ernst and Young, "Turning Tides: EY Attractiveness Program, Africa,"
October 2018, https://www.ey.com/Publication/vwLUAssets/ey-Africa-
Attractiveness-2018/$FILE/ey-Africa-Attractiveness-2018.pdf.

51. Tan Jian, "Remarks at 'China-Africa: People-to-People Exchange for
Mutual Learning' Seminar by Chinese Ambassador Tan Jian" (speech at
"China-Africa: People-to-People Exchange for Mutual Learning" seminar, Addis Ababa, Ethiopia, February 2, 2018), http://et.china-embassy.
org/eng/zagx/t1534986.htm.

52. Aaron Maasho, "Ethiopia Loosens Throttle on Many Key Sectors, but
Privatization Still Far Off," Reuters, June 6, 2018, https://www.reuters.
com/article/us-ethiopia-privatisation/ethiopia-loosens-throttle-on-
many-key-sectors-but-privatization-still-far-off-idUSKCN1J21QV.

53. Quoted in Dereje Feyissa, "Aid Negotiation: The Uneasy 'Partnership'
between EPRDF and the Donors," *Journal of Eastern African Studies* 5
(2011): 795.

54. Lishan Adam, *Risks and Opportunities of Late Telecom Privatization: The
Case of Ethio Telecom* (Cape Town: Research ICT Africa, 2019), 8, https://
researchictafrica.net/wp/wp-content/uploads/2019/02/2019_After-Access-
Steps-and-issues-in-the-privatisation-of-the-telecommunication-sector-in-
Ethiopia.pdf.

55. Katrina Manson, "Ethiopia's Leader Aims to Maintain Tight Rein on
Key Businesses," *Financial Times*, May 27, 2013, http://www.ft.com/intl/
cms/s/0/c0985378-c5ef-11e2-99d1-00144feab7de.html.

56. Meles Zenawi, "FT Interview: Meles Zenawi, Ethiopian Prime Minister,"
interview by William Wallis, *Financial Times*, February 6, 2007, https://
www.ft.com/content/4db917b4-b5bd-11db-9eea-0000779e2340.

57. Tewodros W. Workneh, "State Monopoly of Telecommunications in
Ethiopia: Origins, Debates, and the Way Forward," *Review of African Political Economy* 45, no. 158 (2018): 592–608.

58. Mesfin Belachew, "Investment in Broadband Infrastructure in Ethiopia"
(paper presented at UN-OHRLLS Regional Meeting for African LDCs,
Dakar, Senegal, March 15, 2017), http://unohrlls.org/custom-content/

uploads/2017/03/Presentation-on-BB-in-Ethiopia.pdf; International Telecommunications Union, "Country ICT DATA (Until 2018): Fixed-Telephone Subscriptions," accessed December 20, 2019, https://www.itu.int/en/ITU-D/Statistics/Pages/stat/default.aspx.

59. Janelle Plummer, *Diagnosing Corruption in Ethiopia* (Washington, DC: World Bank, 2012), 356, https://openknowledge.worldbank.org/bitstream/handle/10986/13091/699430PUB0Publ067869B09780821395318.pdf?sequence=1&isAllowed=y.

60. Zhao Lili, "Contributing to the Development of Ethiopia with Wisdom and Strength," ZTE, https://www.zte.com.cn/global/about/magazine/zte-technologies/2009/6/en_414/172517.

61. Lili.

62. The mobile penetration rate is the number of SIM cards or mobile devices divided by the total population and can exceed 100 percent.

63. Adam, *Risks and Opportunities of Late Telecom Privatization*, 5–6.

64. Ewan Sutherland, "China and Africa: Alternative Telecommunications Policies and Practices," *African Journal of Information and Communication* 17 (2016): 181–182.

65. Tokunbo Ojo, "Political Economy of Huawei's Market Strategies in the Nigerian Telecommunication Market," *International Communication Gazette* 79, no. 3 (2017): 327.

66. Benjamin Tsui, "Do Huawei's Training Programs and Centers Transfer Skills to Africa?" (Policy Brief no. 14, China Africa Research Initiative, Washington, DC, 2016), https://static1.squarespace.com/static/5652847de4b033f56d2bdc29/t/578e94e83e00be65954fe b3f/1468962026573/Tsui+brief+v.5.pdf; Alemayehu Geda and Atenafu G. Meskel, "Impact of China-Africa Investment Relations: The Case of Ethiopia" (Policy Brief no. 11, Africa Economic Research Consortium, Nairobi, July 2013), https://aercafrica.org/wp-content/uploads/2018/07/CA_11_GedaMeskel.pdf.

67. Tom Gardner, "Ethiotel Strives for Better Signal," *Africa Report*, May 3, 2018, https://www.theafricareport.com/667/ethiotel-strives-for-better-signal/.

68. Felix Horne and Cynthia Wong, "They Know Everything We Do: Telecom and Internet Surveillance in Ethiopia," Human Rights Watch, March 25, 2014, https://www.hrw.org/report/2014/03/25/they-know-everything-we-do/telecom-and-internet-surveillance-ethiopia#.

69. Tewodros W. Workneh, "Chinese Multinationals in the Ethiopian Telecom Sector," *Communication, Culture & Critique* 9, no. 2 (February 2016): 138, https://academic.oup.com/ccc/article/9/1/126/3979314.

70. Michael Kovrig, "China Expands Its Peace and Security Footprint in Africa," International Crisis Group, October 24, 2018, https://www.crisisgroup.org/asia/north-east-asia/china/china-expands-its-peace-and-security-footprint-africa.

71. Joan Tilouine and Ghalia Kadiri, "In Addis Ababa, the Seat of the African Union Spied On by Beijing" (in French), *Le Monde*, January 27, 2018, https://www.lemonde.fr/afrique/article/2018/01/26/a-addis-abeba-le-siege-de-l-union-africaine-espionne-par-les-chinois_5247521_3212.html.

72. World Bank, *Project Appraisal Document on a Proposed Regional IDA Grant in the Amount of SDR 16.5 Million (US$25 Million Equivalent) to the African Union Commission for the Support for Capacity Development of the African Union Commission and Other African Union Organs Project* (Washington, DC: World Bank, 2014), http://documents.worldbank.org/curated/en/205721468194353464/pdf/816180PAD0P126010Box385177B00OUO090.pdf.

73. Huawei, "Desktop Cloud Draws Praise in Africa," July 25, 2013, https://e.huawei.com/en/case-studies/global/older/hw_201214.

74. Danielle Cave, a researcher at the Australian Strategic Policy Institute, was among the first to make these connections. See Cave, "The African Union Headquarters Hack and Australia's 5G Network," *The Strategist* (Australian Strategic Policy Institute), July 13, 2018, https://www.aspistrategist.org.au/the-african-union-headquarters-hack-and-australias-5g-network/; African Union, "AUC Signs MoU with Huawei for Partnership on ICT," February 3, 2015, https://au.int/en/newsevents/29758/auc-signs-mou-huawei-partnership-ict.

75. Deng Yingying, "China's National Innovation System (NIS) in the Making: Case Studies of Three Indigenous Chinese Companies" (master's thesis, University of Massachusetts–Lowell, 2003), 11, 45–46.

76. Christopher Balding and Donald C. Clarke, "Who Owns Huawei?," SSRN, April 17, 2019, https://papers.ssrn.com/sol3/papers.cfm?abstract_id=3372669.

77. Reuters, "China Rejects Claim It Bugged Headquarters It Built for African Union," *Guardian*, January 29, 2018, https://www.theguardian.com/world/2018/jan/30/china-african-union-headquarters-bugging-spying.

78. Cave, "African Union Headquarters Hack."

79. Chinedum Uwaegbulam, "West Africa: New Ecowas Abuja Headquarters Project Throws Up Consultancy Jobs," *AllAfrica*, March 11, 2019, https://allafrica.com/stories/201903110079.html.

80. Jonathan E. Hillman, *Influence and Infrastructure: The Strategic Stakes of Foreign Projects* (Washington, DC: Center for Strategic and International Studies, 2019), 14, https://csis-prod.s3.amazonaws.com/s3fs-public/publication/190123_Hillman_InfluenceandInfrastructure_WEB_v3.pdf.

81. Elaine Sciolino, "The Bugged Embassy Case: What Went Wrong," *New York Times*, November 15, 1988, https://www.nytimes.com/1988/11/15/world/the-bugged-embassy-case-what-went-wrong.html.

82. Sutherland, "China and Africa," 184.

83. Hua Jingyi, "Huawei ZTE Won the Bid for Kenya Optical Cable Backbone Construction Project" (in Chinese), *OFweek*, September 4, 2007, https://fiber.ofweek.com/2007-09/ART-210007-8110-10671001.html.

84. James A. Lewis, "5G: The Impact on National Security, Intellectual Property, and Competition" (testimony before the Senate Committee on the Judiciary, Washington, DC, May 14, 2019), 7, https://csis-prod.s3.amazonaws.com/s3fs-public/congressional_testimony/190514_Jim_Lewis_Testimony.pdf.

85. GSM Association, "Case Study: RuralStar Huawei Safaricom," January 10, 2019, https://www.gsma.com/futurenetworks/wiki/ruralstar-huawei-safaricom-case-study/#87b0f37ea57dc3bb8bf3db501600eb3e.

86. Lauder Institute, *Lauder Global Business Insight Report 2009: First-Hand Perspectives on the Global Economy* (Philadelphia: Lauder Institute, Knowledge@Wharton, 2009), https://docplayer.net/23954919-Lauder-global-business-insight-report-2009.html; Christine Chang, Amy Cheng, Susan Kim, Johanna Kuhn-Osius, Jesús Reyes, and Daniel Turgel, "Huawei Technologies: A Chinese Trail Blazer in Africa," *Knowledge@Wharton*, April 20, 2009, http://knowledge.wharton.upenn.edu/article/huawei-technologies-a-chinese-trail-blazer-in-africa/.

87. Lauder Institute, *Lauder Global Business Insight Report 2009*.

88. Mao Tse-Tung, *Selected Works of Mao Tse-Tung*, vol. 4 (Beijing: Foreign Languages Press, 1961), 157.

89. Okuttah Mark, "Safaricom Hands Over CCTV System to Police This Week," *Business Daily Africa*, November 22, 2015, https://www.businessdailyafrica.com/Corporate-News/Safaricom-hands-over-CCTV-system-to-police-this-week/539550-2967242-slf222z/index.html.

90. Donal Power, "Global Smart Cities Market to Reach a Whopping $3.5 Trillion by 2026," *ReadWrite*, January 7, 2017, https://readwrite.com/2017/01/07/smart-cities-market-will-grow-3-5-trillion-worldwide-2026-cl4/.

91. Huawei, "Safe City: Kenya," April 10, 2018, https://e.huawei.com/en/videos/global/2018/201804101038.

92. Matthew Dalton, "Telecom Deal by China's ZTE, Huawei in Ethiopia Faces Criticism," *Wall Street Journal*, January 6, 2014, https://www.wsj.com/articles/telecom-deal-by-china8217s-zte-huawei-in-ethiopia-faces-criticism-1389064617.

93. "Bone and Structure of Sh45 Billion Safarigate Scandal," *Nairobi Law Monthly*, March 10, 2016, http://nairobilawmonthly.com/index.php/2016/03/10/bone-and-structure-of-sh45-billion-safarigate-scandal/.

94. Edith Mutehya, "Kenya and Huawei Sign Agreement for Digital Transformation," *China Daily*, May 16, 2017, http://www.chinadaily.com.cn/world/2017-05/16/content_29372143.htm.

95. World Bank, *The Economics of Rail Gauge in the East Africa Community* (Washington, DC: World Bank 2013), https://africog.org/wp-content/uploads/2017/06/World-bank-Report-on-the-Standard-Gauge-Railway.pdf.

96. Uhuru Kenyatta, "Speech at the Jamhuri Day 50th Independence Anniversary Celebrations," Nairobi, Kenya, December 12, 2013, http://www.kenyabrussels.com/ckfinder/userfiles/files/news%20&%20events/2013/Pres_Kenyatta_speech_50th_Anniversary.pdf.

97. Victor Wahome, "Impact of the Standard Gauge Railway (SGR) and Lapsset Development Corridor to the Kenyan Economy," Kenya Railway Corporation, March 26, 2015, https://web.archive.org/web/20160705134949/http://www.isk.or.ke/userfiles/SGR_Presentation_March_2015.pdf; A. Dreher, A. Fuchs, B. C. Parks, A. M. Strange, and M. J. Tierney, "China EXIM Bank Loans USD 1.633B for Nairobi-Mombasa Railway Section (Link to Project #31777 and #47025)," AidData, 2017, https://china.aiddata.org/projects/37103.

98. Office of the President of the Republic of Kenya, "President Kenyatta Delivers the SGR, His Biggest Promise to Kenyans," May 31, 2017, http://www.president.go.ke/2017/05/31/president-kenyatta-delivers-the-sgr-his-biggest-promise-to-kenyans/.

99. Paul Wafula, "Revealed: SGR Workers Treated Badly by Chinese Masters," *Standard Media*, July 8, 2018, https://www.standardmedia.co.ke/article/2001287179/revealed-sgr-workers-treated-badly-by-chinese-masters.

100. Xinhua, "Kenya's New Railway Builds Ties between Ordinary Kenyans, Chinese," *Xinhuanet*, June 17, 2018, http://www.xinhuanet.com/english/2018-06/17/c_137260738.htm.

101. Lily Kuo, "Kenya's $3.2 Billion Nairobi-Mombasa Rail Line Opens with Help from China," *Quartz Africa*, June 2, 2017, https://qz.com/africa/996255/kenyas-3-2-billion-nairobi-mombasa-rail-line-opens-with-help-from-china/; Xinhua, "Experts Envisage Integrated High Speed Railway Network in Africa," China.org.cn, April 10, 2019, http://www.china.org.cn/world/Off_the_Wire/2019-04/10/content_74667099.htm.

102. Quoted in Miller, *Lunatic Express*, Kindle loc. 4761–4790.

103. Quoted in Miller, Kindle loc. 5668.

104. Njuguna Ndung'u, "M-Pesa—A Success Story of Digital Financial Inclusion" (Practitioner's Insight, University of Oxford Blavatnik School of Government, Oxford, UK, July 2017), https://www.bsg.ox.ac.uk/sites/default/files/2018-06/2017-07-M-Pesa-Practitioners-Insight.pdf.

105. Duncan Miriri, "Kenya's Safaricom FY Earnings Jump on Upbeat M-Pesa Growth," *Business Report*, May 4, 2019, https://www.iol.co.za/business-report/international/kenyas-safaricom-fy-earnings-jump-on-upbeat-m-pesa-growth-22440491.

106. Cynthia Ilako, "Mobile Cash Transactions Averaged Sh15 Million per Minute in 2018," *Star*, April 2, 2018, https://www.the-star.co.ke/business/2019-04-02-mobile-cash-transactions-averaged-sh15-million-per-minute-in-2018/.

107. For the projected share, see Japan International Cooperation Agency, *Project for Master Plan on Logistics in Northern Economic Corridor: Final Report, Annex—Data Book* (Nairobi: Japan International Cooperation Agency, March 2017), https://www.works.go.ug/wp-content/uploads/2017/11/EI-JR17053-NECMP-DB-vol1-01.pdf.

108. Patrick Beja, "State Orders Ship Agents to Transport Goods on SGR," *Standard Media*, February 24, 2018, https://www.standardmedia.co.ke/article/2001270942/state-orders-ship-agents-to-transport-goods-on-sgr.

109. World Bank, Africa Transport Unit, "The Economics of Rail Gauge in the East Africa Community," August 8, 2013, https://africog.org/wp-content/uploads/2017/06/World-bank-Report-on-the-Standard-Gauge-Railway.pdf.

110. George Omondi, "Kenya to Start Repaying the Sh319bn SGR Loan in 2023," *Business Daily Africa*, August 9, 2017, https://www.businessdailyafrica.com/corporate/shipping/Kenya-start-repaying-Sh319bn-SGR-2023/4003122-4051318-s1paamz/index.html.

111. "Report: Kenya Risks Losing Port of Mombasa to China."

112. Claire Munde, "China Will Not Take Over Port of Mombasa, Ignore Propaganda—Uhuru," *Star*, December 29, 2018, https://www.the-star.co.ke/news/2018-12-29-china-will-not-take-over-port-of-mombasa-ignore-propaganda-uhuru/; George Omondi, "Mombasa Port at Risk as Audit Finds It Was Used to Secure SGR Loan," *East African*, December 20, 2018, https://www.theeastafrican.co.ke/business/Mombasa-port-SGR-loan-default-Chinsa/2560-4903360-clh5nn/index.html.

113. U.S. Department of State, Bureau of African Affairs, "U.S. Relations with Kenya," September 4, 2018, https://www.state.gov/u-s-relations-with-kenya/.

114. James Baraza, "Lamu Port Hits Key Milestone with First Berth Completion," *Construction Kenya*, August 29, 2019, https://www.constructionkenya.com/5293/lamu-port-project/.

115. Joseph Kahn, "China Has an Ancient Mariner to Tell You About," *New York Times*, July 20, 2005, https://www.nytimes.com/2005/07/20/world/asia/china-has-an-ancient-mariner-to-tell-you-about.html.

116. Charles Clover, "South China Sea Island-Maker Seeks Foreign Flotation," *Financial Times*, June 11, 2015, https://www.ft.com/content/2bd0b16a-0f51-11e5-897e-00144feabdc0.

117. Otsieno Namwaya and Aditi Shetty, "'They Just Want to Silence Us': Abuses against Environmental Activists at Kenya's Coast Region," Human Rights Watch, December 17, 2018, https://www.hrw.org/report/2018/12/17/they-just-want-silence-us/abuses-against-environmental-activists-kenyas-coast.

118. Adam Moore, "The U.S.'s Overlooked Counter-terrorism Outpost in Kenya," *Conflict Geographies* (blog), November 16, 2016, https://

conflictgeographies.com/2016/11/29/the-u-s-s-overlooked-counter-terrorism-outpost-in-kenya/.

119. Jane Mugambi and Weldon Kipkemoi, "Chinese Firm Halts Work at Lamu Port," *Standard*, January 8, 2020, https://www.standardmedia.co.ke/article/2001355693/chinese-firm-halts-work-at-lamu-port.

120. Japan Port Consultants Ltd. and BAC/GKA JV Company, "LAPSSET Corridor and New Lamu Port Feasibility Study and Master Plans Report," May 2011, https://drive.google.com/file/d/0B7w3900K6lYnSndkdEtjNXJXbnc/view.

Chapter Ten. Refining the Blueprint

1. Presidency of the Republic of Turkey, "A New Era Will Be Heralded in Our Region Based on Stability and Prosperity," May 14, 2017, https://www.tccb.gov.tr/en/news/542/75199/a-new-era-will-be-heralded-in-our-region-based-on-stability-and-prosperity.

2. Shohret Hoshur, "Around 120,000 Uyghurs Detained for Political Re-education in Xinjiang's Kashgar Prefecture," Radio Free Asia, January 22, 2018, https://www.rfa.org/english/news/uyghur/detentions-01222018171657.html; Stephanie Nebehay, "U.N. Says It Has Credible Reports That China Holds Million Uighurs in Secret Camps," Reuters, August 10, 2018, https://www.reuters.com/article/us-china-rights-un/u-n-says-it-has-credible-reports-that-china-holds-million-uighurs-in-secret-camps-idUSKBN1KV1SU.

3. SPA, "Saudi, Chinese Officials Meet at Belt and Road Forum in Beijing," *Arab News*, April 26, 2019, http://www.arabnews.com/node/1488556/saudi-arabia; Xinhua, "Xi Jinping Met with Foreign Leaders Attending the Second Belt and Road Forum for International Cooperation," Belt and Road Portal, April 29, 2019, https://eng.yidaiyilu.gov.cn/qwyw/rdxw/87410.htm.

4. Philip Hammond, "Belt and Road Forum: Philip Hammond's Speech" (speech at the Second Belt and Road Forum for International Cooperation, Beijing, April 26, 2019), https://www.gov.uk/government/speeches/belt-and-road-forum-philip-hammonds-speech.

5. China Economic News, "The Complete Speech of Prime Minister Imran Khan at the Belt and Road Forum 2019," CPEC Info, April 26, 2019, http://www.cpecinfo.com/news/the-complete-speech-of-prime-minister-imran-khan-at-the-belt-and-road-forum-2019/Njk5OQ.

6. Mahathir Mohamad, "Speech at the High-Level Meeting of Belt and Road Forum for International Cooperation" (speech at the Second Belt and Road Forum for International Cooperation, Beijing, April 26, 2019), Prime Minister's Office of Malaysia, https://www.pmo.gov.my/2019/04/speech-at-the-high-level-meeting-of-belt-and-road-forum-for-international-cooperation/.

7. Prime Minister's Office of Malaysia, "Press Statement by YAB Prime Minister Tun Dr. Mahathir Bin Mohamad on East Coast Rail Link (ECRL) Project," April 15, 2019, https://www.pmo.gov.my/2019/04/press-state ment-by-yab-prime-minister-tun-dr-mahathir-bin-mohamad-on-east-coast-rail-link-ecrl-project/.

8. Web Desk, "Pakistan Received $2.1 Billion Loan from China," *News*, March 25, 2019, https://www.thenews.com.pk/latest/448668-pakistan-received-21-billion-loan-from-china.

9. Xi Jinping, "Working Together to Deliver a Brighter Future for Belt and Road Cooperation" (speech at the Second Belt and Road Forum for International Cooperation, Beijing, April 26, 2019), https://www.fmprc.gov.cn/mfa_eng/zxxx_662805/t1658424.shtml.

10. Advisory Council of the Belt and Road Forum for International Cooperation, "Belt and Road Cooperation: For a Better World, Report on the Findings and Recommendations from the First Meeting of the Advisory Council of the Belt and Road Forum for International Cooperation," Belt and Road Portal, April 10, 2019, 32, https://eng.yidaiyilu.gov.cn/wcm.files/upload/CMSydylyw/201904/20190428015 2042.pdf.

11. Xi, "Working Together."

12. Stephanie Petrella, "What Is an Economic Corridor?," Reconnecting Asia, Center for Strategic and International Studies, March 27, 2018, https://reconnectingasia.csis.org/analysis/entries/what-economic-corridor/.

13. Jonathan Hillman, "China's Belt and Road Is Full of Holes," Center for Strategic and International Studies, September 4, 2018, https://www.csis.org/analysis/chinas-belt-and-road-full-holes.

14. Yun Sun, *Africa in China's Foreign Policy* (Washington, DC: Brookings Institution, April 2014), https://www.brookings.edu/wp-content/uploads/2016/06/Africa-in-China-web_CMG7.pdf; Wendy Leutert, "Challenges Ahead in China's Reform of State-Owned Enterprises," *Asia Policy* 21 (January 2016): 87, https://www.brookings.edu/wp-content/uploads/2016/07/Wendy-Leutert-Challenges-ahead-in-Chinas-reform-of-stateowned-enterprises.pdf; Sabine Mokry, "Chinese Experts Challenge Western Generalists in Diplomacy," *Diplomat*, August 15, 2018, https://thediplomat.com/2018/08/chinese-experts-challenge-western-generalists-in-diplomacy/.

15. Sun, *Africa in China's Foreign Policy*; Denghua Zhang and Graeme Smith, "China's Foreign Aid System: Structure, Agencies, and Identities," *Third World Quarterly* 38, no. 10 (2017): 2330–2346.

16. Denghua Zhang, "China's New Aid Agency Won't Change Much," East Asia Forum, March 9, 2019, https://www.eastasiaforum.org/2019/03/09/chinas-new-aid-agency-wont-change-much/.

17. Nadege Rolland, "Beijing's Response to the Belt and Road Initiative's 'Pushback': A Story of Assessment and Adaptation," *Asian Affairs* 50, no. 2 (2019): 216–235, https://www.tandfonline.com/doi/full/10.1080/0306837 4.2019.1602385.

18. Zhang, "China's New Aid Agency Won't Change Much."

19. Jonathan Hillman, "China's New Silk Road Conundrum," *Washington Post*, February 14, 2018, https://www.washingtonpost.com/news/theworldpost/wp/2018/02/14/cpec/?utm_term=.84d01780c373.

20. S. A. M. Adshead, *Central Asia in World History* (New York: Palgrave, 1993), 89.

21. Austin Ramzy, "He Needed a Job. China Gave Him One: Locking Up His Fellow Muslims," *New York Times*, March 2, 2019, https://www.nytimes.com/2019/03/02/world/asia/china-muslim-detention-uighur-kazakh.html.

22. Xinhua, "Xi Calls for Building 'Great Wall of Iron' for Xinjiang's Stability," *Xinhuanet*, March 10, 2017, http://www.xinhuanet.com//english/2017-03/10/c_136119256.htm.

23. Adrian Zenz, "Xinjiang's Re-education and Securitization Campaign: Evidence from Domestic Security Budgets," *China Brief* 18, no. 17 (November 5, 2018), https://jamestown.org/program/xinjiangs-re-education-and-securitization-campaign-evidence-from-domestic-security-budgets/.

24. Xi Jinping, "Work Together to Build the Silk Road Economic Belt and the 21st Century Maritime Silk Road" (speech at the Belt and Road Forum for International Cooperation, Beijing, May 14, 2017), *Xinhuanet*, May 16, 2017, http://www.xinhuanet.com//english/2017-05/16/c_136287878.htm.

25. J. A. Hobson, *Imperialism: A Study* (New York: James Pott, 1902); Vladimir Il'ich Lenin, *Imperialism, the Highest Stage of Capitalism: A Popular Outline* (New York: International, 1939); Edward W. Said, *Culture and Imperialism* (London: Chatto and Windus, 1993); Uday Singh Mehta, *Liberalism and Empire: A Study in Nineteenth-Century British Liberal Thought* (Chicago: University of Chicago Press, 1999).

26. "Imperialism, n.," *OED Online*, Oxford University Press, accessed January 17, 2020, https://www.oed.com/view/Entry/92285?redirectedFrom=imperialism&.

27. Howard W. French, *China's Second Continent: How a Million Migrants Are Building a New Empire in Africa* (New York: Random House, 2014), 260–261.

28. Francis Fukuyama, Michael Bennon, and Bushra Bataineh, "How the Belt and Road Gained Steam: Causes and Implications of China's Rise in Global Infrastructure" (CDDRL Working Papers, Freeman Spogli Institute for International Studies, Stanford, CA, May 2019), https://cddrl.fsi.stanford.edu/publication/how-belt-and-road-gained-steam-causes-and-implications-china%E2%80%99s-rise-global.

29. Robert M. Orr Jr., *The Emergence of Japan's Foreign Aid Power* (New York: Columbia University Press, 1990).

30. George Friedman and Meredith Lebard, *The Coming War with Japan* (London: St. Martin's, 1991).

31. European Commission, *EU-China Connectivity Platform Short-Term Action Plan* (Brussels: European Union, 2018), https://ec.europa.eu/transport/

sites/transport/files/2018-07-13-eu-china-connectivity-platform-action-plan.pdf.

32. Andrew Small, "A Slimmer Belt and Road Is Even Scarier," *Bloomberg*, April 24, 2019, https://www.bloomberg.com/opinion/articles/2019-04-24/a-slimmed-down-belt-and-road-will-increase-china-s-influence.

33. Warren Buffet, "Berkshire's Corporate Performance vs. the S&P 500," Berkshire Hathaway, 2001, http://www.berkshirehathaway.com/2001ar/2001letter.html.

Acknowledgments

THANK YOU TO MY colleagues at the Center for Strategic and International Studies (CSIS). John Hamre created the Reconnecting Asia Project, Craig Cohen and Josiane Gable nurtured it, and Matthew Goodman has been its champion. Emily Tiemeyer produced the maps in this book, demonstrating again that Andrew Schwartz, Rebecka Shirazi, and Paul Franz have built the best media team in the think-tank business. Maesea McCalpin led a talented group of researchers who provided critical support, especially John McHugh and Sebastian He.

Many experts, within and outside CSIS, provided feedback on drafts: Noah Barkin, Jude Blanchette, Cat Chiang, Judd Devermont, Daniel Headrick, Murray Heibert, Chris Miller, Vasu Mohan, Andrew Small, and Tom Zoellner. I also benefited from the deep expertise of the Reconnecting Asia Project's nonresident scholars, Bushra Bataineh, Mike Bennon, Agatha Kratz, and Peter Raymond, as well its advisory board: Victor Cha, Edward Cho, Alexander Cooley, Alexander Diener, Michael Green, Scott Kennedy, Sarah Ladislaw, Jeffrey Mankoff, Scott Miller, Richard Rossow, Daniel Runde, and Amy Searight. The staff at the Rockefeller Archive Center and the Richard Nixon Library helped track down documents about early U.S. involvement in Pakistan. I am also indebted to numerous former U.S. officials who shared their thoughts privately as well as two anonymous reviewers of the manuscript.

The book would not have been possible without the generous support of the Smith Richardson Foundation (SRF) and the Alfred

P. Sloan Foundation. Allan Song at SRF challenged me to focus on carefully describing China's Belt and Road as it is, rather than jumping ahead to consider how the United States and others should respond. Doron Weber at Sloan pushed me to focus on China's technology, an area that I plan to continue exploring.

Several editors generously provided opportunities to write and sharpen my thinking: Andrew Hill, James Kynge, Gwen Robinson, and Stefan Wagstyl at the *Financial Times* and *Nikkei Asian Review*, Adam Kushner at the *Washington Post*, Peter Mellgard and Kathleen Miles at the *WorldPost*, and Chris Russell at *Axios*.

Toby Mundy, literary agent and advocate of big ideas, encouraged me to tackle this project, helped lift it for a broader audience, and found it a home. Every author needs an editor like Jaya Chatterjee at Yale University Press: strategic, smart, and responsive from beginning to end. Mary Pasti and Eva Skewes masterfully kept all the parts of the manuscript moving toward production. Andrew Katz provided a careful and critical eye, just when my own vision was starting to get blurry. Enid L. Zafran efficiently created the index. This is my first book, and hopefully not the last, but I suspect I have been spoiled.

I also owe a personal debt to several teachers and mentors. A decade ago, Douglas Blum, Linda B. Miller, and Claudia Elliott taught me how to turn evidence into arguments, arguments into essays, and essays into chapters. I learned much about China's rise as a research and teaching assistant to Graham Allison, and I remain a student. Working for Michael Froman, one of the few true practitioners of both economics and national security, I learned how to think about economic power. Leslie H. Gelb, who passed away while this book was being edited, challenged me to write more and better. I can still hear his voice: provocative to grab your attention, brutally direct to point out what you are missing, encouraging to inspire action and a better outcome, and always honest.

Finally, thank you to friends and family for enduring my stories about infrastructure projects and understanding when I needed to disappear to visit a strange place or into a quiet room to write. My parents never wavered in their encouragement along the path that led from Massachusetts to New Mexico, New York, Rhode Island, Kyrgyzstan, and eventually to this book. Liz, my wife and partner in all things, is a constant source of inspiration. This book is for her, and I smile when thinking that one day, our daughter, Harper, might read it.

Index

Maps are indicated by italicized page numbers.